WILLIAM FAULKNER'S CRAFT OF REVISION

The Snopes Trilogy
"The Unvanquished"
and "Go Down, Moses"

WILLIAM FAULKNER'S CRAFT OF REVISION

The Snopes Trilogy,
"The Unvanquished"
and "Go Down, Moses"

by Joanne V. Creighton

Wayne State University

Wayne State University Press
Detroit   1977

Library of Congress Cataloging in Publication Data

Creighton, Joanne V   1942–
    William Faulkner's craft of revision.

    Bibliography: p.
    Includes index
    1. Faulkner, William, 1897–1962—Technique.
I. Title.
PS3511.A86Z775   813'.5'2   76-51441
ISBN 0-8143-1572-0

This book is published with the support of a grant from the American Council of
Learned Societies for publication of first or second books by scholars in the fields
of the humanities.

To Tom

CONTENTS

ACKNOWLEDGMENTS

I would like to express my thanks to Professor Lyall Powers whose enthusiasm for Faulkner inspired my own and who has been a mentor and friend over the years; to Professor Joseph Prescott who provided valuable encouragement and advice with the manuscript; to Wayne State University which awarded me two Grants-in-Aid to help finance my research expenses; to the staff of the Manuscripts Department of the Alderman Library, The University of Virginia, who have been unfailingly courteous in their management of the magnificent Faulkner collection, and to Mrs. Marguerite C. Wallace, Wayne State University Press, who helpfully and competently edited the manuscript. I appreciate the permission to quote from the Faulkner collection granted by the Alderman Library and Mrs. Jill Summers, Executrix of the Faulkner estate, from the published texts granted by Random House, Inc., and from *Faulkner in the University* granted by The University Press of Virginia. Revised and incorporated into this study is material which appeared in three articles: "Suratt to Ratliff: A Genetic Approach to *The Hamlet*," *Michigan Academician* 6 (Summer 1973): 101–12; "Revision and Craftsmanship in the Hunting Trilogy of *Go Down, Moses*," *Texas Studies in Literature and Language* 15 (Fall 1973): 577–92; and "Revision and Craftsmanship in Faulkner's 'The Fire and the Hearth,' " *Studies in Short Fiction* 11 (Spring 1974): 161–72. I thank the editors of these journals both for publishing my work and for their kind permission to reprint it, allowing me to expand these earlier investigations into the larger design of this book. Finally, I feel a special debt of gratitude to that master craftsman himself, William Faulkner, whose works have buoyantly withstood my painstaking examination of them and have only increased in their capacity to awe and delight me.

Textual Note

All quotations from Faulkner's unpublished works in my text are
verbatim. I did not take the liberty
to correct his typographical errors.

INTRODUCTION

This is a study of the process of revision and composition under-taken by William Faulkner when he incorporated preexistent short stories into longer works. The Snopes Trilogy, *The Unvanquished*, and *Go Down, Moses* provide the focus of the investigation. Al-though some of his other works also incorporate a story or two, the revision, for the most part, is less extensive and less revealing of Faulkner's method.[1] My primary objective is to gain insight into the structural designs of these works. Sprawling and amalgamative, they have puzzled and sometimes annoyed commentators. But clearly Faulkner was not restricted by the principles of a well-made novel when putting together these works, nor should we be in assessing them. A study of his revisions illuminates the kind of structure he was attempting to create. Developing a sense of what Faulkner had in mind must precede an evaluation of these unusual works. I am much less concerned with arriving at conclusions about Faulkner's craft of revision in general—although some conclusions are inevi-table—than I am with studying closely and sometimes minutely the gradual evolution of the final work.

My method is strictly inductive, based on a word-by-word comparison of multiple versions of the texts. In other words, I first recorded the textual changes between an earlier and later version of a story and then attempted to explain the apparent rationale behind them. What did Faulkner have to do to satisfy himself that he had incorporated an independent story into a larger context? What do his changes reveal about the ideas and the structure he was trying to implement in the evolving larger work? The answers to these ques-tions lie in materials that surprisingly have been untapped as a source of investigation. Not only have many of Faulkner's published stories been incorporated into longer published works but a wealth of unpublished manuscripts and typescripts is also available, allowing one to reconstruct the stages of composition and revision. Frequently, several drafts of both the original stories and Faulkner's recasting of them for longer works are available. For example, at least seven different versions (with six different titles) of the spotted horses story are available for comparison with the version eventually included in *The Hamlet*. One can follow the transformation of three simple comic stories as they become assimilated into "The Fire and the Hearth" and the even more complex structure of *Go Down, Moses*.

Analysis of the relationship between the original story and the longer work into which it was later incorporated yields perspective upon both the works under study and the part-whole duality inherent in all of Faulkner's Yoknapatawpha County fiction. Faulkner's protean characters, stories, and myths create the uniquely interconnected world of his fiction and invalidate the new critical premise that each work of literature is totally autonomous and self-contained. Faulkner's works reflect on each other. *Meaning* in his fiction is always contingent upon how much the reader knows; and how much he knows depends, sometimes, on how much he brings to the work. Because many of Faulkner's characters recur from work to work, their very introduction in a novel or a story evokes—to the well-versed reader of Faulkner—history, personality, and associations that may not be explicitly developed in that particular work. In "Wash," Sutpen appears to be a landed aristocrat because we see him as Wash does. In *Absalom, Absalom!* we discover with Quentin Compson that Sutpen is actually a self-made man. Correspondingly, Quentin of *Absalom, Absalom!* appears to be the one character who can completely understand Sutpen and thus understand himself. If we approach *Absalom, Absalom!* after reading *The Sound and the Fury*, however, we are likely to be haunted by Quentin's subsequent suicide and likely to moderate our view of how much Quentin's understanding of himself implies acceptance of himself. Like life itself, Faulkner's fictional world expands in richness and complexity as more of the past and future is brought to bear upon the present.

Yet one cannot say that because Faulkner created characters and situations which exist beyond the boundaries of individual works that he was unconcerned with those boundaries. Although the Yoknapatawpha County fiction becomes a kind of "meta-novel" that exists above and beyond the individual stories and novels which inform it, Faulkner, for the most part, approaches each story and novel as a self-contained unit with an autonomous shape and significance. Where this concern with the boundaries of a work can be most closely observed is in a comparison of the different uses he makes of the self-contained episode. For this reason I concentrate on the "story" as a unit rather than on "character" or "idea" or "myth," because I am particularly interested in observing the way that Faulkner works against the autonomous structure and meaning of the short story when he incorporates it into a larger aesthetic whole with a differing structure and meaning. A comparison of the two versions of the Wash-Sutpen story is a small illustration of the kind of structural craftmanship practiced by William Faulkner which I think merits careful study.

Basically the same episode in which Wash kills Sutpen in revenge for his callous treatment of his granddaughter and her child is presented in both "Wash" and *Absalom, Absalom!* But the short story, told from Wash's perspective, is drawn along class-conflict lines. Because the reader sees the events as Wash sees them, Sutpen is indistinguishable from other Southern gentlemen. When this "gentleman," whom Wash had so admired, exploits his granddaughter and shirks responsibility, Wash feels betrayed by the Sutpens of the world who "set the order and rule of living" and who will forever tread on the humanity of his kind. In the novel, however, the class conflict is muted, because Wash is unknowingly betrayed by one of his own kind. Sutpen has risen from the poor-white status he at one time shared with Wash. The rather dispirited and broken old man of the story is seen now as the madly purposeful self-made man who is worried that he may not have enough time to accomplish his design in the person of an acceptable son and a salvaged plantation. The sex of the child, immaterial for the story's meaning, is now all-important, since Sutpen is implementing with Milly the breeding experiment that so outraged Miss Rosa. The logic is simple: if it was a boy he would have married her; since it is not, he need not.

Furthermore, Sutpen's poor-white origins form the basis of some ironic parallels in the novel. The affront to his dignity that Sutpen suffers as a child from the "monkey-nigger" at the door of the plantation mansion is exactly duplicated by the affront that Wash feels at the door of Sutpen's house when he is turned away by Clytie. The rather simple class-conflict becomes part of a complex mythic treatment of transcendent moral retribution working itself out in human affairs. Sutpen's inhumanity reaps its own reward in the form, appropriately enough, of his own scythe wielded by an affronted member of his own class.

Faulkner's astute perception of the interdependency of technique and meaning is also evidenced in the dramatic structure of "Wash" and the multiple narration of *Absalom, Absalom!* The climax of the short story is heightened by presenting it first. The story begins—without explanation—at the very moment when Wash overhears Sutpen's callous rejection: "Well, Milly . . . too bad you're not a mare. Then I could give you a decent stall in the stable."[2] The scene is left as a dramatically poised tableau while the narrator fills in with expository summary in part two. The suspended moment provides the fulcrum for the action in part three, which builds in tension as Wash moves slowly, quietly, and methodically to effect the violent anticlimax. After murdering Sutpen, he beheads his granddaughter and great-granddaughter with a butcher knife, sets his shack afire, and runs out to "the curious, and the vengeful: men of Sutpen's own kind" (W. pp. 546–47) with raised scythe in hand. In contrast to the short story's taut dramatic structure is the distorted, incomplete, and repetitive treatment of the story in the novel. Not only is the story told twice,[3] but the events are first mentioned in fragmentary allusions. The radically differing points of view, of course, are responsible for this divergence in shape as well as in meaning.

The Wash-Sutpen story in the novel is related many years after the events through both the thoughts of Quentin Compson and his extended conversation with his Harvard roommate, Shreve. While meaning in the short story is to be found in the knowable facts as they are reported by the reliable narrator, in the novel it requires the perspective of time; the shifting through of multiple, conflicting, and incomplete points of view; and the use of conjecture, logic, and imagination. The locus of the novel is ultimately within the mind of Quentin Compson to whom Sutpen's history is more than the life of one man. In a broader sense in *Absalom, Absalom!* Sutpen and Wash are one in their mutual duping by the discriminatory standards and hollow splendor of the antebellum South. To understand what went wrong with Sutpen's "design" and with his "logic and morality" is to understand what went wrong with the antebellum South. Only through this understanding will Quentin Compson gain some insight into "a barracks filled with stubborn back-looking ghosts" (AA. p. 12), that is, himself.

"Wash" and *Absalom, Absalom!* depict a familiar pattern in

Faulkner's canon. He frequently reused a single episode, first publishing it as a short story and then incorporating it into a longer work. But, like here, reuse is seldom mere reiteration. The works to be examined in this study all commonly incorporate preexistent short stories, but they offer interesting and illuminating contrasts, growing out of remarkably different geneses and taking markedly different shapes.

In spite of the relatively late publication dates of the novels of The Snopes Trilogy, the origin of the Snopes saga is part of Faulkner's earliest inspiration for the Yoknapatawpha County world of his most successful fiction. Faulkner claimed that the idea of the Snopeses came to him "at once like a bolt of lightning lights up a landscape and you see everything,"[4] and indeed the unpublished "Father Abraham" (1926–27), the first Snopes story, outlines much of the pattern of the Snopeses' invasion of Frenchman's Bend and Jefferson that gives shape to the trilogy. The Snopeses were conceived as a family existing within a prescribed economic, social, and moral context, and much of their history was similarily prescribed by Faulkner's "bolt of lightning" conception. Yet Faulkner first wrote the Snopes story "in pieces," composing several short stories long before he began to pull the material together for the first volume of The Snopes Trilogy, *The Hamlet,* published in 1940. He continued to use stories some thirty years after they were first written when he composed *The Town* and *The Mansion* in the 1950s. The task not only of welding together the discrete stories with the governing design of the saga but also of creating separate novelistic structures for the three units of the trilogy no doubt tested Faulkner's skill much more severely than the composition of *The Unvanquished,* the second work under study.

Like The Snopes Trilogy, *The Unvanquished* reiterates material that had been part of Faulkner's earliest evocation of the Yoknapatawpha County world. *The Unvanquished* is composed of tales of the Sartorises, that family of brave, reckless, and suicidal aristocrats who people another part of Faulkner's legendary South. Faulkner apparently created the Sartorises and the Snopeses at approximately the same time, working on both parts of his "little postage-stamp world" simultaneously until late 1926 or early 1927 when he abandoned the unfinished Snopes story to work on *Flags in the Dust* (completed September 29, 1927)[5], later revised and published as *Sartoris* in 1929. So, unlike the saga of the Snopeses, that of the Sartorises was first presented in novelistic form; only later did Faulkner write separate short stories about this family, many of which were elaborations of incidents first mentioned in the novel. That Faulkner from the first envisioned these separate stories as a "long series"[6] makes *The Unvanquished* the simplest work under study, since the stories are about the same characters and take place in discontinuous chronological time. Yet Faulkner made some noteworthy revision and addition when composing *The Unvanquished,* and the work is important as his first effort to create a short story composite, a form between that of the novel and the collection of short stories which could accommodate his dual focus on the past and the present, the individual and the tradition, the episode and the historical context.

Go Down, Moses, however, is a much more ambitious attempt to fashion this kind of structure. Unlike *The Unvanquished* or The Snopes Trilogy, this work grew out of neither single inspiration nor a single family of characters. Rather, in an audacious attempt at collage, Faulkner brought together stories from markedly dissimilar origins. Hunting stories about a courageous dog and a hard-to-kill old bear are coupled with the story of a young white man's rejection of his inheritance and with tales of a black man's grief for his dead wife and a black grandmother's grief for her executed grandson. Stories of a wily black man with a penchant for moonshining and gold-divining are coupled with another view of this same man who as a mulatto is related to his white landlord whom he fears is sexually using his wife. *Go Down, Moses* incorporates ten short stories—eight published— about a multivarious group of individuals from unrelated families: the Compsons, Sartorises, Sutpens, McCaslins, and Beauchamps. If nothing else, *Go Down, Moses* would be a startling attempt to bring together disparate materials. Although its experimental structure seems fairly obvious, surprisingly few studies have been made of these stories as a means towards elucidating Faulkner's plans for the final volume. Fortunately, a large number of the early drafts of the stories and the preliminary drafts of the composite are on deposit in the Alderman Library. Tracing the evolutionary development of the manuscript forms the largest part of this study. Because so many versions of the stories and drafts of "The Fire and the Hearth" are available, I have made a close textual and stylistic analysis of it.

In this study I seek neither to trace the genesis of characters and ideas in the author's mind nor to examine the reuse of characters and tales apart from structural principles.[7] One can never really know when and how creative ideas occurred to William Faulkner. He himself, in fact, often stated that he was unconcerned about the origin of characters or stories. Nothing is sacred about the genesis of Ike McCaslin, for example. He appears to have been first conceived as an old hunter.[8] Only later, with the composition of *Go Down, Moses* was he fitted with the sensitive boyhood that was originally a part of another character's being, Quentin Compson. When and why Faulkner made this change is less significant than how he worked it out on the page. His talent is primarily in his structural craft, only secondarily in his protean characters whom he used and reused, cut, shaped, and discarded to suit his purposes. In the discussions which follow, I catalogue the changes that Faulkner made in the process of revision and composition, attempt to determine the governing artistic purposes which inspired the changes, and offer my critical evaluation of the success or failure of Faulkner's craftsmanship.

THE SNOPES TRILOGY:
1 STORIES INTO NOVELS

Faulkner's statements about the conception and evolution of the Snopes saga and the supporting evidence indicate that the relationship between the early short stories and the three novels of the trilogy is a complex and interdependent one. The publication of *The Hamlet* was preceded by the publication of five Snopes stories[1] and by several unpublished versions of the spotted horses story. Yet Faulkner insists that he "thought of the whole story at once"[2] and envisioned it from the start as a novel.[3] Evidence to substantiate his claim can be found both in *Flags in the Dust* (1927), the unpublished earlier draft of *Sartoris* (1929), and in "Father Abraham," apparently the earliest unpublished Snopes manuscript, probably written around 1926–27 or before.[4] In *Flags in the Dust* and *Sartoris* brief allusion is made to the clan's invasion of Frenchman's Bend, to Flem's rise from store clerk to plant manager to vice-president of the bank, and to the association of Montgomery Ward Snopes with Horace Benbow in the W.M.C.A. during the war.[5] Byron Snopes is a significant minor character (developed more fully in *Flags in the Dust*) who writes vulgar love notes to Narcissa Benbow, and who robs the Sartoris bank and then flees town. In "Father Abraham" Flem's presidency of the bank is alluded to and his marriage to Eula Varner is summarily treated before the more detailed treatment of the spotted horses story. Clearly, at a relatively early date, long before the publication of *The Hamlet* (1940), Faulkner sketched the Snopes story as a single entity, even though when he wrote, the result was isolated episodes that took the form of short stories.

Recently released materials—both the variously titled typescripts depicting Faulkner's several attempts to cut out of "Father Abraham" a publishable spotted horses story and the Ober-Faulkner correspondence documenting Faulkner's desperate financial need to publish stories[6]—reveal that the immediate pressure on Faulkner was to create stories rather than a novel. But since the Snopes material itself is essentially episodic, the intricate and unified structure of *The Hamlet* and to a lesser degree of *The Town* and *The Mansion* is a credit to his mastery of formal organization. That mastery of organization can be closely observed in the reworking into novels of previously autonomous stories. The way that he worked against the autonomy of the short story in his revision illuminates the overall design of the trilogy and the specific themes and structures of each of the three novels. Of course, the material from pre-existent short stories forms a relatively small part of the three novels, and I make no attempt here at a comprehensive analysis of the novels.[7] But the richness and complexity of The Snopes Trilogy have worked against a careful examination of the individual episodes in critical studies of the works; just such a careful examination of several episodes I hope to give here.

Much more overtly than his treatment of other Yoknapatawpha County families, Faulkner defines the Snopeses within a prescribed sociological, symbolical, and moral context. The sociological milieu is explicitly elaborated in "Father Abraham," where certain moral inadequacies are concomitant with the anomalous social standing of these "shiftless tenant farmers," who like mold on cheese are parasites rather than constructive members of society.

> The Snopes sprange untarnished from a long line of shiftless tenant-farmers—a race that is of the soil and yet rootless, like mistletoe; owing nothing to the soil, giving nothing of it and getting nothing in return; using the land as a harlot instead of an imperious and abundant mistress, passing on to another farm. Porlific and rootless and clannish, they move and marry and multiply and move and marry and multiply like rabbits: magnify them and you have political hangerson and petty dishonest officeholders; reduce the perspective and you have mold on cheese, steadfast and gradual and implacable: theirs that dull provincial cunning that causes them to doubt anything that does not jibb with their preconceived and arbitrary standards of verity, yet which permits them to be taken in by the most barefaced liar who is as all plausible. [TS, pp. 8–9][8]

Disrespect for the land, rootlessness, clannishness, opportunism, dishonesty, distrustfulness, gullibility, cunning, and expedient morality are qualities that cling to the Snopeses in stories and novels to come; in fact, ultimately they are conjured up by the very name Snopes, although perhaps the mercenary opportunism untempered with any conscience for the exploited, illustrated later in the story in Flem's covert role in the sale of the spotted horses, becomes the most obvious hallmark of Snopesism. Symbolically, the Snopeses are seen as an ironic replica of the modern age and the modern mind. Democracy, the great leveler, has made possible Flem's phenomenal success—from tenant farmer to bank president—and Flem's ascendancy ironically suggests that he is the representative *man* of this inglorious age, as Roland, the Old Frenchman, and Abraham were of theirs:

> He is a living example of the astonishing byblows of man's utopian dreams actually functioning; in this case the dream is Democracy. He will become legendary in time, but he has always been symbolic. Legendary as Roland and as symbolic of a form of behavior; as symbolic of an age and a region as his predecessor, a portly man with a white imperial and a shoestring tie and a two gallon felt hat, was; as symbolic and as typical of a frame of mind as Buddha is today. With this difference: Buddha contemplates an abstraction and derives a secret amusement of it; while he, behind the new plate glass of his recently remodelled bank, dwells with neither lust nor alarm on the plump yet still disturbing image of his silkclad wife passing the time of the day with Colonel Doxey in front of the postoffice. . . . This, behind its plate glass, these quiet unwinking eyes, this mouth like one of those patent tobacco pouches that you open and close by ripping a metal ring along the seam, this is the man. It boots not that for thirty years the town itself saw him not four times a year, that for the next fifteen years the bank knew him only on the customers' side of the savings window; this was and is and will be, the man. Jehovah said once to Moses: "I AM that I AM" and Moses argued with the good God; but when he spoke to one of his tribe, that one said immediately: "Here am I, Uncle Flem." He chews tobacco constantly with a slow thrusting motion, and no one ever saw his eyelids closed. He blinks them of course, like everybody else, but no one ever saw him do it. This is the man. [TS, pp.1–2]

In fact, the ironic parallel to the biblical Abraham that is developed in "Father Abraham" and alluded to in *Flags in the Dust* and *Sartoris*[9] (but dropped in The Snopes Trilogy) suggests that Flem, the sterile father of them all, is establishing a modern age Snopes dynasty equivalent to that of Abraham of old. Secretive, unwinking, implacable, Flem is the super-Snopes who owes his success to his working assumption that man's behavior and ethics are a matter of mere expediency: "For Flem had reduced all human conduct to a single workable belief: that some men are fools, but all men are no honester than circumstance requires." [TS, p. 8]

Although Faulkner amplified and refined his conception of the Snopeses and his characterization of their titular head, Flem, he did not stray from initial conception of them. When he attempted, however, to incorporate stories such as "Fool About a Horse" and "The Hound" that were not originally about Snopes characters, some un-Snopesian qualities adulterate the purity of generic Snopesism and complicate what is for the most part the almost categorically unsympathetic treatment of them as human beings.

"THE HAMLET"

Extensive experimentation with the arrangement of parts in *The Hamlet* and considerable reworking of scenes and episodes attest to Faulkner's careful craftsmanship. Far from a mere composite of loosely related episodes, *The Hamlet* is intricately organized structurally, thematically, symbolically, and tonally. In fact, the evolution of the novel offers revealing perspective on the interrelationship of what Coleridge calls the primary and secondary imaginations. Because if "Father Abraham" can be viewed as a close approximation of how the Snopes chronicle first presented itself to Faulkner's mind—and he has suggested as much—then it is fascinating to see when he altered that initial conception and when, faced with a problem of presentation, he returned to it.

"Father Abraham" begins with the two-paragraph, tongue-in-cheek description of Flem as symbolic and representative of the age of democracy, quoted in part above, which finds no part in *The Hamlet* in its final form. In the novel no omniscient narrator introduces Flem and sketches his symbolic and legendary significance. A fortunate choice of Faulkner's "secondary imagination" was to reinforce the enigmatic role of Flem by restricting the point of view. The narrator places the reader in the same position in relation to the Snopeses as that of the community of Frenchman's Bend. Like the residents of this country hamlet, the reader first learns of the Snopeses when Ab approaches Joby Varner for a tenant's lease. Like the residents, he picks up some background about the Snopeses from the itinerant sewing-machine agent, Ratliff, who draws from gossip and prior experience. Like the residents, he gradually forms his own assessment of who and what the Snopeses are and represent. Never, except with the unsnopesian Snopes, Mink, is an interior view of them revealed. Like the residents of Frenchman's Bend and Jefferson, the reader sees them only as they approach and invade. This perspective reinforces the picture of them as outsiders, parasites of an established society.

The Hamlet begins with a description of Frenchman's Bend, its people and its history, a descriptive survey which resembles the one in "Father Abraham" after the initial two-paragraph description of Flem. This panoramic survey of the rich land with its gutted shell of an enormous antebellum mansion owned by an anonymous Old Frenchman, "His dream, his broad acres were parcelled out now into small shiftless mortgaged farms for the directors of Jefferson banks to squabble over before selling finally to Will Varner,"[10] is an appropriate introduction to a novel which catalogues yet another stage in the changing history of the land and community, the invasion of the Snopeses. As a matter of fact, *The Hamlet* records Flem's "passing through" Frenchman's Bend; for at the end of the novel Flem Snopes, having reaped maximum profits from his use of the inhabitants and the property of the hamlet, is on his way to a bigger and better arena with half ownership of a Jefferson restaurant in his pocket. Moreover, the mention, in the second paragraph of the novel, of the persistent legend that the original owner buried money prepares for the final episode of the novel in which Flem succeeds in using that legend for a shrewd final deal that terminates his ownership of Old Frenchman place and jettisons him into Jefferson. Although Faulkner's choice of opening, then, seems particularly effective in setting up an encompassing frame for the novel—from Flem's entrance to his exit from Frenchmen's Bend—it was no simple choice for Faulkner. He appears to have been particularly obsessed with the problem of where and how to begin the novel.

Extant manuscript and typescript materials indicate, for example, that at one time he intended the novel to begin with what is now the story "Barn Burning."[11] Faulkner claimed that he discovered that "Barn Burning" (and "Wash") "had no place in that book at all."[12] He was obviously right; I cannot agree with Michael Millgate's claim that "there is no doubt that the deeply moving story of 'Barn Burning' would have been in many ways an effective introduction."[13] Not only is the interior view of Sarty in "Barn Burning" contrary to the external perspective of the Snopeses that Faulkner uses in *The Hamlet* but Sarty's character and the serious and tragic tone of this story are also contrary to the nature and the spirit of the Snopes chronicle as it was ordained by Faulkner's "bolt of lightning" inspiration. Sarty is unsnopesian in his concern with personal integrity and with abstract principles of justice and fair play. He is so motivated by this integrity and these principles that he is forced to leave home and family rather than be a party to the barn-burning activities of his vengeful, vindictive, and exploitative father. A powerful and moving story, it is hardly an appropriate introduction to the Snopes saga which has as its germinal idea the tale—told with amusement and detachment—of a tribe of almost subhuman mercenary opportunists who prey on the weaknesses and gullibility of others. The story, in other words, gets Faulkner off onto the wrong track, and he wisely decided to return to the tale as conceived by the "primary imagination."

The barn-burning episode is still included as an extremely important part of *The Hamlet,* but the tone, emphasis, style, and significance of it are completely changed by altering the point of view and the context in chapter one of Book One. Instead of the tragic perspective of sensitive and tortured Sarty Snopes who tries to think well of his barn-burning father, Faulkner employs the witty detachment of Ratliff who covertly enjoys the "shocked and outraged consternation" of Joby Varner as he tells of the infamy of Varner's newest barn-burning tenant farmer and who makes ironic gibes at Joby without breaking his straight-faced mask:

> "The barn burnt all regular and in due course; you'll have to say that for him. This here was just a call, just pure friendship, because Snopes knowed where his fields was and all he had to do was to start scratching them, and it already the middle of May. Just like now," he added in a tone of absolutely creamlike innocence. "But then I hear tell he always makes his rent contracts later than most." But he was not laughing. The shrewd brown face was as bland and smooth as ever beneath the shrewd impenetrable eyes. [H, pp. 14–15]

Told from this perspective, the story functions as a harmonious and integral part of *The Hamlet.* It both establishes a distanced perspective on the antics of the Snopeses which is so important to the comic tone tinged with moral disapproval—that is first created in "Father Abraham" and recreated in *The Hamlet*—and reinforces the important intensification of Ratliff's role as Snopes-watcher and Snopes-antagonist, an intensification that will later be traced in the reworking of each of the early Snopes stories.

The unSnopesian Sarty is almost entirely removed from the novel version except for Ratliff's brief mention of him: "there was another one too, a little one; I remember seeing him once somewhere. He wasn't with them. Leastways he aint now. Maybe they forgot to tell him when to get outen the barn" (H, p. 14). While this account creates none of the pathos of Sarty's tortured departure from his family, it is factually consistent with the separately published story, "Barn Burning." Viewing the events from a distance, Ratliff emphasizes not the tragedy of Sarty Snopes, but the comically bizarre behavior of Ab Snopes. Only the angle is changed; the story is the same. As Faulkner said: "there's not too fine a distinction between humor and tragedy . . . even tragedy is in a way walking a tightrope between the ridiculous—between the bizarre and the terrible."[14] The terrible still remains in Ratliff's account; that is, the vengeful vindictiveness of Ab Snopes still remains, but it becomes much less terrible, as it is registered with the horrified and indignant Joby Varner who stands to lose at most a barn and supplies, than it does with Sarty Snopes who stands to lose, on the one hand, his personal integrity and, on the other, his place in his family. In other words, Joby is threatened economically but not morally, or so at least it seems at this point. For the Snopeses initially are seen as an economic threat; only gradually is the moral dilemma—equivalent to that which Sarty Snopes faces—recognized by some perceptive members of the community.

The groundwork for that moral challenge, however, is clearly laid in the contract between Ab and Joby. Joby's motives in taking on Ab are none-too-honorable and his weakness establishes an important pattern in the novel: the Snopeses prey on the moral vulnerability of others. Joby desires to make a fast buck. When he learns that Ab has a reputation for barn burning, he plans to use the threat of blackmail to swindle Ab Snopes out of his fair share of the profits of the crop. That the Snopeses are more successful at this kind of shoddy mercenary opportunism does not exonerate Varner's behavior. In fact, each stage in the rise of Flem Snopes can be traced to his "trading" in other such moral lapses: from the purchase of a respectable marriage for his pregnant daughter by Will Varner to the purchase of cuckolding rights to that wife by Manfred de Spain. The Snopeses become a grotesque symbol of the expedient morality of the society they exploit.

Other early Snopes stories show the repeated use of a trading context to portray the mercenary opportunism of the Snopeses.

"Spotted Horses" reveals Flem's behind-the-scenes manipulation of his gullible neighbors to purchase wild horses. "Lizards in Jamshyd's Courtyard" twice pits Yoknapatawpha County's shrewdest trader, V. K. Surratt, against Flem, once with regard to the goat purchase and a second time with the planted money on Old Frenchman place. A non-Snopes horse-trading story, "Fool About a Horse," was revised and incorporated into the Snopes chronicle.

In fact, each of the three chapters of Book One, entitled "Flem," are drawn from earlier stories. While Faulkner assimilated aspects of "Father Abraham" and "Barn Burning" into an extremely effective first chapter, "Fool About a Horse," incorporated into the second chapter, is less well assimilated. Depicting "Pap's" duping by the super horse-trader, Pat Stamper, it is the earliest published story reworked for *The Hamlet*. Even after its metamorphosis into a Snopes story, it does perhaps jar slightly with the germinal idea of the Snopeses. Pap, who becomes Ab Snopes in the novel, is a sympathetic—if gullible—human being and the Snopeses are usually not sympathetic. In fact, the original "Pap" of the story was Lem Surratt, V. K.'s father. Only the name was changed, not the characterization. The reader comes to expect much more fundamental differences between Snopeses and ordinary human beings than this story presents. Of course, Faulkner does attempt to minimize this problem by offering Ratliff's glib explanation of Ab's metamorphosis from a sympathetic to a vindictive person: "Old man Ab aint naturally mean. He's just soured" (H, p. 29). Ratliff reminds us of activities of Ab that have been treated elsewhere in Faulkner's canon, such as his horse-and-mule partnership with Miss Rosa Millard. The incident is further woven into the fabric of the novel by the addition of the latter-day meeting of Ratliff and Ab following the store incident. In a mood of good will, affability, and curiosity, Ratliff brings Ab some whiskey. He is met with the humorless, distrustful, self-protective curtness so typical of the Snopeses, particularly the "soured" Ab. The fundamentally differing natures of the two men is clear; the incident prepares for the opposition of Ratliff with another Snopes, Flem, later in the book.

One can follow closely the evolution of "Fool About a Horse" by studying the unpublished materials.[15] The point of view, repeatedly altered, shows an interesting on-again, off-again use of Suratt-Ratliff as narrator. In both the manuscript and typescript versions a nameless twelve-year-old boy narrates the story, but he merely establishes a frame for Suratt's narration:

> Suratt told this one too:—Suratt, who sold or traded (and it was said,
> gambled) sewing machines against whatever the little lost hill cabins in
> our county contained to spare or to swap—the meagre and terrific
> hoards of nickles and dimes and quarters and worn dollar bills in buried
> baking powder cans. . . . He told this one to my grandfather, along with
> the others, the three of us—Grandfather and Suratt and I—sitting in the
> office where Grandfather used to practise law. [Carbon TS, pp.1–2]

This initial description, sketching the character of Suratt and establishing the setting for his narration of the story, covers four-and-a-half
pages of the typescript. Intermittent interruptions of Suratt's narrative later in the story refer us back to this frame situation. The most
interesting of these interruptions is the sketch of Suratt's character as
it relates to his tenant farmer origins:

> So he resumed with no break that you could mark, with something in
> his face now of bemused retrospect, something of the warm and secret
> man himself—the son of a tanant farmer, a race existing in complete
> subjection not to modern exploitation but to an economic system stub-
> bornly moribund out of the dark ages themselves, who had escaped his
> birthright and into independence and even pride. [TS, p. 8]

So the essential character of the man is clearly defined even at this
early draft of the story. Although he comes from the same socio-
economic class as the Snopeses, the warm, secret, witty, and independent Suratt is the humane counterpart of the Snopeses, their
natural antagonist.

　　Since this frame contributes little to the central episode,
Faulkner wisely decided to omit it when the story was published in
Scribner's.[16] The published story is told by a nameless boy who records the antics of his nameless "Pap." Finally, in *The Hamlet,* the
story is returned to Suratt-Ratliff's folklore, but now Ratliff is the
neighbor boy who accompanies Ab Snopes during the horse swapping
fiasco. This use of Ratliff as a Snopes-watcher was concomitant with
the very inception of the Snopeses. Ratliff's wry narration establishes
the comic, distanced, and slightly ironic perspective on the antics of
the Snopeses so basic to the success of *The Hamlet.*

　　Since the episode is frequently closer to the unpublished typescript than to the published story, Faulkner probably returned to it
when rewriting for the novel.[17] Except for the shifts in point of view,
the fuller descriptive detail in the novel, and the innumerable alterations of diction and phrasing from version to version, the story remains

essentially the same. One noteworthy alteration, however, is that in the novel, Mrs. Snopes trades the cow for the milk separator. This minor change improves the credibility and heightens the humor. Since Pat Stamper will not trade back what he has already gained in a previous shrewd deal, it is extremely unlikely that "Mammy" could have succeeded in trading back the team for the separator, as she does in the earlier versions. Now she makes two trips to town, the second with the cow in Odum Tull's wagon. The repeated running through of the one gallon of milk in the separator is consequently more ironic and more humorous. Although she has no cow and only borrowed milk, she stubbornly has her separator and "it looks like she is fixing to get a heap of pleasure and satisfaction outen it" (H, p. 48).

The central incident of the third and final chapter of Book One finds its germ in "Lizards in Jamshyd's Courtyard." In fact, Faulkner incorporated both incidents of the short story, the goat deal and the planted money swindle, into the context of *The Hamlet,* but with considerable elaboration and modification. These two encounters between V. K. Suratt and Flem Snopes are strategically placed, the goat deal in Book One where Ratliff tests his cunning against Flem and loses, and the buried money fiasco as the final scene of the novel where he loses again and makes Flem's triumph over Frenchman's Bend complete. The extent of the complication that Faulkner introduces into these encounters is a measure of the shrewdness he attributes to both Ratliff and Flem, shrewdness the earlier Suratt does not share.

In the short story the goat deal is uncomplicated and shows little perspicacity on the part of either Suratt or Flem. Suratt purchased for twenty dollars a contract from a Northerner to supply a hundred head of goats. But when he went to buy the goats, he found out that Flem had beaten him to the purchase, not surprising since Suratt had indiscreetly talked about the deal in Varner's store. When Snopes buys the goat contract from him for twenty-one dollars, Suratt takes his one-dollar profit with the sardonic reflection, "Well, at least I ain't skunked."[18] Flem's opportunism is perfectly in character; if Suratt had any foresight, he would have expected as much.

Unlike Suratt, Ratliff is more concerned with outsmarting Flem than he is with monetary profits. He deliberately sets up the incident as a test of his cunning against Flem's, a test that he loses because he fails to allow sufficient latitude to Flem's ruthless exploitation of his own kin. The shrewd moves of both men, however, are a credit to their perceptive understanding of each other and to their trading skill, while the incident reveals the fundamentally different sense of values of each man.

First of all, Ratliff decides to undertake the contest with Flem only after some careful and perceptive watching of Flem's methods. The incident in the novel is contained within part two of the three-part chapter. Part one, devoted to Flem's encroaching entrepreneurship, describes Ratliff as a quiet observer. Furthermore, pragmatically and efficiently Ratliff through trades, sales, and debt-collecting remedies a situation in which "he had almost sold himself insolvent in his own bull market" (H, p. 55). By the time the goat contract is mentioned in part two, Ratliff is established as both an experienced Snopes-watcher and a shrewd and pragmatic businessman in his own right. Yet the repeated emphasis on Ratliff's recent illness that interlaces the development of the intricacies of the goat deal acts as ominous foreshadowing of Ratliff's dulled perception and cunning.

Ratliff discovers with a little research in the Chancery Clerk's office that Flem owns two hundred acres of land. He goes to look at the property and finds Mink Snopes name scrawled on the mailbox. On the pretense that he is delivering a sewing machine ordered by an unspecified Snopes, he sparks some revealing antagonism in Mink and his wife toward Flem. With a salesman's closing skill, Ratliff lets the antagonism and the circumstances lead Mink to the decision to keep the machine. To his surprise, however, he acquires two I.O.U. notes for which Flem is allegedly responsible. The first is a promissory note for twenty dollars in six months' time to which Mink cosigns Flem's name. The second, for the ten-dollar down payment, is a note Flem had given Ike Snopes three years earlier in exchange for his ten-dollar inheritance and which Mink had subsequently "bought." Not fooled by Ratliff's pretense ("I don't know what you are up to and I dont care. But you aint fooling me any more than I am fooling you" [H, p. 77]), Mink opportunistically seizes what profit and revenge he can out of the situation. Ratliff, for his part, is seemingly content with the opportunity to confront Flem that the notes offer.

Ratliff next reveals the details of his goat contract to the men in Varner's store. This scene parallels the one in the short story except for the important difference that Ratliff is setting up Flem, while Suratt is stupidly oblivious to Flem's alert ear. Ratliff is so sure of Flem's ear that he boldly sits with his back to the window so that he will not be able to watch Flem's exit to make a quick purchase of goats. Observing the reactions of the other men, he does not need to observe Flem himself. He is pleased with the development of his planned trap: "Because I believe I done it right. I had to trade not only on what I think he knows about me, but on what he must figure I know about him, as conditioned and restricted by that year of sickness and abstinence from the science and pastime of skullduggery. But it worked with Bookwright. He done all he could to warn me. He went as far and even further than a man can let his self go in another man's trade" (H, p. 83).

After waiting a sufficient time and then making the necessary futile gesture to purchase the fifty goats that Flem had already bought, Ratliff is ready for his encounter with Flem. Instead of selling his contract for a one-dollar profit to Flem as Suratt does, Ratliff pretends to bargain with Flem from his position as the apparent underdog: " 'You beat me,' Ratliff said. 'How much?' " (H, p. 85). After rejecting Flem's offer of fifty cents a head (which would leave him with no profit whatsoever, since he paid twenty-five cents for the contract and would get seventy-five cents a head for its fulfillment), Ratliff pulls out his first trump card, the first note. Flem, quick to perceive the situation, asks for a match to burn his bill of sale for the goats—so the goats become Ratliff's property. Then, Ratliff pulls out the other note and succeeds, at least, in stopping Flem's chewing jaw. But when Flem asks Ratliff to wait a minute while he goes out, Ratliff recognizes with horror his error: "Then something black blew in him, a suffocation, a sickness, a nausea. They should have told me! he cried to himself. Somebody should have told me! Then, remembering: Why, he did! Bookwright did tell me. He said Another one. It was because I have been sick, was slowed up, that I didn't—" (H, p. 86). Flem brings in his idiot kinsman, Ike. Ratliff realizes his dilemma: if he collects the note from Flem, he will use it again, and if Ratliff tries to give the money to Ike, Flem will take charge of it as Ike's guardian. Ratliff makes the only decision open to him; he asks Flem to burn the note. The incident reveals how well Flem understood his opponent. In bringing in Ike, Flem knew that Ratliff's humanitarian feelings would effect his decision to destroy the note. If Ratliff were purely opportunistic, it would not matter to him what Flem did with the note after it was returned to him, and he would not care that Ike was being used by his cousin. Flem knew that he would have these scruples and he is unscrupulous enough to use them for his own monetary profits.

Flem outsmarts Ratliff because his shrewdness is unadulter-
ated with even a trace of humanism. As Ratliff realizes: "I quit too
soon. I went as far as one Snopes will set fire to another Snopes's
barn and both Snopeses know it, and that was all right. But I stopped
there. I never went on to where that first Snopes will turn around and
stomp the fire out so he can sue that second Snopes for the reward
and both Snopeses know that too" (H, p. 89). When Ratliff assesses
the monetary damages of his deal, he takes his five-dollar profit
($37.50 for goats, minus $12.50 for the contract, minus $20.00 for
Flem's goats) and the ten dollars plus three years' interest on Flem's
promissory note to Ike and gives them to Mrs. Littlejohn to keep for
Ike. Ratliff's concern for justice, humanity, and decency takes prece-
dence over the profit motive. Beaten in the game of one-upmanship
with Flem, he stands yet in moral opposition to Flem's ruthless rapacity. In asking Mrs. Littlejohn to tell Varner "it aint been proved yet
neither" (H, p. 89), he ironically recognizes his defeat, but seems to
indicate with the "yet" that he will continue to try to outsmart Flem.

Unstopped by Ratliff, Flem in the final few pages of Book One
is shown to be continuing along his relentless rise, replacing Will
Varner as supervisor of the tenants' harvest and even more shock-
ingly as proprietor of the "flour barrel" chair on the porch of Old
Frenchman place, an ominous foreshadowing of his impending ownership of this crumbling property. The ownership is effected by the end
of Book Two, entitled "Eula," which is an expansion of a few paragraphs in "Father Abraham" to over fifty pages. In the original, Eula
is described as "a very popular girl" who attracts "one of the village
young bucks" and who, after this young man "sold his yellow
wheeled runabout and his matched horses, and departed for Texas"
(TS, pp. 6, 7), is married off to Flem Snopes and rushed off to Texas.
The flippant tone and the sketchy descriptive details of the original
are replaced in *The Hamlet* by the unrestrained, loving rhetorical
exuberance of the omniscient narrator who expounds upon Eula's
burgeoning "mammalian maturity" (H, p. 95). The descriptions of her
comically immobile childhood and adolescence in which she listens
"in sullen bemusement . . . to the enlarging of her own organs" (H,
p. 95); her brother's rage at her teeming and unabashed sexuality; her
encounter with the schoolteacher Labove whose "pagan triumphal
prostration before the supreme primal uterus" (H, p. 114) is met with
her priceless rebuff: "Stop pawing me . . . you old headless horse-

man Ichabod Crane" (H, p. 122); and her affair with McCarron whom she assists both by beating back with a whip the would-be protectors of her virginity and by helping her disabled lover to effect her deflowering are all absent from earlier accounts. Thematically, tonally, and symbolically, Faulkner is here adding an important dimension to the novel absent from the early Snopes stories. In fact, most of the major additions not drawn from earlier stories are related to this other core of the novel. For if Flem can be seen as the very embodiment of economic greed, Eula likewise is the incarnation of passionate life. These two basic human drives, money and sex, as other critics have also observed, account for most of the motivating drives in the characters of the novel.

The compelling force of sexuality is present not only in Book Two but also in Book Three "The Long Summer," which relates three interlinking, passionate, and ultimately unhappy affairs: Ike and the cow, Lucy Pate and Jack Houston, and Mink Snopes and his wife. Only one of these episodes,[19] that of Mink, finds its genesis in a story, and then Mink's tormenting passion for his wife is added to the novel. His passion is not the only humanizing trait that makes him an anomaly in his family. Some of these differences can be traced to his evolution from a non-Snopesian character, Ernest Cotton, who murders Jack Houston in "The Hound."[20] Refashioned, this story becomes part of the extended treatment of Mink Snopes's murder of Houston in *The Hamlet* (H, pp. 221–63). Where the short story focuses narrowly upon the complications of getting rid of Houston's body created by its rigor mortis and by Houston's loyal hound, the novel version extends forward and backward in time from the crime, including in its scope Mink's and even Houston's history.

"The Hound," taut, dramatic, and moving, shows Faulkner at his story-telling best. As is so frequent in several of Faulkner's better short pieces, the story begins with the climax that disrupts the life of the protagonist, and the rest of the story traces the reverberations of that incident upon his life. In this case the climax is, of course, Ernest Cotton's killing of Jack Houston. Part one begins with that fatal shot and outlines briefly Cotton's stunned reaction. Part two catalogues the aftermath of the murder where Cotton returns home only to discover that Houston's howling dog acts as a nemesis disturbing his sleep and forcing him out to attempt to quell the dog. Part three centers on a scene in Varner's store where Cotton attempts to remain composed and unsuspected as men discuss Houston's disappearance. After the store interlude, Cotton returns home only to be obsessed again by the howling dog. He goes out, fires at it, and returns home to his sleepless vigil. In part four he denies possession of a gun which the clerk Snopes questions him about and discovers upon returning home that buzzards are circling the sky. That evening he goes to the rotten tree where he has buried the body and attempts to dump it in the river, but his job is compounded by the rigor mortis of the body and the aggression of Houston's incorrigible hound. He manages to free the body and fight off the dog, but when he throws the body in the stream, he discovers it has only three limbs. When he goes back to get the dismembered arm, he is arrested by the sheriff. Finally, the last part of the story depicts the long journey to the jail, including Cotton's foiled attempt to commit suicide. The story ends with Cotton's dismay in jail that they are "going to feed them niggers before they feed a white man."

Although Faulkner retains much of the same basic outline when incorporating this story into *The Hamlet,* the episode is expanded with fuller descriptive detail, flashbacks, and the introduction of new significant characters, including Mink's wife and Lump Snopes. The episode still begins with the fatal shot, but the preceding chapter has depicted the sad and tragic life and love of Houston. So the cardboard figure of pride and arrogance, who is briefly sketched by Cotton, becomes a fully developed human being in *The Hamlet,* compounding our reaction to the characters and events. As a matter of fact, the metamorphosis of the relatively simple and uncomplicated life and character of Ernest Cotton into that of the complex Mink Snopes accounts for much of the difference between the two versions.

The different nature of the two protagonists is signaled by the way each reacts to his role as murderer. Where Cotton has to fight the overwhelming urge to run, Mink would like to gloat and publicize his self-vindication: "It was no blind, instinctive, and furious desire for flight which he had to combat and curb. On the contrary. What he would have liked to do would be to leave a printed placard on the breast itself: *This is what happens to the men who impound Mink Snopes's cattle,* with his name signed to it. But he could not, and here again, for the third time since he had pulled the trigger, was that conspiracy to frustrate and outrage his rights as a man and his feelings as a sentient creature" (H, p. 222). Much more than Cotton, Mink is a man who feels put upon by people and circumstance. The altercation with Houston is the culmination of a series of affronts, insults, and injustices that he has suffered, and he responds to his crime without the slightest remorse or faintheartedness. Much of his frustration stems from his poverty.

Where Cotton is a bachelor who is poor but not destitute, Mink is married with two children, and evidence and reminders of his dire poverty are omnipresent; they exacerbate Mink's feelings that he is victim of forces "leagued against him . . . in the vindication of his rights and the liquidation of his injuries" (H, p. 221). Where Cotton's living accommodations are summarily treated: "He lived in a chinked log cabin floored with clay on the edge of the bottom, four miles away" (TH, p. 266), Mink's oppressive poverty, developed in detail, is made more poignant by being filtered through Mink's consciousness:

> He emerged from the bottom and looked up the slope of his meagre and sorry corn and saw it—the paintless two-room cabin with an open hall-way between and a lean-to kitchen, which was not his, on which he paid rent but not taxes, paying almost as much in rent in one year as the house had cost to build; not old, yet the roof of which already leaked and the weather-stripping had already begun to rot away from the wall planks and which was just like the one he had been born in which had not belonged to his father either, and just like the one he would die in if he died indoors. [H, pp. 222–23].

Where Cotton appears to own his cabin, Mink's frustrations are intensified by the conviction that his cousin Flem owns his shack. Where Cotton has food to eat and money to buy more groceries, Mink eats cold peas and then sustains himself on raw meal and hot water sweetened with sugar. Where Cotton's solitary existence is uncomplicated, Mink's passionate but joyless marriage contributes to his feeling of being driven, affronted, and denied his equal rights. His first sexual experience with his wife made a monogamist of him forever, yet Mink is haunted "by the loud soundless invisible shades of the nameless and numberless men" from her promiscuous past (H, p. 225). Mink's attraction to his wife is "like drink. It's like dope to me" (H, p. 225), yet he beats her and sends her from the house. She declares that she relishes the thought of seeing him hanged, yet she desperately tries to give him money and to aid his escape.

The motivation for Cotton's crime is relatively simple. Although his reaction is extreme, his anger is justifiable and understandable. Houston's hog has wandered on his property. Cotton penned it up and tried to find the owner. Only after he had wintered it on his corn did Houston show up to claim the hog. Although the ensuing court settlement required that Houston pay Cotton for wintering it plus a pound fee of one dollar, he is enraged at the inadequacy of the dollar compensation for his troubles. The wealth and arrogance of Houston contributes to his outrage: "Swelling around like he was the biggest man in the county. Setting that ere dog on folks' stock. . . . A dog that et better than me. I work, and eat worse than his dog" (TH, p. 269). Mink's gripe against Houston has less claim to legitimacy. Now the head of livestock is a "scrub yearling" belonging to Mink who lets Houston pasture and feed it all winter and then tries to claim it. Since Houston will not let him have the bull, Mink takes him to court where he is told that he can have the animal when he pays Houston three dollars pasturage. In other words, where Cotton has a justifiable complaint, Mink is trying to get something for nothing. Only his distorted view of the world allows him to see Houston, the court, his kinsman, his wife, his size, the land, and the weather, indeed all circumstances in a conspiracy leagued against him. While the conflict of the story is focused upon sharply drawn class lines, in the novel Mink sees himself in a cosmic fight against a hostile world which would deny him justice and personal dignity.

Mink is no ordinary Snopes. Indeed, Ratliff clarifies his difference from the Snopes clan when he claims that Mink is "the only out-and-out mean Snopes" with "no profit consideration or hope at-all."[21] Just how far Mink is from generic Snopesism is illustrated in his sharp contrast with Lump Snopes, the clerk of Varner's store. Although an unspecified Snopes also appears as the clerk in "The Hound," his role is minimal. In the novel, Lump has a major role in the action providing, as "normal" Snopes usually do, a humorous view of unmitigated avarice. He gladly becomes an accomplice to the crime, making up a story about the gun to cover for Mink, in order to share in the assumed spoils. He is absolutely amazed that Mink has not even checked the body for the fifty dollars that he is sure Houston was carrying on the day of the murder. He frantically trails his cousin and even consents to a five-hour game of checkers in the vain hope that he will win the fifty dollars a nickel at a time! Then he is afraid that he should have been losing or Mink will never show him where the body is, so he reverses his tactics. Mink is driven to knocking him out to prevent him from following him. Even after he has been knocked out and tied up, Lump lies again to the sheriff, establishing an alibi for Mink in his incorrigible hope for a share of the money. Only by knocking him out a second time does Mink finally manage to get to the body by himself.

So with Lump as a Snopesian norm, Mink appears distinctly unSnopesian. Rather than the profit motive, he is moved by such abstract principles as honor, pride, dignity, and self-vindication. Just as the sympathetic rendering of Ab Snopes in "Fool About a Horse" is somewhat at odds with the categorically unsympathetic treatment of the Snopeses in *The Hamlet*, so too Mink's distorted pursuit of justice and personal dignity makes him an anomaly in his amoral, thick-skinned, and mercenary family. Both of these aberrations from the Snopesian norm are created by grafting non-Snopes stories into the structure of *The Hamlet*. One could simply credit these seeming inconsistencies to Faulkner's failure to assimilate the two stories totally into the Snopes chronicle. But as the eventual instrument of the demise of Snopesism, that is, as the eventual murderer of Flem, Mink is a special Snopes and the evolution of this character from Ernest Cotton to the gutsy and steadfast old man of *The Mansion* reveals a great deal about Faulkner's evolving design for the trilogy. In *The Hamlet* Mink is mean; he has exaggerated and distorted the forces conspiring against him. His tense, humorless, vicious, vengeful, and unloving over-reaction to life's inequities and injustices is antithetical to the light-hearted, humanistic, and sympathetic tone that infuses *The Hamlet*. Yet, it is not difficult to see how Mink eventually becomes the sympathetic old man of *The Mansion* who ironically earns his right to be a "champion" by murdering his kinsman. Faulkner frequently displays sympathy for the down-and-outs, the people who are driven to dire extremes to vindicate themselves for injustices and indignities imposed upon them. Mink has two qualities that Faulkner ranks high: the ability to endure and pride in himself. Just as the denied love of the Snopes family flowers in misshapen and pathetic form in the person of Ike, an idiot who falls in love with a cow, so too the Snopesian denial of the dictates of abstract moral principles takes grotesque form in the fanatical seeker of justice, Mink. It is appropriate to the moral pattern of the trilogy that Snopesism is destroyed from within by its own exploitative inhumanity. Because Flem acted unlovingly toward Mink, Mink becomes Flem's destructive nemesis. While Mink has exaggerated and distorted Flem's responsibility for his situation, yet Flem has failed to respond compassionately and humanely to his cousin, and for this failure, he is destroyed. Apparently forseeing Mink's role in the total design of the Snopes saga, Faulkner prepares for Mink's eventual act of revenge against Flem while simultaneously weaving Mink's story into the fabric of *The Hamlet*. Early in the novel Ratliff's ploy with the sewing machine reveals Mink's envious hostility toward Flem and frustrated expectations of kinship. Later in an epilogue to the Mink-Houston episode, Mink tediously waits in jail for assistance from his kinsman through the long fall and winter of Flem's Texas sojourn. Finally near the end of the novel—in his indomitable expectation of kinship from his unloving cousin—he watches futilely and constantly the rear of the courtroom while his trial and sentencing take place.

Mink is not the only character whose revenge against Flem is unassuaged by the end of *The Hamlet*. He is joined by a good share of the Frenchman's Bend "peasants," including Ratliff. The final book of the novel, "The Peasants," is centered on two incidents which originated in earlier stories, the sale of the spotted horses and of the Old Frenchman place. In the first, Flem dupes the local residents; in the second, he crowns his success with the addition of V. K. Ratliff.

Incompletely told in "Father Abraham," spotted horses is the earliest Snopes tale. It has a complicated history of titles and versions—as least seven different versions (with uncountable drafts of each) and six different titles[22]—before it found its most successful form and place in *The Hamlet*. With faith in the perpetual elasticity of his stories, Faulkner expanded and contracted them to suit his purposes. But contraction, I contend, is less characteristic of his method and less conducive to successful results. Faulkner's several efforts to carve out a publishable spotted horses story from the long and unfinished "Father Abraham" were notable failures.

Faulkner's apparently earliest effort to reshape "Father Abraham" for short story publication was "Abraham's Children."[23] This story is very similar in many respects—especially tone and language—to "Father Abraham" (in fact, at one point Faulkner merely renumbered pages from the "Father Abraham" typescript and inserted them into the new story),[24] but he was obviously attempting to prune the story both by condensing the initial background data about Flem and his relationship with Frenchman's Bend, and by deleting some of the florid rhetoric of the original. Another major difference is the deleting in the latter typescript of the Henry Armstid story.[25] In "Abraham's Children" a man named Henry bids on the horses, but all further references to him are dropped so that we no longer have his wife's pleading, the return of his money by Buck and Flem's expropriation of it, his disastrous attempt to catch his horse and the subsequent broken leg, Suratt's chiding of Flem about the Armstids, and Mrs. Armstid's meek attempt to regain the five dollars from Flem, which is met with Flem's offer of five cents' worth of "sweetening for the chaps." This version ends rather with Jody Varner violently ejecting the hulking boy "Cla'ence" from behind the candy counter. I think that Faulkner was attempting to focus exclusively upon the comic oddity of the Snopeses and their antics and to play down the more serious implications of Flem's behavior. Now less about "father" Abraham, Flem, and more about his "children," the story is weakened rather than improved by such a diminishing of Flem's role and of the moral implications of his behavior. Faulkner apparently came to this conclusion because all of the later versions give Henry Armstid's predicament prominent focus.

Very interestingly Faulkner titled two other versions of the spotted horses story "As I Lay Dying." Although the story has earlier claim to the title than does the novel of the same name,[26] it is hard to guess what connection Faulkner saw between it and the spotted horses episode. Joseph Blotner claims that Faulkner identified the source of the title as ghostly Agamemnon's speech to Odysseus in the eleventh book of *The Odyssey*: "As I lay dying the woman with the dog's eyes would not close my eyelids for me as I descended into Hades."[27] No one in the spotted horses story is dying or dead (Henry Armstid is even less likely to die from his broken leg than Cash in *As I Lay Dying*[28]), although the lack of compassion that Agamemnon laments in the woman with the dog's eyes is paralleled in Flem's behavior toward the Armstids. Perhaps it is wisest to concede that Faulkner's eclectic choice of titles at times seems merely whimsical and defies ready explanation.

One form of the "As I Lay Dying" story, a seventeen-page complete typescript, is told entirely through dialogue in poor white dialect with no authorial commentary whatsoever. In fact, some ambiguity exists at times as to who exactly is speaking. The story begins with Suratt's coming to town. He and the local residents quip back and forth (sample: "Whut you hitchin whar we spittin fer, V. K.?" [TS, p. 204]), and reminisce upon the sale of the spotted horses. Suratt dwells upon the gullibility of the townfolks, relates his encounter with the horse in the house, and elaborates upon the predicament of Henry Armstid. Flem is silent throughout the scene ("settin in his cheer in the do' " [TS, p. 204]) except for a single disclaimer ("Twarn't none of my hosses" [TS, p. 210]). It is I. O. who assumes the role of Flem's defender: "Henery Armstid's a bawn fool. Always was. I haint no patience with a fool" (TS, p. 215). The story ends with Mrs. Armstid's request for her five dollars, Flem's five-cent gift of candy, and Suratt's final commentary: "Well, long's she owns a spotted hoss and a sack of candy, she wont need no shoes. I bet Flem could buy that hoss back from her fer a bottle of snuff too" (TS, p. 220). Although the dialogue achieves moments of humor and verisimilitude, the spotted horses story suffers loss of immediacy from the narration of reminiscence. Similarly, the other version of "As I Lay Dying" also suffers from second-hand narration.

This version, a twenty-two page complete typescript, narrated in the first person by an unidentified boy, is radically different in tone and language. The boy, self-consciously a "citified" outsider in this country town, is at times whimsically imaginative (and one might add unconvincingly so). For example, when he and his uncle (a judge on a "quadriennial vote-garnering itinerary" [TS, p. 3], who might be an early version of Gavin Stevens) confront a wild mustang, one of the spotted horses, on the road, he describes it as follows: "It looked like a goblin, like something unbelievable out of a nightmare; between the rearing lunge of our team I had a flying picture of something resembling a patchwork quilt in a cyclone or a Fourth of July pinwheel seen by daylight and magnified out of all reason and outraging very credibility" (TS, p. 1). The two had heard of the horse sale fiasco which had taken place four days earlier from a farmer they had stayed with on route. Now upon entering Frenchmen's Bend, they learn more from Suratt and the men gathered in Varner's store. Needless to say, the story suffers loss of immediacy from the complicated method of narration and the additional superfluous frame characters.

Yet another rendition of the story (a sixteen-page complete typescript), "Aria Con Amore," also has a seemingly inappropriate title because the story is most decidedly neither a song nor about love. Narrated in the first person by Suratt, it is closer to the version eventually published as "Spotted Horses" than the others, but still very different. It begins with the discussion between Mrs. Littlejohn and Mrs. Armstid, as they wash dishes, about the five dollars Flem owes the latter. Here, through Suratt's narration both to the men gathered in Varner's store and more generally to the reader is a fuller treatment of the actual auction, of Henry's bidding, and of Flem's expropriation of the money than in the other attenuated versions.

The inevitable conclusion from the perusal of Faulkner's unsuccessful attempts to make the spotted horses episode a publishable short story is that the effort weakens the artistry of the original. In my opinion Faulkner was more skillful when he used his craftsmanship to expand and enrich, not to condense and contract. It was detrimental to the spirit, tone, language, and characterization of the original "Father Abraham" story to make a brief short story from the episode. In fact, in the version titled "Spotted Horses" that was finally published, Faulkner condenses much of that larger story into a few sentences. Only with the stories like "Spotted Horses" can I agree with Alfred Kazin's claim that Faulkner's interest in "folks" sometimes "gets too big for the mold to which stories are fitted."[29] In "Spotted Horses" Suratt does not tell us only about the sale of spotted horses, but he briefly sketches Flem's family background and his rise to prominence as Varner's clerk; tells of Eula Varner and her popularity, of her quick marriage to Flem, and of their exit to Texas; and wryly comments upon the size of their child.[30] While "Father Abraham" also has a wide-ranging scope, it is a long story, whereas "Spotted Horses" is a comparatively short short story encompassing much of the Snopes saga; in descriptive detail it is disappointingly sparse.

What makes both the "Father Abraham" and *The Hamlet* versions of the episode (H, pp. 275–326) so delightful is the creation of an almost surrealistic world of madness, motion, disorder, and enchantment. A whimsical description of fecund springtime, a full moon, and an idyllically untroubled countryside serves as a mood-setting prelude to the spotted horses episode in "Father Abraham":

> Then it turned April. Peach and pear and apple bloomed yet, and blackbirds swung and stooped with raucous cries like rusty shutters in the wind, and like random scraps of burned paper, slanted across the fields and the new-fledged willow-screens beyond which waters chucked and murmured with the grave and endless irrelevance of children; and behind surging horses and mules men broke the land anew and the turned earth smelled darkly rich and sweet like new calves in a clean barn, and sowed it; and nightly the new moon stood longer and longer in the windless west and soon by day stood, yet incomplete, in the marbled zenith.
>
> Thus the world, and on a day Flem drove up the road in a covered wagon, accompanied by a soiled swaggering man in a clay-colored Stetson hat. [TS, p. 12]

As the duping proceeds, the omniscient narrator repeatedly sketches a dreamlike atmosphere created by the full moon and the strange horses and punctuated by the ironically appropriate cry of a lone mockingbird:

> The houses were all dark by this hour, and soon the last straggler had betaken his shadow away through the silver dust, and there was no sound anywhere save a sorrowful occasional dog down the valley or in the fixed far hills, and the mockingbird's senseless silver reiteration from the dreaming apple tree, and at intervals an abrupt squeal or a thudding muffled blow from the livery stable lot. [TS, pp. 20–21]

In *The Hamlet,* even more attention is given to this atmosphere, and the diction is elevated:

> The moon was almost full then. When supper was over and they had gathered again along the veranda, the alteration was hardly one of visibility even. It was merely a translation from the lapidary-dimensional of the day to the treacherous and silver receptivity in which the horses huddled in mazy camouflage, or singly or in pairs rushed, fluid, phantom, and unceasing, to huddle again in mirage-like clumps from which came high abrupt squeals and the vicious thudding of hooves. [H, p. 280]

Later, the omniscient narrator of "Father Abraham" describes how the "pearly" quality of the night reduces the horses to "stamping shapes":

> Evening was completely accomplished. The sparrows had retired, the final cloud of swallows had swirled into a chimney somewhere, and the ultimate celestial edges of the world rolled on into vague and intricate subtleties of softest pearl. The apple tree was a ghost in pearl also, gustily and hauntingly sweet, and the horses tethered beneath it and beneath the locust trees were stamping shapes without bulk or emphasis. [TS, pp. 45–46]

The description in the novel is less whimsical but more precise in defining the strangely unreal quality of the night and the strangely disemboweled appearance of the spotted horses:

> And now night had completely come. The light itself had not changed so much; if anything, it was brighter but with that other-worldly quality of moonlight, so that when they stood once more looking into the lot, the splotchy bodies of the ponies had a distinctness, almost a brilliance, but without individual shape and without depth—no longer

horses, no longer flesh and bone directed by a principle capable of calculated violence, no longer inherent with the capacity to hurt and harm. [H, p. 304]

Because of Suratt's narration and the condensing of "Spotted Horses," such descriptive passages are entirely omitted from the short story, and the special fantasy-world of the original story is lost. Suratt mentions the full moon and the surging ponies all right, but his conversational diction and folksy metaphors create an entirely different effect:

> You-all mind the moon was nigh full that night, and we could watch them spotted varmints swirling along the fence and back and forth across the lot same as minnows in a pond. And then now and then they would all kind of huddle up against the barn and rest themselves by biting and kicking one another. We would hear a squeal, and then a set of hoofs would go Bam! against the barn, like a pistol. It sounded just like a fellow with a pistol, in a nest of cattymounts, taking his time. [SH, p. 587]

Even this kind of description is limited; Suratt concentrates almost exclusively on the human drama being enacted. Even so, some of the best scenes and most vivid characters are so summarily treated in the short story that they lose much of their effectiveness. Some of the most noticeable and detrimental condensing has to do with the horse-selling dude, Buck. Slightly characterized, Buck is little more than functional in "Spotted Horses," and several amusing scenes involving him are reduced to cryptic summary. For example, Suratt tells of Buck's bravado with the ponies which resulted in a severed vest ("when that Texas man got down offen the wagon and walked up to them to show how gentle they was, one of them cut his vest clean offen him, same as with a razor" [SH, p. 586]), but the scene is shown in vivid detail in both "Father Abraham" and the novel, and the humor in the latter is spiced by Quick's wry comment:

> "Them's good, gentle ponies," the stranger said. "Watch now." He put the carton back into his pocket and approached the horses, his hand extended. The nearest one was standing on three legs now. It appeared to be asleep. Its eyelids drooped over the cerulean eye; its head was shaped like an ironingboard. Without even raising the eyelid it flicked its head, the yellow teeth cropped. For an instant it and the man appeared to be inextricable in one violence. Then they became motionless, the stranger's high heels dug into the earth, one hand gripping the animal's nostrils, holding the horse's head wrenched half around while

it breathed in hoarse, smothered groans. "See?" the stranger said in a panting voice, the veins standing white and rigid in his neck and along his jaw. "See? All you got to do is handle them a little and work hell out of them for a couple of days. Now look out. Give me room back there." They gave back a little. The stranger gathered himself then sprang away. As he did so, a second horse slashed at his back, severing his vest from collar to hem down the back exactly as the trick swordsman severs a floating veil with one stroke.

"Sho now," Quick said. "But suppose a man dont happen to own a vest." [H, p. 277]

The transfer of the ponies from the wagon to the lot involves several pages in both "Father Abraham" and *The Hamlet* and includes some extremely amusing description, for example, that which depicts Buck's skillful and lucky dexterity while the freed horses madly slam into the fence (H, p. 279). This scene in the short story is condensed into a few words which fail to evoke any of the humor of the original (SH, p. 587).

Where Buck is individualized in "Spotted Horses" so slightly as to be a rather indistinct stereotype of the Texan, in "Father Abraham" he is a good-natured, pleasantly conversational, relaxed man who skillfully exhorts the locals to buy his horses. In the novel, however, he is less amiable and more obviously manipulative, hard, and shrewd. While in "Father Abraham" he roves "his hearty inviting eye from one grave face to another" (TS, p. 22), in *The Hamlet* "when he look directly at anyone, his eyes became like two pieces of flint turned suddenly up in dug earth" (H. p. 276). In the novel he is successfully unresponsive to all leading questions. When Freeman asks him if he is going to wait for Flem, he responds: "Why? . . . There was nothing, no alteration, in the Texan's voice" (H, p. 289). When someone asks him about the horse that cut off his vest, "the Texan looked toward the sound, bleak and unwinking. 'What about it?' he said. The laughter, if it had been laughter, ceased" (H, p. 290). Even his humor is not really funny in this serious business of selling: " 'Naturally they got spirit; I aint selling crowbait. Besides, who'd want Texas crowbait anyway, with Mississippi full of it?' His stare was still absent and unwinking; there was no mirth or humor in his voice and there was neither mirth nor humor in the single guffaw which came from the rear of the group" (H, p. 289). The change in Buck can be traced to another unpublished version of the spotted horses story, "The Peasants."[31] This fifty-nine page typescript was apparently Faulkner's relatively late attempt at a more leisurely rendition of the episode as an isolated story, and it includes a more realistic, less whimsical presentation of other characters as well as Buck.[32] *The Hamlet,* in my opinion, is a successful, selective fusion of the realism of "The Peasants" version with the pastoral lyricism of "Father Abraham." Perhaps Faulkner decided that any partner of Flem Snopes, however transient, would have to be "harsh, ready, forensic" (H, p. 290) rather than cheerful and pleasant. This change is in keeping with the more serious ramifications of trading in *The Hamlet.*

Moreover, the scene between Flem and Buck after the sale is entirely rewritten for the novel. Where Buck trades two horses for a wagon to make his exit from Frenchman's Bend in "Father Abraham" and in "Spotted Horses," the buggy is apparently part of the prearranged deal in *The Hamlet.* The buggy, however, "was the one with the glittering wheels and the fringed parasol top," a buggy which occasions several sarcastic retorts by the Texan: "Only I ought to have a powder puff or at least a mandolin to ride it with" (H, p. 302). Also added to this scene is Flem's decision to ride as far as Varner's store with Buck. Flem's actions give the locals further opportunity to speculate upon his part in the shady deal, and their assumption that Flem will demand most of the money is expressed in sardonic reflection: " 'He'll be lighter when he get there,' Freeman said. . . . 'Yes,' Bookwright said. 'His pockets wont rattle' " (H, p. 303). So, not only is Buck more coldly professional and more slick but Flem's manipulation of Buck is also more evident. The inclusion of the final remarks by the local residents underscores growing appreciation in Frenchman's Bend of the limitless aplomb of Flem's mercenary opportunism.

Suratt-Ratliff's activities in all versions are essentially the same. He will have nothing to do with the spotted horses and chides the people of Frenchman's Bend for their gullibility. In all versions he has the humorous encounter with the horse in Mrs. Littlejohn's boarding house. But Ratliff of the novel is more disdainful of the horse trading and more subtle and effective in his confrontations with and implicit condemnation of Flem than Suratt of the stories. The most substantial addition in the novel to the original "Father Abraham" version is a four-page passage (H, pp. 280ff.) which relates some sarcastic comments of Ratliff as he expounds upon Flem's probable role in the horse trade, chides the other men for their gullibility, and listens silently to their conversation as they talk themselves into the duping:

Ratliff, invisible in the shadow against the wall, made a sound, harsh,
sardonic, not loud.

"Ratliff's laughing," a fourth said.

"Dont mind me," Ratliff said. The three speakers had not
moved. They did not move now, yet there seemed to gather about the
three silhouettes something stubborn, convinced, and passive, like children who have been chidden. [H, pp. 281–82]

Ratliff's wry commentary and disapproving detachment underscore
the threat that he sees in Flem's easily engineered duping of the
villagers: "A fellow can dodge a Snopes if he just starts lively
enough. In fact, I dont believe he would have to pass more than two
folks before he would have another victim intervened betwixt them.
You folks aint going to buy them things sho enough, are you?" (H,
p. 281).

"Spotted Horses" does not display this clear separation of
Ratliff from the local residents that is sketched in "Father Abraham"
and developed in *The Hamlet*. His narration of "Spotted Horses"
decidedly weakens both the separation of Suratt-Ratliff from the
townspeople and the opposition of Flem and V. K. The loss of Suratt's folksy diction is lamented by Watkins and Young,[33] but they fail
to observe that the first person point of view is inappropriate for
Ratliff's role as the subtle and inscrutable opponent of Flem in the
novel. Since Suratt presents himself as a shrewd trader as well, he
cannot help but be sardonically envious of the superior business acumen of Flem: "Why, that fellow could make a nickel where it wasn't
but four cents to begin with. He skun me in two trades, myself, and
the fellow that can do that, I just hope he'll get rich before I do; that's
all" (SH, p. 586). Even though his sarcasm frequently implies disapproval of Flem's methods, he hardly presents himself as a moral
opponent to Flem's opportunism as Ratliff does.

The most revealing scene highlighting the difference between
Suratt and Ratliff is the final one in which several people are
gathered together in Varner's store. Lump Snopes replaces I. O.
Snopes of the short story as clerk of the store, and he is much more
defensive about his cousin's behavior. Lump is no match for Ratliff
who traps him into an admission that Flem owned the horses (H,
p. 315). Whereas Flem is in the store through the entire scene in
"Spotted Horses," in the novel he comes in during Ratliff's ironic
monologue about the losses of Eck and Henry Armstid, giving Ratliff an opportunity to demonstrate his imperturbable composure:

"He ceased, though he said, 'Morning Flem,' so immediately afterward and with no change whatever in tone, that the pause was not even discernible" (H, p. 316).

Suratt good-humoredly chides Flem: "Flem's done skun all of us so much . . . that we're proud of him. Come on, Flem . . . How much did you and that Texas man make offen them horses?" (SH, p. 595). In the novel, in contrast, it is Lump who attempts to initiate an altercation between the men: "You're just in time . . . Ratliff here seems to be in a considerable sweat about who actually owned them horses" (H, p. 316). In fact, Ratliff fails to confront Flem directly at all. Rather, he subtly implicates Flem in damages that resulted from the horse fiasco by ironically disclaiming Flem's responsibility: " 'Of course there's Mrs Tull,' Ratliff said. 'But that's Eck she's going to sue for damaging Tull against that bridge. And as for Henry Armstid—' " (H, p. 317). Lump's heated response to this insinuation, "If a man aint got gumption enough to protect himself, it's his own look-out," is a variant on a sarcastic remark made by Suratt himself (SH, p. 595). The transfer of this remark to Lump gives Ratliff the opportunity to agree in a "dreamy, abstracted tone" where he seems to dismiss Henry's damages as he in fact underscores them: "And as for that broke leg, that wont put him out none because his wife can make his crop" (H, p. 318). He implies that the Armstids are lazy, provoking a rebuttal by one of the other men in the store. In other words, he cleverly involves the others in a defense of Henry so that his duping is made more inhumane, an underhanded blow to a man already hard pressed by circumstances and bad luck. His indirect incrimination of Flem gets bolder and bolder as his narration proceeds ("this country [is] still more or less full of them uncaught horses that never belonged to Flem Snopes" [H, p. 319]).

Ratliff's refusal to confront Flem directly with the sarcastic accusations of Suratt prevents the bald denials of Flem from establishing his superior control. With his ironic detachment, Ratliff is as cool as Flem. Any admiration that Suratt, the trader, grudgingly gives to the super-trader, Flem, is erased from Ratliff's ironic commentary. Ratliff concentrates more upon the inhumanity of Flem than he does on the monetary profits he has made. Much more than Suratt, Ratliff is a humanist concerned with the moral implications of Flem's actions. Later, when Bookwright asks him if he gave Henry Armstid his lost five dollars, Ratliff's moral outrage and frustration break through: "I could have . . . But I didn't. . . . I never made them Snopeses and I never made the folks that cant wait to bare their backsides to them. I could do more, but I wont. I wont, I tell you!" (H, p. 326). How different this remark is from Suratt's final word on this subject in "Spotted Horses" where he sarcastically recognizes that Flem's sheer nerve outclasses his own trading skill: "I be dog if he ain't [a sight]. If I had brung a herd of wild cattymounts into town and sold them to my neighbors and kinfolks, they would have lynched me. Yes, sir" (SH, p. 597). The humor of the incident is modified by Ratliff's keen cognizance of the moral implications of Flem's behavior.

Because Faulkner has carefully developed and nurtured the opposition of Flem and Ratliff in the revisions of stories incorporated into *The Hamlet* and pitted the humane outlook of Ratliff against the cold greed of Flem, it is shocking and disappointing that Ratliff could be taken in by the lure of buried money and by Flem's none-too-subtle plant as he is in the final episode of the novel. Nevertheless, as the goat deal in "Lizards in Jamshyd's Courtyard" foreshadows Suratt's ultimate demise, just so it does for Ratliff in *The Hamlet*. Ratliff is humane, but he is also human and therefore vulnerable. Flem's inhumanity makes him a superior opponent. Ratliff's guilty involvement is essential to the novel's moral pattern; Flem's cold-blooded progress exploits the greed and weakness of others. The inclusion of Ratliff in the company of those duped makes Flem's success total. But although he is duped, Ratliff is much less a fool than Suratt.

In "Lizards in Jamshyd's Courtyard" Suratt's "peasant's mind" rather simplistically and illogically insists upon the actuality of the buried treasure at Old Frenchman place: "Folks wouldn't keep on digging for it if it wasn't there somewhere. It wouldn't be right to keep on letting them. No, sir" (L, p. 52). Ratliff is less moved by a sense of "rightness" than he is by the evidence for the existence of the buried money. Even the skeptical Bookwright is convinced by Ratliff's logical and reasonable conjecture, especially since Ratliff expresses some reluctance to involve Bookwright (H, p. 341). Where Suratt discovers Flem's digging and devotes four nights without sleep (to Armstid and Tull's two nights) to the venture, in the novel Henry Armstid initiates the midnight forays two weeks earlier. In fact, much of Suratt's urgency and frenzy is transferred to Armstid, making Ratliff much more restrained and thoughtful about his participation in this undertaking.

Since Ratliff does not waste his time on fruitless sarcasm, confrontations with Flem in the short story are either moderated or omitted in the revision. Suratt blurts out his erroneous suppositions to Flem in exaggerated sarcasm: " 'Flem,' he said, 'you sholy ain't going to unload that Old Frenchman place on a poor fellow like Eustace Grimm? Boys, we hadn't ought to stand for it' " (L, p. 57). Ratliff learns more through greater subtlety and indirection, although he like Suratt misconstrues what he learns. The sole meeting between Flem and Ratliff over this incident takes place on the road between Frenchman's Bend and Varner's place. Ratliff goes out to trade with Flem and makes no attempt to disguise the fact. Suratt, in contrast, tries to pretend that only the apparent interest of Eustace Grimm in the property inspires his own interest. That there is much less pretense between the two men in the novel is indicative of their mutual understanding and intelligence. Where Suratt carries out the pretense that he wants a place to settle down, Ratliff volunters no explanations. When Flem asks him what he wants with the land, Ratliff replies, "To start a goat-ranch . . . How much?" (H, p. 361). Both men realize the irony of this remark; not only is it a reference to Flem's duping of Ratliff in the past, but it is the equivalent of saying that's *my* business.

In both versions, Suratt-Ratliff fights the other two men for shovels as the men hastily dig for the treasure. Yet, Ratliff belatedly gains some perspective on his actions that causes him to shudder at his own greed: "Then Ratliff seemed to realize what he was doing. He released the shovel; he almost hurled it at Bookwright. 'Take it,' he said. He drew a long shuddering breath. 'God,' he whispered. 'Just look at what even the money a man aint got yet will do to him' " (H, p. 349). Unlike Suratt, Ratliff maintains some dignity and control.

One final way that Ratliff retains more stature than Suratt is in his realization of the swindle. In the story Vernon Tull speculates about Grimm's kinship to the Snopeses, and neither he nor Suratt reaches any immediate conclusions about it. In contrast, Ratliff is troubled by a "clicking" in his mind (H, p. 357) about Grimm's lineage. When he asks Bookwright about it he learns that "Eustace's ma was Ab Snopes's youngest sister" (H, p. 367); he realizes immediately the duping and goes off to examine the money and to laugh at their gullibility. The opposition of Ratliff and Flem is underscored at the end of the novel by a spectator of Henry Armstid's solitary dig-

ging: "Anybody might have fooled Henry Armstid. But couldn't nobody but Flem Snopes have fooled Ratliff" (H, p. 372). Although a
similar remark is made about Suratt, undoubtedly it is more true of
Ratliff. In Faulkner's revisions Suratt, the shrewd trader, becomes
Ratliff, the intellectual and moral opponent of Snopesism. Although
Faulkner claimed that he changed Suratt's name to Ratliff merely to
avoid confusing the character with an actual person,[34] he need not be
taken at his word. Whether or not Faulkner was consciously aware of
the transformation, Ratliff is very different from Suratt. In fact, perhaps the most significant aspect of Faulkner's revisions of these early
stories when incorporating them into *The Hamlet* was the increased
emphasis on the opposition of Flem and Ratliff as traders and as men.

Flem is the undisputed victor in this muted conflict between
Ratliff and Flem that begins, ends, and interlaces *The Hamlet,* yet
this opposition is continued in the next two books of the trilogy. For
although *The Hamlet* is a structurally autonomous work, it only presents the first incomplete part of the total Snopes chronicle. The fact
that Faulkner placed "end Volume One" at the end of the typescript
setting copy shows his reluctance for the reader to think of *The Hamlet* as complete in itself. The battle of wits between Flem and Ratliff is
one of the many pieces of unfinished business that Faulkner did not
return to until seventeen years later. He says the reason why he
waited so long to continue to work on the Snopes chronicle was "that
it's more fun doing a single piece which has the unity and coherence,
the proper emphasis and integration, which a long chronicle doesn't
have. That was the reason. Though it had to be done before I did stop
writing."[35] He masterfully creates unity and coherence, emphasis and
integration in the disparate pieces worked into *The Hamlet,* but in the
larger view Flem is not to have the final victory; the portrayal of his
final defeat, in fact, "had to be done before I did stop writing."
Ultimately, Ratliff will triumph over Flem, but he needs the help of
"Fate, and destiny, and luck, and hope, and all of us mixed up in it—
us and Linda and Flem and that durn little half-starved wildcat down
there in Parchman, all mixed up in the same luck and destiny and fate
and hope until cant none of us tell where it stops and we begin."[36]
That "durn little half-starved wildcat" is, or course, Mink Snopes,
and Faulkner has also providently sown the seeds for his future role
in this impressive first volume of a trilogy which remained incomplete
for nineteen years.

"THE TOWN"

No doubt *The Hamlet* is better structured than the other two volumes of the trilogy. One probable cause is the long delay in returning to this material which was no longer fresh for Faulkner. The garrulous re-telling of Snopes tales, so much more effectively presented in *The Hamlet,* is annoying to the reader who expects the trilogy to read as a single crafted whole. But Faulkner fashioned different structural designs for each of the novels. Restricted to the points of view and the language of Charles Mallison, Gavin Stevens, and V. K. Ratliff, *The Town* lacks the pastoral lyricism, dramatic immediacy, or descriptive detail evoked by Faulkner's flexible rhetorical voice in *The Hamlet.* But to be fair, he was here cataloguing another stage of his Snopes chronicle, where such a mode was inappropriate. *The Town* is really an extended conversation of Gavin, Ratliff, and Charles with each other and with the reader. Alert now to the dangers of the Snopeses, Gavin and Ratliff are obsessive Snopes-watchers and long-winded tellers of Snopes-lore. Charles, a latter-day resident of Jefferson and relative of Stevens, is largely a recipient of handed-down tales of the public and private drama provoked by the Snopeses in the town and in his Uncle Gavin.

The first of three self-contained episodes incorporated into *The Town,* "Centaur in Brass,"[37] was revised to become chapter one. Although "Centaur in Brass" was published in 1932, more than twenty years before it was incorporated into *The Town,* and although it even preceded the publication of *The Hamlet* by eight years, its basic outline, the characters and their interrelationships are retained in *The Town.* It further evidences the scope of Faulkner's early plan for the Snopes chronicle. Like so many of these early Snopes stories, it begins with a rehearsal of Flem's history; his infamous horse-stealing father, Ab; his rise from store clerk to his marriage to the "belle of the countryside"; the exit of her suitors; their move to Texas; their return with a "well-grown baby"; Flem's covert role in the sale of wild spotted horses; his purchase of Suratt's half of a restaurant business and elimination of his partner. The narrator also mentions the town's awareness of an illicit relationship between Mrs. Snopes and Major Hoxey and strongly implies that a causal relationship between this affair and the newly created job for Flem as water-plant supervisor exists.[38]

This same capsule history of Flem is expansively told at the beginning of chapter one of *The Town*. This summary is a way of indicating that by now the Snopeses have become absorbed into the communal consciousness of the town. Their history is commonly known, their peculiarities duly noted. The question is no longer who or what they are, but what is the town going to do about them. Or as Ratliff puts it: "we got them now; they're ourn now; I don't know jest what Jefferson could a committed back there whenever it was, to have won this punishment, gained this right, earned this privilege. But we did. So it's for us to cope, to resist; us to endure, and (if we can) survive" (T, p. 102). Indeed, the importance of the town's role in *The Town* has been augmented by a complicated revision of point of view from short story to novel. In fact, most of the differences between the two versions of the brass-stealing incident can be traced to changes either in point of view or in theme: Flem's brass-filled watertower changes from the "monument" of the short story to the "footprint" of the novel with far reaching ramifications.

A combination of first person singular, first person plural, and omniscient narration, the point of view of "Centaur in Brass" is, to say the least, fuzzy. Although the narrator speaks collectively for the town, cataloguing its knowledge, opinions, and prejudices in relation to Flem's mounting career and to Major Hoxey and Mrs. Snopes's covert relationship, he occasionally refers to himself in the first person ("Perhaps, as I said, this was the fault of the town" [CB, p. 151]; "In the very quiet hearing of it I seemed to partake for the instant of Turl's horrid surprise" [CB, p. 162]; "The first thing I wanted to know was, what Tom-Tom used in lieu of the butcher knife which he had dropped" [CB, p. 165]). He does not identify himself as a specific person, however, and indeed he later tells us of incidents and information that could not possibly be known by either a single person or by the town. For example, he relates a domestic scene between Tom-Tom and his wife that has no outside witness; he comments upon the significance of Flem's "monument" even though he told us at the beginning of the story that "only four people, two white men and two Negroes, know that it is his monument, or that it is a monument at all" (CB, p. 149). Presumably these people are Snopes, Harker, Tom-Tom, and Turl. Although the narrator does rely in large part on direct transcription of the accounts of the eyewitnesses like Harker and Turl, nevertheless some blurring of focus results from the inconsistent point of view.

In the novel Faulkner seeks to retain the advantages of the narration that is at once first person singular, first person plural, and omniscient, but he takes pains to establish the credibility of this point of view by adding additional perceivers. The person who immediately relates the story to us, Charles Mallison, is identified by the appearance of his name captioning the chapter, as each subsequent chapter is labeled to signify the point of view of Charles, Gavin, or Ratliff. In this book then, as in so many of Faulkner's major novels, unbiased omniscient narration is nonexistent. All information is filtered through limited narrators and the reader can register and discount his bias as he goes along. But Charles's narration is special because, particularly in the beginning, he is at a greater distance from the events and the people. By the time he hears of the incidents, they have become assimilated into the collective consciousness of the town: "So when I say 'we' and 'we thought' what I mean is Jefferson and what Jefferson thought" (T, p. 3). He is also cognizant of his uncle's personal involvement with the Snopeses, functioning as a bridge between public and private drama. Ratliff, who has a comparatively minor narrative role, serves as an occasional commentator who understands so well, but remains uninvolved, unlike the well-meaning, bungling Gavin who tries to save the Snopes women from Flem.

Charles has not even been born when Flem's brass-stealing takes place. He gets most of his information from either his cousin Gowan, who as assistant plant manager is added to the cast of characters, or from his Uncle Gavin.[39] Snatches of conversation between Gavin and Ratliff intersperse Chick's commentary, emphasizing the dominant role of these men as Snopes-watchers and as transmitters of Snopes-lore to Chick. Charles documents his information no matter how circumlocutiously it may have come to him: "And now there was some of it which Mr Harker himself didn't know until Uncle Gavin told him after Tom Tom told Uncle Gavin" (T, p. 19). Like the narrator of the short story, he relies in large part on the direct accounts of eyewitnesses (and these portions of the story have undergone only minor revision), but when he has not a direct source, he makes clear that he is imaginatively recreating the scene: "Only we had to imagine this part of it of course. Not that it was hard to do" (T, p. 20).

This careful documentation of point of view necessitates an alteration of the angle of vision for some of the incidents. For example, rather than directly rendering Tom Tom's discovery of his wife's infidelity as is done in the short story, the particulars of this scene are left to the reader's imagination. Where Tom Tom does not show up for work, the reader anticipates with horror the shock to be experienced by the unsuspecting Turl when he finds Tom Tom at home. Where no one witnesses the centaur-like phenomenon of Tom-Tom on Turl's back in the short story, in the novel Harker sees them as he rushes to Tom Tom's in an attempt to avert the anticipated disaster, and he later narrates this part of the story. Another result of filtering the narration through the accounts of witnesses is to lessen the focus on the drama of the three blacks; the short story supplies fuller particulars about them. Since Faulkner has tailored the story to become an integral part of the Snopes chronicle, what hapens to Tom Tom, his wife, and Tomey's Turl is minor and tangential and appropriately condensed.

Flem is both more dominant and more formidable in the novel version. In the short story Flem experiences a double indignity. While he forks over the money for the missing brass only once in the novel, in the short story he pays twice, once again when the auditors discover an error in their original estimate. Furthermore, Flem's prospects of future success seem quite remote at the end of the story as he sits idly in his slum neighborhood: "they would see him quite often in his tiny grassless and treeless side yard. It was a locality of such other hopeless little houses inhabited half by Negroes, and washed clay gullies and ditches filled with scrapped automobiles and tin cans, and the prospect was not pleasing. Yet he spent quite a lot of his time there, sitting on the steps, not doing anything" (CB, p. 168). Since the story was published in 1932, well after the writing of "Father Abraham," Faulkner apparently intended that Flem would get over this set-back and go on to become president of the bank of Jefferson, but this story gives no indication of that. Rather, Flem is depicted as a somewhat ordinary and petty thief who merely attempts to seize what advantage happens to come his way: "His vision at first, his aim, was not even that high; it was no higher than that of a casual tramp who pauses in passing to steal three eggs from beneath a setting hen" (CB, p. 153). All such disparaging asides where the narrator mocks, through homey metaphors, Flem's petty and foiled plans are expunged in the revised version where Flem's methods—however unsuccessful—are not to be dismissed with ridicule. One such deleted passage is the following where both Harker and the narrator relish Flem's folly:

> Then the next Summer came, with Harker still laughing at and enjoying what he saw, and seeing so little, thinking how they were all fooling one another while he looked on, when it was him who was being fooled. For in that Summer the thing ripened, came to a head. Or maybe Snopes just decided to cut his first hay crop; clean the meadow for reseeding. Because he could never have believed that on the day when he sent for Turl, he had set the capital on his monument and had started to tear the scaffolding down. [CB, p. 158]

In fact, the difference between the two views of Flem hinges in large part on two different words to describe the brass-filled water tower. In the short story it is labeled a monument; in the novel, a footprint. The monument of the short story attests to Flem's total defeat. He is outsmarted by his own too-clever machinations, and in his silent contemplation of the tower at the end of the story, the narrator expounds upon Flem's defeat:

> So they wondered what Snopes was looking at. They didn't know that he was contemplating his monument: that shaft taller than anything in sight and filled with transient and symbolical liquid that was not even fit to drink, but which, for the very reason of its impermanence, was more enduring through its fluidity and blind renewal than the brass which poisoned it, than columns of basalt or of lead. [CB, p. 168]

The effect of the revisions of this final scene for the novel, however, is to militate against the finality of this temporary setback. Clarifying the difference between a footprint and a monument, Charles makes clear that Flem will undoubtedly move again:

> So he could sit all day now on the gallery of his little backstreet rented house and look at the shape of the tank standing against the sky above the Jefferson roof-line—looking at his own monument, some might have thought. Except that it was not a monument: it was a footprint. A monument only says *At least I got this far* while a footprint says *This is where I was when I moved again.* [T, p. 29][40]

The incorrigibility of Flem's opportunism is highlighted with added commentary by Ratliff and Gavin at the end of the chapter:

"Not even now?" Uncle Gavin said to Ratliff.

"Not even now," Ratliff said. "Not catching his wife with Manfred de Spain yet is like that twenty-dollar gold piece pinned to your undershirt on your first maiden trip to what you hope is going to be a Memphis whorehouse. He dont need to unpin it yet." [T, p. 29]

Ratliff sees that Flem still has his trump card, or twenty-dollar gold piece if you will, and he is unscrupulous enough to wait until he can reap maximum profit from it. Later he uses the exposure of his own cuckoldry to catapult himself into the presidency of the bank, a move which has for its side effects Manfred de Spain's exit from Jefferson and Eula's tragic suicide. The effect of ending the chapter with this snatch of dialogue, then, is to heighten the reader's anticipation of Flem's next inevitable step. By calling attention to the profit value of the adulterous relationship, Faulkner is neatly tying up the causal connection between Flem's water superintendent job and the affair of Eula and Manfred de Spain. Although this connection is made in the short story as well, nothing is said of it after Flem's defeat.

The town's attitude towards the adulterous affair between Mrs. Snopes and Major Hoxey/Manfred de Spain also is changed. In the short story the town is outraged not so much by adultery as by Flem's failure to do anything about it: "the idea of their [Snopes and Hoxey] being on amicable terms outraged us more than the idea of the adultery itself. It seemed foreign, decadent, perverted: we could have accepted, if not condoned, the adultery had they only been natural and logical and enemies" (CB, p. 151). In the novel, the town clandestinely champions the affair:

> We were on his [Manfred's] side. We didn't want to know. We were his allies, his confederates; our whole town was accessory to that cuckolding. . . . Nor were we really in favor of adultery, sin: we were simply in favor of De Spain and Eula Snopes, for what Uncle Gavin called the divinity of simple unadulterated uninhibited immoral lust which they represented: for the two people in each of whom the other had found his single ordained fate; each to have found out of all the earth that one match for his mettle; ours the pride that Jefferson would supply their background. [T, pp. 14–15]

The town is not outraged by the affair, but some individuals are puzzled by Flem's failure to put a stop to it. Gavin Stevens asks Ratliff: "This town aint that big. Why hasn't Flem caught them?" (T, p. 15). Ratliff, with characteristic insight into Flem's behavior, responds "He dont need to yet." That the town secretly champions the affair has important ramifications later in the novel when Flem finally "needs to" catch them. The moral hypocrisy of the town is exposed. What they could accept as an open secret, they cannot accept as public fact, especially since public exposure would threaten their economic well-being: "the very rectitude and solvency of a bank would be involved in their exposure" (T, p. 307). That the town responds with self-interest disguised as moral self-righteousness to the exposure of the affair, then, unites them with the Flem Snopeses of the world who "set the cold stability of currency above the wild glory of blood" (T, p. 308), and they share his responsibility for the resultant suicide of Eula. Indeed, all of Flem's successes are built upon the moral weaknesses—particularly the greed—of others.

So Faulkner has molded an earlier short story into an effective opening chapter of a much later novel. It might seem an odd choice to begin a novel depicting Flem's immitigable success with an episode that shows his temporary defeat, his one and only failure to reap maximum monetary profits from a situation. But by turning the "monument" into a "footprint," by showing how Flem is undaunted and indeed strengthened by his defeat—in the same way an insect that develops an immunity to a pesticide is strengthened—and by strongly intimating that he will continue to exploit his fortuitously profitable cuckoldry, Faulkner turns a casual egg-stealing tramp into a frighteningly incorrigible opportunist.

The Town records the seemingly indomitable drive of Flem from waterplant supervisor to bank president, a rise necessitating a change in his tactics. As Ratliff discovers long before anyone else, Flem has learned that he has got to have respectability and so he must rid himself of the unsavory relatives who have trailed into Jefferson in his footprints. The antics of these "unvarnished" Snopeses are described in considerable detail by the bemused Snopes-watchers. In this volume Faulkner adds immeasurably to his wonderfully comic invention both by creating new mutations of Snopesishness and by enriching and embellishing the eccentrics and their oddities introduced in *The Hamlet* and elsewhere. Despite the unevenness in synthesis and integration of the novels of the trilogy, undoubtedly the whole is greater than the parts, for it provides both a densely rich sense of the Snopeses and a complete chronicle of their experiences in a way that no single volume—even the superb *The Hamlet*—can.

Some of Faulkner's comic tales about the peripheral members of the clan lay dormant in short stories written long before *The Town*. In integrating one such story, "Mule in the Yard,"[41] into the dominant structural patterns of the novel, Faulkner also renders it more skillfully. "Mule in the Yard," like "Centaur in Brass," is a humorous episode with a similar theme: the too-clever mercenary machinations of a Snopes result in frustration and financial loss. In this instance the Snopes is I. O., and the action centers around his attempt to recover from Mrs. Hait some of the money that he feels is owed him out of the profitable mule-killing set-up he had arranged with the now deceased Mr. Hait. Mr. Hait secretly affixed Snopes's mules to the railroad ties. After their inevitable deaths, Snopes collected sixty dollars a head from the railroad and paid Hait ten dollars a head for his assistance. Only the last time Hait failed to remove himself from the tracks, and then—much to Snopes's consternation—Mrs. Hait collected eight thousand five hundred dollars for her dead husband and for the mules she claimed for her own.

The central incident of the short story has to do with the confusion engendered by one of Snopes's unmanageable mules which reels around Mrs. Hait's yard, runs through the open door of her basement, knocks over a live scuttle of ashes, and sets her house on fire. After the fire Mrs. Hait attempts to buy the mule from Snopes for ten dollars—claiming he still owes her fifty dollars for the five mules Mr. Hait successfully had killed along with himself. The ironic twist to the story is that Snopes indignantly refuses to make the sale until he discovers that Mrs. Hait shot the mule in reparation for its destruction of her house. She refuses to refund the ten dollars after he has discovered the dead mule, and his frustration reaches a climax at the end of the story: "They could see him in silhouette, as though framed by the two blackened chimneys against the dying west; they saw him fling up both clenched hands in a gesture almost Gallic, of resignation and impotent despair" (MY, p. 264).

Although the basic outlines of the story are retained in the revision for the novel, some important changes in characterization, plot, and descriptive detail are made. The characterization of both I. O. Snopes and old Het in the novel more closely parallels that in the manuscript-typescript than in the published story.[42] I. O. Snopes has a somewhat different nature and significantly different motivation in each version. Although in all versions he is the same harried, petty opportunist who arranges for his mules to be tied to the railroad tracks and resents Mrs. Hait's eight thousand percent profit for her husband's death, he is weaker and less vindictive in the published story where his mules accidentally get into Mrs. Hait's yard. Deathly afraid of the mules and tortured by the chase, he is at least apologetic to Mrs. Hait for the accident: "Fore God, Miz Hait! I done everything I could!" (MY, p. 255). How different this is from the novel version where Snopes expressly releases the mules and suffers the tortures of his fright of the animals, for the exquisite, vindictive pleasure of troubling Mrs. Hait. Instead of apologizing he screams: "Where's my money? Where's my half of it? . . . Pay me my money! Pay me my part of it!" (T, p. 239). While the unpublished story offers conjecture rather than verifiable fact about Snopes's motivation, it at least leaves open the possibility of Snopes's deliberate vindictiveness:

> This is what the town saw two or three times each year from behind adjacent windows and from front and back porches and the sidewalk and even from halted cars and wagons, and which after repetition began to assume in the town's eyes the grim quality of a duel between two humans in the center of a mad vortex of mules, and which after more years still began to take on another quality—a quality fatal, futile, furious and in miniature, like two bugs imprisoned in a bottle by diabolic boys. They wondered many and diverse things—if perhaps Snopes did not actually drive the mules onto her premises, or it Mrs. Hait did not believe that he did anyway; and if in either case, why she did not build a fence about her yard or appeal to law. [TS, pp. 11–12]

As a matter of fact, Faulkner tones down the role of ironic fatality and plays up Snopes's deliberate vindictiveness in the changes made from manuscript to typescript and in turn from typescript to novel. Where the manuscript makes repeated references to the "dark author" who manipulates Snopes and Mrs. Hait and the mules in an almost ritualized "comedy," some of these references are crossed out in the typescript and all such allusions are dropped in the novel in which I. O. is moved not by a "dark author" but by his own distorted sense of justice and retribution.

Another difference is the obsessively proverbial rhetoric that becomes his hallmark in the novel, but is absent from the earlier characterizations. Of course, I. O. is a character who extends beyond the borders of the mule-in-the-yard episode in the novel, and Faulkner has opportunities to elaborate on his "snarling and outraged babble" in which he jumbles and twists familiar clichés elsewhere:

"cash on the barrelhead is the courtesy of kings, as the feller says, not to mention the fact that beggars' choices aint even choices when he aint even got a roof to lay his head in no more. And if Lawyer Stevens has got ara thing loose about him the vice presi-dent might a taken a notion to, he better hold onto it since as the feller says even a fool wont tread where he jest got through watching somebody else get bit" (T, pp. 253–54). To be sure, that I. O.'s outrageous rhetoric does not emerge until later in the chapter—which was extensively revised from earlier accounts—might suggest that Faulkner has not consistently transformed the earlier rather weak-willed I. O. into the more aggressive and brash I. O. of the novel, but this is a discrepancy of diction alone. Furthermore, at one point Ratliff offers an excuse for the inconsistency by arguing that I. O. did not sound like himself: "Ratliff said he didn't sound like I. O. Snopes anyway because whenever I. O. talked what he said was so full of mixed-up proverbs that you stayed so busy trying to unravel just which of two or three proverbs he had jumbled together that you couldn't even tell just exactly what lie he had told you until it was already too late. But right now Ratliff said he was too busy to have time for even proverbs, let alone lies" (T, p. 242). This probably is not a sufficient excuse for the inconsistent diction, but at least it is an attempt at one.

In all versions old Het is a cheerful old Negress who makes weekly forays from the poorhouse to the homes of the white housewives of the village, but in the unpublished and novel versions more is made of her "implacable rounds": "For twentyfive years women, seeing her through a front window or perhaps hearing her stromg, loud, cheerily adjurant voice from the street or from the house next door, fled to bathrooms. But even this did no good unless they had first thought to lock the house doors" (TS, p. 1). Apparently Faulkner decided to condense the published story by minimizing the role of old Het in the drama. While the short story has a dramatic immediacy that the two other versions lack because the action is presented directly with a minimum of extraneous background, it loses in the delightful characterization of old Het.

The unpublished version treats old Het's poverty more seriously than either of the two later accounts: "tall, lean: voluble, timeless, and cheerful save to that few who looked beyond the loose mouth and the wordy opportunism and saw in the baffled and bewildered eyes that terror and dread of hunger which not even the security of a poorhouse can efface from the eyes of old negroes" (TS, pp. 1–2). By omitting this passage Faulkner perhaps decided that the serious view it gives of old Het's poverty is at odds with the essentially cheerful and comic characterization. She, in fact, takes a more comic and prominent role in the novel. For example, in a conversation with Gavin Stevens added to the novel, she ingeniously expounds upon her service to Jefferson as the perpetual benefactress:

> There's some folks thinks all I does, I tromps this town all day from can-see to cant, with a hand full of gimme and a mouth full of much oblige. They're wrong. I serves Jefferson too. If it's more blessed to give than to receive like the Book say, this town is blessed to a fare-you-well because it's steady full of folks willing to give anything from a nickel up to a old hat. But I'm the onliest one I knows that steady receives. So how is Jefferson going to be steady blessed without me steady willing from dust-dawn to dust-dark, rain or snow or sun, to say much oblige? [T, p. 245]

Her more pronounced presence, however, is due largely to the filtering of much of the action through her eyewitness account.

Faulkner's careful documentation of point of view is again apparent. The omniscient point of view of the short story is replaced by Charles's narration of the episode in the novel. Although one might expect that omniscient narration would allow for more precisely rendered scenes, actually old Het's homey and colorful language— recreated by Charles—more vividly captures the turmoil of the mule in the yard. In fact, many descriptive flourishes of the short story are overly-ingenious and rather abstract analogies that compare unfavorably with the specificity of old Het's eyewitness account. For example, when the mule encounters some chickens the narrator grandly elaborates: "Then for an instant its progress assumed the appearance and trappings of an apotheosis: hell-born and hell-returning, in the act of dissolving completely into the fog, it seemed to rise vanishing into a sunless and dimensionless medium borne upon and enclosed by small winged goblins" (MY, p. 251). But old Het's explanation more effectively captures the almost sinister and supernatural quality of the mule which appears suddenly out of the fog and collides with the chickens: "Old Het said it looked just like something out of the Bible, or maybe out of some kind of hoodoo witches' Bible: the mule that came out of the fog to begin with like a hant or a goblin, now kind of soaring back into the fog again borne on a cloud of little winged ones" (T, p. 238). In another parallel descriptive passage, the frightened cow is described with the same similies, but the elevated diction of the narrator of the short story is reduced to the simplicity and directness of old Het's language:

> The cow's head likewise had a quality transient and abrupt and unmundane. It vanished, sucked into invisibility like a match flame, though the mind knew and the reason insisted that she had withdrawn into the shed, from which, as a proof's burden, there came an indescribable sound of shock and alarm by shed and beast engendered, analogous to a single note from a profoundly struck lyre or harp. [MY, p. 251]

> Anyway, old Het said the cow snatched her face back inside the shed like a match going out and made a sound inside the shed, old Het didn't know what sound, just a sound of pure shock and alarm like when you pluck a single string on a harp or bango. [T, pp. 237–38]

That the cow and the mule look like "two-mismatched book-ends" as they confront one another enhances the comedy of the scene in the novel, but the verbose elaboration of this analogy in the short story is unnecessarily complicated: "they looked like two book ends from two distinct pairs of a general pattern which some one of amateurly bucolic leanings might have purchased, and which some child had salvaged, brought into idle juxtaposition and then forgotten" (MY, p. 256). Other analogies of the short story likewise are dropped for the directness of old Het's observations in the novel. Such innumerable parallel passages show that Faulkner carefully worked over the details of the story for its incorporation into the novel. Contrary to the myth that he liked to have perpetuated about himself—that he wrote only in the heat of inspiration and had neither time nor inclination to polish his work stylistically—he expended a great deal of energy on such polishing.

Old Het's narrative function in the novel is complemented by Ratliff's and Gavin Stevens's new roles as secondary perceivers. Again, Charles reminds us of his dependency on these two men as Snopes-watchers. In fact, the chapter begins with an unequivocal statement of that dependency: "This is what Ratliff said happened up to where Uncle Gavin could see it" (T, p. 231). Charles repeatedly credits information and commentary to them throughout the episode. For example, in the short story the "town wag" ironically comments that Mrs. Hait sold her husband to the railroad for "eight thousand percent profit" but in the novel Ratliff makes this comment. Faulkner seeks to keep these two men in view because, despite their humorous commentary, they function as the chief antagonists of Snopesism in Jefferson. In keeping with the pattern of *The Town,* Gavin gets drawn into the action while Ratliff remains an aloof and all-seeing observer.

Gavin gets personally involved, because the action is complicated in the novel by the introduction of Flem and his legalistic and opportunistic maneuvering. While in the short story Mrs. Hait outsmarts I. O. Snopes, now Flem Snopes is the super-manipulator who outsmarts both Mrs. Hait and I. O., and the unfolding of the action demands Stevens's legal services. Stevens's services, in fact, are called upon by both Mrs. Hait and Flem. Mrs. Hait seeks Stevens to witness her purchase of the house-burning mule from I. O., and Flem seeks him to witness his ridding the town of I. O. But Flem's involvement in this episode extends beyond merely seeking to rid the town of an unsavory relative. I. O. reveals Flem's covert role in—and large profits from—the handling of Mrs. Hait's insurance. Using blackmail and persuasive reasoning, he got half of her eight-thousand-dollar profit and paid one hundred dollars out of his share to keep I. O. quiet:

> All legal and open: I could keep my mouth shut and get a hundred dollars, where if I objected, the vice presi-dent his-self might accidently let out who them mules actively belonged to, and wouldn't nobody get nothing, which would be all right with the vice presi-dent since he would be right where he started out, being as he never owned Lonzo Hait nor the five mules neither. [T, p. 249]

Faulkner's successful interpolation of Flem into the episode is typical of the protean flexibility of his stories in his imagination. No hack job, Faulkner's revisions not only improve the story but mold it into an important and integral part of the continuing saga of Flem Snopes. Flem's behavior here is completely in character. He steps in and exploits for monetary profits the moral vulnerability of others, in this case of Mrs. Hait and of I. O., and he also uses the situation to advance his own incorrigible drive to the presidency. In the brief conversation between Ratliff and Charles that follows the episode, Ratliff wisely and accurately comments upon Flem's behavior. Although Gavin Stevens "missed it" and continues to miss the point throughout much of the novel, Ratliff understands that Flem has discovered that he has to have "respectability":

When it's jest money and power a man wants, there is usually some
place where he will stop; there's always one thing at least that ever—
every man wont do for jest money. But when it's respectability he finds
out he wants and has got to have, there aint nothing he wont do to get it
and then keep it. [T, p. 259]

So Flem's buying of I. O.'s mules on the grounds that he leave Jefferson forever—a twist that is added to the episode—signals this important development of the major plot of the novel.

"The Waifs," the final self-contained story incorporated into
The Town, forms its last episode. It depicts the hilarious but sinister
destructive activity of the half-Indian, totally wild children of Byron
Snopes who are shipped to Flem by Byron from Texas and, after a
great deal of trouble, shipped back to Byron by Flem. In so doing,
Flem succeeds finally in effecting "the last and final end of Snopes
out-and-out unvarnished behavior in Jefferson" (T, p. 370). Unlike
the other two short stories which were written much earlier and extensively revised for the novel, "The Waifs" was published in the
same year as *The Town,*[43] and it is essentially the same in both versions, making "The Waifs" a story that probably either grew out of,
or was carved out of, a novel in progress.

Since the episode is self-contained, it readily adapts itself to
publication as a separate story, but this strange tale nevertheless
profits from the larger context of the novel, and it functions as a
particularly appropriate finale to the volume. For the Snopes Indians
exemplify the animalistic core of Snopesism. Their "unvarnished"
behavior is not generically different from Flem's varnished behavior.
Like Flem, they are basically subhuman; they grab what they can get;
they have no moral scruples; they are secretive, quiet, and deadly
threatening in their behavior. As in the mule-in-the-yard episode,
Flem must again pay for the unvarnished Snopesism of his relatives:
here he dishes out five hundred dollars for the pedigreed dog that his
cousins ate, but again he gains from his purchase. He succeeds in
making the final payment on his coveted respectability.

In summary, the three stories incorporated into *The Town* are
well-integrated into its structural patterns. Filtered through the per-
spectives of Gavin, Ratliff, and Charles, they become part of the
extended conversation which gives shape to the novel. They are

tales further attesting to the infinite variety but unchanging core of Snopesism. But through skillful refashioning and strategic placement within the dominant plot, they are also integral pieces of the portrayal of Flem's immitigable drive to success. That Faulkner managed to integrate these isolated episodes into a meaningful novelistic design is a credit to his organizational skill. To be sure, *The Hamlet* is a volume of greater integration and intensity, perhaps in part because it sustains a comic perspective upon the not-quite-human antics of the Snopeses who invade the idyllic and folksy world of Frenchman's Bend. In *The Town,* the tone is more varied, and generally more somber. The Snopeses become an increasingly serious threat, and the inhabitants of Jefferson are more realistically drawn. The love-goddess, Eula, becomes demythologized; the romantic drama of Gavin and Linda is on an entirely different plane from the comic tales of Snopesian enterprise that intersperse it. But the humor of the centaur-in-brass episode is moderated by the inevitability of Flem's next footprint, the humor of the mule-in-the-yard episode by the horrible limitlessness of Flem's ambition, and the humor of the waifs episode by the disturbing parallels between the Snopes Indians and the Snopes president of the Bank of Jefferson. If *The Town* fails to measure up to *The Hamlet,* its failure lies less with the preexistent Snopes episodes incorporated into it than with the stilted treatment of its nonepisodic parts, particularly the interminable attitudinizing of Gavin Stevens and his "adolescence-in-reverse" relationship, first with Eula and then with Linda Snopes. With Gavin and Linda, in particular, Faulkner is moving dangerously far from the "bolt of lightning" which inspired his Snopes saga.

"THE MANSION"

The Mansion has for the most part a sustained narrative rather than an episodic structure, although, like most of Faulkner's major fiction, the novel is sectioned into parts. Most of Books One and Three, titled "Mink" and "Flem" respectively, are told from an omniscient narrator's point of view. Like *The Town,* the chapters of Book Two,

"Linda," are told from the points of view of Ratliff, Charles, and Gavin. Book One begins with the verdict of "Guilty" at Mink's trial and concentrates on Mink's mounting resentment and revenge against Flem over the years. Book Two builds up a sense of Linda and her mounting antagonism toward her "father" Flem. Finally, Book Three portrays the conspiring both of transcendent forces, "fate, and destiny, and luck, and hope," and of individuals, Mink, Linda, Ratliff, and Gavin, to put down Snopesism by murdering Flem. Snopesism is no longer viewed with humorous tolerance; it is an evil which must be eradicated, and Linda and Mink in particular are deadly serious, actually fanatical, in their pursuit of that end.

Chapter one retells the story of Mink's killing of Jack Houston. In its third telling, Faulkner elaborates in much greater detail the frustration that led up to the killing. Conversely, he does not relate again the problems after the crime created by the rigor mortis of the body and the ferocity of Houston's hound. Nor does he detail Mink's passionate bondage to his wife which ties his story into the thematic context of *The Hamlet*. The details of the story are changed again, including the disputed animal—now a cow—and the negotiations over it are much more complicated than in the earlier versions. Alluding to factual discrepancies like these, Faulkner in the prefatory note to the volume claims:

> The purpose of this note is simply to notify the reader that the author has already found more discrepancies and contradictions than he hopes the reader will—contradictions and discrepancies due to the fact that the author has learned, he believes, more about the human heart and its dilemma than he knew thirty-four years ago; and is sure that, having lived with them that long time, he knows the characters in this chronicle better than he did then.

He certainly gives the reader the opportunity to know Mink better, creating a powerful and moving portrait of this intractable little man.

In *The Mansion* the emphasis is upon Mink's unflagging endurance of the exasperating hardships and bad luck that have plagued him throughout his life and upon his unreconciled pride which demands revenge first upon Houston and ultimately upon his kinsman, Flem. The chapter begins with the verdict of guilty and Mink's preoccupation in the courtroom with his absent kinsman so that the ensuing retelling of Mink's murder of Houston is clearly set within the larger pattern of revenge yet to be effected, his murder of Flem.

The narrative voice effectively both summarizes and comments upon Mink's recording consciousness, sympathetically cataloguing Mink's "bad luck" which "had all his life continually harassed and harried him into the constant and unflagging necessity of defending his own simple rights" (M, p. 7). His experience with his cow is typical of his bad luck and his testing by "*them—they—it,* whichever and whatever you wanted to call it, who represented a simple fundamental justice and equity in human affairs, or else a man might just as well quit" (M, p. 6). His cow had failed to freshen, and although he had paid for a bull fee, it remained barren. Now he faces the prospect of wintering it again with neither calf nor milk for compensation. When his cow wanders into Houston's herd, he intends at first to recover her, but then, unable to resist the advantages of the arrangement and already antagonized by Houston's wealth and arrogance (who had rudely forced Mink off the road earlier as he galloped by on his stallion), he lets the cow stay and fabricates a lie about having sold the animal. Later, when he attempts to recover his cow, now fattened by Houson's feed and impregnated by his bull, he is met with Houston's resistance, and he takes the case to Will Varner for settlement. Varner decides that Mink must pay one-half the current market value of the cow. Since Mink does not have the money, he is to work it out at fifty cents a day digging postholes for Houston. Although Mink accepts the arrangement without argument, and although he throws himself into the work, "his pride still was that he would not be, would never be, reconciled to it" (M, p. 18). In fact, first Houston and later Varner become apprehensive over Mink's dogged acceptance of this task. Both try to get him to take cash for the cow, and Varner tries to give him the cow outright, but Mink, stubborn and patient in his pride and curiously respectful of the letter of the law, refuses. His intractability makes Varner "suddenly afraid, afraid for the peace and quiet of the community which he held in his iron usurious hand, buttressed by the mortgages and liens in the vast iron safe in his store" (M, p. 19).

Described in detail is Mink's anticipation of the receipt of his cow on the last day of his labor, but these feelings of satisfaction and elation are squelched by Houston's incredible insistance that he is owed two more days labor for the pound fee. When Mink checks with Varner and discovers that this fee is indeed legal, he is determined again to fulfill his legal obligation, even though Varner, enraged at Houston's arrogance, tries to pay it for him. He completes the final

two days of work, but he also plots the murder of Houston. Again he
has to endure the inevitable obstacles which complicate his life. For
example, he takes a five-dollar bill saved for an emergency to buy
shells for his gun, loses the money on the way to town, accuses a man
of stealing it, and fights with him over it, even though his small size
insures his defeat. When Ike McCaslin refuses to give him buckshot
shells, he must rely on two other shells from his meager stock. He has
to wait days in ambush for Houston to ride past and even then the
first shell fails to go off—"*And even now. They still aint satisfied yet*"
(M, p. 39). Even when the second shell fires, he feels cheated of the
chance to say to Houston before his death:

> I aint shooting you because of them thirty-seven and a half four-bit
> days. That's all right; I done long ago forgot and forgive that. Likely
> Will Varner couldn't do nothing else, being a rich man too and all you
> rich folks has got to stick together or else maybe some day the ones
> that aint rich might take a notion to raise up and take hit away from
> you. That aint why I shot you. I killed you because of that-ere extry
> one-dollar pound fee. [M, p. 39]

The story of Mink's killing of Houston in *The Mansion* bears
only a slight resemblance to that of Cotton in "The Hound," for
Faulkner has not only changed the character but he has altered the
focus also, expanding now upon the causes rather than the consequences of the crime. It is characteristic of his method to move toward greater complexity: to fill out the past that informs the present,
to affix to one-dimensional characters fully realized psyches, and to
describe profusely earlier sketchy details. He does that masterfully
here, through both the retelling of the Houston killing and the continued amplification of Mink's story detailed throughout *The Mansion*.
Each telling of the Houston killing is superbly effective. "The
Hound" is one of Faulkner's best short stories. It is skillfully woven
thematically and narratively into *The Hamlet*. Finally, it functions in
The Mansion as a poignant and sympathetic introduction to the gutsy
little man whose role as a murderer the reader uncomfortably champions. Faulkner wisely decided to humanize this Snopes, to portray him
uncharacteristically from the "inside," and to show that his very
insistence upon equal rights as a human being—however madly he
construes them—destroys the mercenary inhumanity of Snopesism.
Ironically, destruction is Mink's only means of self-assertion. We
champion him because in his own mad way he is seeking the eternal

verities: "the courage and honor and hope and pride and compassion and pity and sacrifice which have been the glory"[44] of man's past, whereas the only eternal verity Flem recognizes is greed.

Faulkner was less successful in his attempt to weave two extraneous comic Snopes stories into *The Mansion*. "Hog Pawn" and "By the People" were revised and incorporated into the novel, although "Hog Pawn" had not been previously published.[45] Both episodes stand out as unassimilated lumps of material. The tall tale quality is at odds with the essentially realistic portrayal of character and event in the novel as a whole. The minor Snopeses seem incidental to the major business of destroying the super-Snopes, Flem. Nevertheless, there are reasons to justify the inclusion of the two episodes in *The Mansion*.

First, in keeping with the overall eradication of Snopeses from Jefferson, both episodes depict the defeat of a Snopes in a scheming enterprise. Orestes Snopes is foiled in his land speculation and in his revenge tactics against old Otis Meadowfill (M, pp. 322–49); Clarence Snopes is foiled forever in his attempt to secure political glory (M, pp. 294–321). Furthermore, our ever-vigilant Snopes-watchers, Gavin Stevens and V. K. Ratliff, each play an instrumental role in this eradication: Gavin watches for and then prevents Orestes's hog pawn booby-trap from injuring the irascible Meadowfill, and Ratliff initiates the scheme to turn Clarence into a "dog post office." Here is the humorous dimension to a serious theme, discussed by Charles and Gavin in explicit terms at the end of the Clarence Snopes episode: "So what you need is to learn how to trust in God without depending on Him. In fact, we need to fix things so He can depend on us for a while. Then He wont need to waste Himself being everywhere at once" (M, p. 321). The hog pawn episode, however, seems unnecessarily digressive. Orestes Snopes's "evil," if you can call his desperate greed that, is not any worse than Meadowfill's spiteful and vindictive meanness. Old Meadowfiill is every bit as obnoxious as Snopes, and one does not champion one man or the other in their childish games over the land and the hog. But the patterning of events does serve to reinforce a major theme of the novel, that Snopesian behavior is not restricted to the Snopes family. What Meadowfill and Orestes do is cancel each other out—with the help of Gavin Stevens—making room for the success of the good people, Meadowfill's daughter and her husband. Jefferson succeeds again in this book of vigilant defensive action by the "good guys" to hold "its own in what Charles's uncle would call the Snopes condition or dilemma" (M, p. 322).

The most successful change Faulkner made when reworking the hog-pawn episode was the encasing of the story into a larger framework of land speculation and double-dealing, centering around the battle of wits between Flem Snopes and Jason Compson. The bringing together of these two most villainous of Faulkner's characters was a stroke of genius. While the two men are soul brothers, guided "by their mutual master, the Devil" (M, p. 326), the villainy of Jason—every bit as opportunistic and self-serving—is the foil that highlights Flem's superior scheming and control. For Jason tries to set up Flem by buying back the Compson land that was sold to send Quentin to Harvard and then spreading rumors about "advance unimpeachable information that an air-training field was to be located in Jefferson" (M, p. 323). After Flem seemingly falls for the trap and buys the land, Jason relishes his apparent victory by ironically commiserating with Flem over the stupidity of a government that does not see the advantages of a hilly airfield:

> Because then Jason began to commiserate with Mr Snopes in reverse, by delivering long public tirades on the government's stupidity; that Mr Snopes in fact was ahead of his time but that inevitably, in the course of time as the war continued and we all had to tighten our belts still further, the Snopes concept of a flying field composed of hills would be recognised as the only practical one and would become known throughout the world as the Snopes Airport Plan, since under it runways that used to have to be a mile long could be condensed into half that distance, since by simply bulldozing away the hill beneath it both sides of the runway could be used for each takeoff and landing, like a fly on a playing card wedged in a crack. [M, pp. 325–26]

But Flem as usual is three steps ahead of his opponent. He foresaw the baby boom and the consequent lucrative housing boom that would follow the war. Jason is left as usual in impotent frustration trying vainly to bribe Gavin Stevens to find or to create a flaw in the title he conveyed to Flem. Flem outSnopes his opponent, but Jason's behavior, coupled with that of Meadowfill, demonstrates that Snopesism is not restricted to the clannish family. Indeed, the reverberations of evil in *The Mansion* extend in scope and locale from Meadowfill's meanness in his scrawny orchard to Franco's political tyranny in Spain.

The only other change of substance from the story is that in the novel the antagonism between Orestes and Meadowfill over Orestes's hog lot predates the antagonism generated by Meadowfill's refusal to sell his corner of land thus preventing Orestes from selling his piece. This change in the novel puts Snopes "under a really impossible handicap: his hog lot had forever interdicted him from approaching old Meadowfill in person, of having any sort of even momentary civilised contact with him" (M, p. 335). The rest of the story—the deliberate release of Orestes's hog into Meadowfill's worthless orchard; Meadowfill's potshots at it; the developing romance and industry of Meadowfill's daughter Essie and her Marine boyfriend; the trapping of Gavin by Orestes for the legal advice to give the hog away; the watch for trouble by Gavin and Charles outside Meadowfill's house; the successful prevention of the booby-trap attached to Meadowfill's screen from seriously injuring him; and the confrontation of Snopes with his handiwork by Gavin—is basically the same in both versions except for extensive expansion of descriptive detail and revision of the language throughout the novel. Only in the novel are the contrasting attitudes of the two prominent Snopes-fighters highlighted at the end. Gavin, who tends to despair at the enormity of the task of Snopes eradication, says: "You see? . . . It's hopeless. Even when you get rid of one Snopes, there's already another one behind you even before you can turn around." Ratliff, who has come to respect man's capacity to help himself, minimizes the difficulty of coping with Snopesism: " 'That's right,' Ratliff said serenely. 'As soon as you look, you see right away it aint nothing but jest another Snopes' " (M, p. 349). He, in fact, counters Gavin's defeatism ("You cant beat him") with this optimism repeatedly throughout the preceding chapter in which he effectively "eliminated Clarence," the political demagogue.

This hilarious tall tale in which Clarence Snopes is turned into a "dog post office" and Will Varner withdraws his support for him ("I aint going to have Beat Two and Frenchman's Bend represented nowhere by nobody that ere a son-a-bitching dog that happens by cant tell from a fence post" [M, p. 319]) is in basic outlines the same in both the short story "By the People," published in 1955,[46] and in the novel, published in 1959. Because of the relatively late publication date of the story, Ratliff is no longer Suratt, the one-dimensional trader. He is the same humanist he is in The Snopes Trilogy. In the introductory exposition of the short story (which does not find a parallel in the novel), the narrator expounds upon his wisdom, tolerance, and affirmative view of human nature:

> He was a universal: among men a man, among ladies a gentleman: sitting among the guffaws now because there was that about him too: still affable, still bland, but discoursive now, with a humor which was not sardonic so much as tolerant, and an aptness which quite often was not just wit but wisdom too. . . . the wit itself and the wisdom which it did not always conceal was that of any man who had watched human folly yet still remained capable of believing in human aspiration. [B, p. 86]

Instead of this summary of the character of Ratliff, a much more extensive exposition of the character and history of Clarence Snopes precedes the account of the specific incident in the novel (M, pp. 295–98). In this section the connection between Clarence's political career and Will Varner's support is repeatedly emphasized. Although it is made in the short story as well, the added emphasis is one of the many ways in *The Mansion* that Snopesism is shown to be a moral disease that is not restricted to the Snopes family. The implication is that Clarence Snopes by himself is harmless; it is his patronage which is alarming and reprehensible:

> So what Charles's Uncle Gavin really wanted to know was not so much what had happened to Clarence, as what had happened to old Will Varner. Because whatever eliminated Clarence from the congressional race would have to impact not on Clarence but on old Will; it wouldn't have needed to touch Clarence at all in fact. Because nobody really minded Clarence just as you dont mind a stick of dynamite until somebody fuses it; otherwise he was just so much sawdust and greasy paper that wouldn't even burn good set on fire. He was unprincipled and without morals of course but, without a guiding and prompting and absolving hand or intelligence, Clarence himself was anybody's victim since all he had was his blind instinct for sadism and overreaching, and was himself really dangerous only to someone he would have the moral and intellectual ascendency of, which out of the entire world's population couldn't possibly be anybody except another Snopes. [M, pp. 297–98]

Set squarely in the modern world, the story even makes mention of actual political figures and organizations, like Huey Long and the Ku Klux Klan, to create a sense of contemporary relevancy to this story of demagoguery and intolerance. The short story, however, is set in the 1950's; Devries is a veteran of both the Korean War and World War II.

The episode in the novel takes place in 1945; Devries volunteered for two tours of duty before his missing leg prevented further participation, and Charles and other veterans do not return to Jefferson until September when their liberal vote is no longer needed to defeat Clarence because he has already been defeated by Ratliff. Charles's point of view in the short story becomes that of an omniscient narrator in the novel; conversations between Charles and Gavin are transferred to Ratliff and Gavin, emphasizing Ratliff's repeated unwillingness to accept Gavin's dismal view of the inevitability of Clarence's success, an unwillingness which foreshadows the subversive role he plays in putting down Clarence. When Gavin suggests sardonically that since they cannot beat Clarence they should join him, Ratliff says:

> There must be some simpler way than that. It's a pure and simple proposition; there must be a pure and simple answer to it. Clarence jest purely and simply wants to get elected to Congress, he dont keer how; there must be some pure and simple way for the folks that purely and simply dont want him in Congress to say No to him, they dont keer how neither. [M, p. 313]

Another added passage shows that while many of the good people were innocently duped by Clarence, Gavin and Ratliff never were:

> Clarence had engorged the country whole . . . the doomed handful of literate liberal underpaid white-collar illusionees who had elected him into the state senate because they thought he had destroyed the Ku Klux Klan, plus the other lesser handful of other illusionees like Charles's Uncle Gavin and Ratliff, who had voted for Clarence that time as the lesser of two evils because he had come out against the Klan and hence were even more doomed since where the school- and music-teachers and other white-collar innocents who learned by heart President Roosevelt's speeches, could believe anew each time that honor and justice and decency would prevail just because they were honorable and just and decent, his uncle and Ratliff never had believed this and never would. [M, p. 304]

Although both men realize that "just to hate evil is not enough. You—somebody—has got to do something about it," the important difference is that Gavin feels "it's too late for us now. We cant now; maybe we're just afraid to stick our necks out again. Or if not afraid, at least ashamed. No: not afraid: we are just too old" [M, p. 307], whereas Ratliff accepts the moral responsibility.

While the credibility of the tall tale of Ratliff's abolition of Clarence Snopes might be questioned, and while the digressive nature of the hog-pawn episode might be criticized, both function as humorous counterparts to the serious business of another act to rid Jefferson of Snopeses, the murder of Flem. Both Ratliff and Gavin act as accessories to Flem's murder. Ratliff suspects Linda's murderous machinations when he signs for Mink's release from prison; Gavin is forced later to recognize her probable motivation. Both men bring money to Mink from Linda after the murder. Gavin is horrified at his own participation in this venture, but he nonetheless did participate; he has violated his stance of detachment and committed himself to moral, responsible, and guilty involvement. Ratliff never loses faith in man's capacity to do good: "I mind I used to think that hope was about all folks had, only now I'm beginning to believe that's about all anybody needs—jest hope" (M, p. 347). The pattern of confrontation that began in the early Snopes stories as the battle of wit between two shrewd and subtle traders, Flem Snopes and V. K. Suratt, has evolved into a moral and philosophical antagonism. Ultimately, Ratliff's life-affirming commitment to moral and responsible action triumphs over Flem's life-denying opportunism, and, it might be added, over Gavin's self-defeating detachment and disillusionment.

"THE UNVANQUISHED": REVISION, 2 RETROSPECTION, AND RACE

The Unvanquished has never enjoyed unquestioned critical acceptance as a major achievement in Faulkner's canon. Allegations of "slick plots," "grating sentimentality," "stereotyped characters," and "stock situations" are apparently reinforced by the fact that six of the seven stories were published earlier in popular magazines (five in *Saturday Evening Post* and one in *Scribner's*[1]). Except for the cautious claim of Edward M. Holmes "that the additions to the text frequently emphasize and underline the themes that recent critics have found in the book," critics have either ignored or been unimpressed with the revision that Faulkner made when incorporating these stories into the larger volume.[2] To be sure, most of the significant revision takes place in the first three stories, and only relatively minor changes—that for the most part improve stylistics rather than alter meaning and execution—are made in the latter three. Nevertheless, these changes, along with the important addition of the seventh and final story, "An Odor of Verbena," newly written for the larger volume, made the total volume vastly different from the sum of the earlier magazine stories. Critical controversy about the unity of *The Unvanquished* is also compounded since it is neither a novel nor a collection of short stories (although it has been called both) but a hybrid form, a short story composite in which the stories profit from mutual illumination and contribute to a larger whole, without losing their identities as separable and distinct stories. Indeed, Faulkner claimed that he saw the book "as a long series. I had never thought of it in terms of a novel, exactly. I realized that they would be too episodic to be what I considered a novel, so I thought of them as a series of stories . . ."[3] The revision of the first three stories maintains this episodic framework by retaining the plots as the basic structural units. Like their magazine counterparts, a large element of lightness and humor is characteristic of these plots: two overly zealous boys shoot a Yankee horse, but the Yankee Colonel turns out to be a gentleman; a small Confederate band and two boys ambush an entire Yankee regiment; a grandmother and two boys recover ten chests of silver, 110 mules, and 110 Negroes for the loss of one chest, two mules, and two slaves. Although *The Unvanquished* retains these sometimes humorous and incredible happenings of wartime, a more serious and complex view of character and event is interjected through two major kinds of revision: alteration of the perspective and diction of the narrator, and heightening of the issue of race.

Alteration in perspective and diction changes the effect and the emphasis of the stories. The narrator of the magazine stories is an adolescent, while the narrator of the revised stories is a man looking back upon his childhood experiences. This change interjects into *The Unvanquished* an important element of retrospective, adult evaluation in keeping with the intelligent and thoughtful Bayard who narrates "An Odor of Verbena." The revised "Ambuscade," for example, is not the sentimental and uncritically nostalgic picture of the past that many critics would make it. The narrator is poignantly aware of the gap between his boyhood perceptions and his adult awareness.[4] He frequently observes that the glamorized images of war and heroes were the stuff boys' dreams were made of and had very little to do with actuality as it can be seen from the retrospective perspective of time. Indeed, that very point is made with the alteration and expansion of the first scene of "Ambuscade" in which Ringo and Bayard play at war. The first version reads:

> Behind the smokehouse we had a kind of map. Vicksburg was a handful of chips from the woodpile and the river was a trench we had scraped in the packed ground with a hoe, that drank water almost faster than we could fetch it from the well. This afternoon it looked like we would never get it filled.[5]

The revision reads:

> Behind the smokehouse that summer, Ringo and I had a living map. Although Vicksburg was just a handful of chips from the woodpile and the River a trench scraped into the packed earth with the point of a hoe, it (river, city, and terrain) lived, possessing even in miniature that ponderable though passive recalcitrance of topography which out-

weighs artillery, against which the most brilliant of victories and the most tragic of defeats are but the loud noises of a moment. To Ringo and me it lived, if only because of the fact that the sunimpacted ground drank water faster than we could fetch it from the well, the very setting of the stage for conflict a prolonged and wellnigh hopeless ordeal in which we ran, panting and interminable, with the leaking buckets between wellhouse and battlefield, and the two of us needing first to join forces and spend ourselves against a common enemy, time, before we could engender between us and hold intact the pattern of recapitulant mimic furious victory like a cloth, a shield between ourselves and reality, between us and fact and doom. This afternoon it seemed as if we would never get it filled.[6]

The man relating the events is aware, as the boy of the *Post* story is not, that the real Vicksburg was as precariously shielded from "fact and doom" as the boy's make-believe one. The double perspective— what he thought as a boy and what he now perceives as a man— creates an incessant thoughtful ambivalence in his report of event and character entirely absent from the first "Ambuscade."

This changed perspective contributes to fuller characterization. The narrator is more aware of his own motivation as well as that of others, more aware of how his child's perspective in the past colored his picture of others. For example, in the magazine story Bayard vehemently dismisses Loosh's insinuations about the defeat of Vicksburg and diverts attention from it by throwing dust at Ringo. But in the revision he is much more aware of the unarticulated uneasiness behind his reaction: "But I was just talking too, I knew that, because niggers know, they know things; it would have to be something louder, much louder, than words to do any good. So I stooped and caught both hands full of dust and rose: and Ringo still standing there, not moving, just looking at me even as I flung the dust" (U, p. 7).

The most lengthy additions to "Ambuscade" are passages relating the impression of the father's return upon the boy. Whereas in the original the father's entrance is handled in a few sentences and his entire stay in approximately eight hundred words, his visit is elaborated in over four thousand words in the revision. The boy's vivid impression of his father is shown in the precise rendering of his appearance as he rides up. The older narrator tries to understand why his father was so impressive. Since he was neither big nor unique, perhaps it was just his closeness to them: "He was not big; it was just the things he did, that we knew he was doing, had been doing in Virginia and Tennessee, that made him seem big to us. There were others besides him that were doing the things, the same things, but maybe it was because he was the only one we knew, had ever heard snoring at night in a quiet house . . ." (U, p. 10). This discounting of the boy's glamorized view of his father is underscored in another addition with his thoughts about his father's "odor": "that odor in his clothes and beard and flesh too which I believed was the smell of powder and glory, the elected victorious but know better now: know now to have been only the will to endure, a sardonic and even humorous declining of self-delusion which is not even kin to that optimism which believes that that which is about to happen to us can possibly be the worst which we can suffer" (U, p. 11). Although the boy reports that "Father was everywhere" (U, p. 13) as they build a pen, he admits that part of his impressiveness had to do with the built-in authority of his position: "not that Father worked faster and harder than anyone else, even though you do look bigger (to twelve, at least, to me and Ringo at twelve, at least) standing still and saying 'Do this or that' to the ones who are doing it; it was the way he did it" (U, p. 13). The man, then, relates the boy's impressions, but he is unwilling to accept them completely at their former value; he feels the need to explain and in the explanation is a repudiation of sentimental distortion.[7] The man underscores the dreamlike quality of his experiences as a boy ("perhaps we were the two moths, the two feathers again or perhaps there is a point at which credulity firmly and calmly and irrevocably declines" [U, p. 20]), without now believing in the dream. It is difficult to see how Michael Millgate can characterize the revisions of "Ambuscade" as stylistic,[8] since this retrospective awareness alters drastically its meaning. From the cursory treatment of the boy-father relationship in the *Post* story is fashioned a major focal point for the larger volume. If in this story the man is attempting to come to terms with his boyhood impressions of his father whose very odor is evocative of "the will to endure," then the volume comes full circle when the odor of verbena comes to stand for sheer inflexible willfulness. Capsulized in the narrator's ambiguous impression of his father—the boy's impression of glamor, strength, and will and the man's recognition of his simultaneous smallness, autocratic privilege, and defeat—is Bayard's uneasy relationship to the Old South whose traditions he is expected to uphold and defend.

Although this element of retrospective evaluation is most pronounced in the reworking of "Ambuscade," revisions of "Retreat" and "Raid" moderate the tone and effect of several events in those stories as well. This evaluative voice is the most pronounced when events are the most extraordinary and unreal and when the feats of John Sartoris are related. When Sartoris's band and the two boys ambush the sleeping Yankees, a passage is inserted highlighting the boy's incredulity: "There is a limit to what a child can accept, assimilate; not to what it can believe because a child can believe anything, given time, but what it can accept, a limit in time, in the very time which nourishes believing of the incredible" (U, p. 75). The seven-page story of the railroad in "Raid" (U, pp. 106–12) is another major addition. (Part of this passage is curiously linked to the Negro movement, to be discussed later.) Fascinated and amazed by the railroad incident, Bayard and Ringo enviously regret their absence from the last valiant but futile run of the Confederate locomotive before the Yankees tore up the tracks: "It was like the meeting between two iron knights of the old time, not for material gain but for principle— honor denied with honor, courage denied with courage—the deed done not for the end but for the sake of the doing—put to the ultimate test and proving nothing save the finality of death and the vanity of all endeavor" (U, p. 111). But lest one feel that this scene sentimentalizes the war, our discerning narrator makes clear that this meeting of iron knights was one isolated incident in a war that was for the most part very unglamorous indeed:

> Father (and other men too) return home, afoot like tramps or on crowbait horses, in faded and patched (and at times obviously stolen) clothing, preceded by no flags nor drums and followed not even by two men to keep step with one another, in coats bearing no glitter of golden braid and with scabbards in which no sword reposed, actually almost sneaking home to spend two or three or seven days performing actions not only without glory (ploughing land, repairing fences, killing meat for the smoke house) and in which they had no skill but the very necessity for which was the fruit of the absent occupations from which, returning, they bore no proof—actions in the very clumsy performance of which Father's whole presence seemed (to us, Ringo and me) to emanate a kind of humility and apology. [U, pp. 107–8]

Partly because the revised stories are told from the point of view of an older narrator, the style, diction, syntax, and transition are improved. The intelligent man ruminating upon his experience recreates it with a sense of vivid and clearly articulated detail which is sparse in the original stories. For example, in the original Louvinia "looked taller than a ghost" and the particulars are left unspecified.

In the revision the narrator completes the picture: "in one dimension like a bolster case, taller than a bolster case in her nightgown; silent as a ghost on her bare feet which were the same color as the shadow in which she stood so that she seemed to have no feet, the twin rows of her toenails lying weightless and faint and still as two rows of faintly soiled feathers on the floor about a foot below the hem of her nightgown as if they were not connected with her" (U, p. 46). In a similar manner, the trunk stuffed behind Granny's bed is given explicit elaboration (U, p. 47). Whereas the journey of Ringo and Bayard, after being dispossessed of wagon, mules, and silver, and separated from Granny, is related matter-of-factly in the original "Raid," the eery slowness and dreamlike strangeness of the journey is recreated in the revision (U, pp. 68–69). Perhaps the account of the swarming Negroes is the most improved in vivid and explicit detail (U, pp. 116–22). Again the emphasis in the revision is upon the incredibility of such an experience for a young boy. Of course, because the narrator keeps insisting that many of his boyhood experiences during the war were incredible, the possible objection of the reader on this point is countered. Insisting that the dream was indeed reality to a young boy growing up during violent civil disorder, he both recreates the dreamlike quality of his experiences and evaluates them from the prespective of time. Because the magazine stories lack both this qualification and this critical evaluation, the same plots seem slick and the tone sentimental.

The second major kind of revision is a heightening of the significance of race. This heightening is both intriguing and puzzling, because it raises more questions than it answers and provokes complexity of theme that may not be dealt with totally satisfactorily in the complete short story composite. For one, the slaves' family relationships and individual personalities are more clearly delineated in the revision. Passages added or rewritten increase the sense of familiarity within the extended family of slaves and owners. For example, a humorous expansion is the confrontation of Joby and Granny over the trunk. Bayard explains that "they were like a man and a mare, a blooded mare . . . and Granny always beat him, not bad; just exactly enough" (U, p. 50). Of course, part of the reason she always beats him is that she is the white boss and he the black slave, but Bayard suggests that her superiority is merely through her stronger obstinacy and willfulness.

The enigmatic character of Ringo particularly is given more

prominence in the revision. In the revised "Raid," for example, Ringo is preoccupied with the railroad. Bayard senses a correspondence in the motion of the locomotive and the black people: "It was as if Ringo felt it too and that the railroad, the rushing locomotive which he hoped to see symbolised it—the motion, the impulse to move which had already seethed to a head among his people, darker than themselves, reasonless, following and seeking a delusion, a dream, a bright shape . . ." (U, pp. 91–92). If Ringo senses this correspondence, however, then surely he would be more interested in the people themselves: "I been having to hear about niggers all my life . . . I got to hear about that railroad" (U, p. 103). Never once identifying with the blacks seeking Jordan, he apparently thinks of himself only as an appendage to the Sartoris family. When they acquire 110 slaves from Colonel Dick, his interest in them is totally administrative: "The main thing now is, whut we gonter do with all these niggers" (U, p. 130). Although several times in the revisions Bayard mentions that Ringo is smarter than he, Ringo apparently is not troubled by slavery during the war or interested in its abolition after the war. In fact, appearing more amused by the abolition of slavery than interested in its personal application ("I ain't a nigger any more. I done been abolished" [U, p. 228]), Ringo shares John Sartoris's disdain for Yankee meddlers: "Used to be when you seed a Yankee you knowed him because he never had nothing but a gun or a mule halter or a handful of hen feathers. Now you don't even know him and stid of the gun he got a clutch of this stuff [new paper money] in one hand and a clutch of nigger voting tickets in the yuther" (U, p. 229).

Not only is Ringo given a more prominent—if ambivalent—role in the revisions but the closeness of his relationship to Bayard is also given increased emphasis. Bayard claims in the revised "Ambuscade," that "Ringo and I had been born in the same month and had both fed at the same breast and had slept together and eaten together for so long that Ringo called Granny 'Granny' just like I did, until maybe he wasn't a nigger anymore or maybe I wasn't a white boy anymore, the two of us neither, not even people any longer: the two supreme undefeated like two moths, two feathers riding above a hurricane" (U, pp. 7–8). At the same time that Bayard asserts the equality of Ringo and himself, however, he relates the inequity of their play activities. He gets to be General Pemberton twice in a row (while Ringo must be Grant) before Ringo can be General Pemberton once.

Indeed, Ringo has achieved this much equality only through standing on his rights and refusing to play. Bayard does not seem to notice as a child or as a man the ironic perspective placed by this war to free the slaves on the relationships between slaves and owners in his own family. In a passage added to "Raid" he explains that it matters little if he and Ringo are of different races, or if they are of unequal intelligence (with Ringo a little smarter), or if one is a slave and the other is not. All that matters is a kind of one-upmanship; Bayard has seen a locomotive and Ringo has not (U, p. 91). Now, it can be believed that children can be removed from the concerns and categorical thinking of adults, but what is a little disconcerting is that this retrospective narrator, who is otherwise so perceptive, fails to see that the existence of slavery does color even this boyhood friendship. He shows that race is a factor in their relationship without even registering the fact: he has the upperhand in play activities; he is quelled by the fact that "niggers know things" that he does not; he observes that his father's "position" makes him seem more imposing.

In "An Odor of Verbena," the two young men—although still close—have gone their separate ways both ideologically and occupationally. Both experience grief at the death of John Sartoris, but Bayard is determined to act on principle, whereas Ringo would be content to implement again the revenge code they followed when avenging Granny's death: "But I reckon that wouldn't suit that white skin you walks around in" (U, p. 251). Bayard observes that Ringo "had changed even less than I had since that day when we had nailed Grumby's body to the door of the old compress" (U, p. 248). Ringo has an "outrageous assurance gained from too long and too close association with white people" (U, p. 250). He is clearly aligned with the ways and the code of the past. While the closeness of their relationship in the past will prevent Bayard from ever being "The Sartoris" to Ringo, he acquiesces with no apparent protest to being Bayard's "boy" who stays home while Bayard goes to law school.

No doubt the thrust of the revisions makes race more of an issue in *The Unvanquished* than in the magazine stories, but the issue is clouded with ambiguity and inconsistency. I think that one of the purposes of the revisions is to show—with an unmistakable Southern bias—that inhumanity to the slaves was not characteristic of Southern families like the Sartorises. Faulkner takes pains in the revisions to show the camaraderie between Ringo and Bayard, the mutual concern of blacks and whites, the sense of "family" in the extended family. In other words, many of the revisions emphasize the positive aspects of antebellum life which are being threatened by the disruptions of war and abolition. Of course, that Loosh is involved with the fredom movement damages the perfect picture of one big happy family. But his dazed stupor (which is augmented in a couple of passages in the revision), his desertion of his "family," and his exposure of the Sartoris silver to the Yankees (which are the same in the original story) are related in such a way that he is seen as a misled traitor who has lost his head in false promises. The swarming blacks trying to get to Jordan are characterized as following a "delusion, a dream, a bright shape." Their movement is seen as self-destructive, an inexplicable denial of security and family for "hope and doom." On the other hand, in the poignancy of Loosh's reply to Granny's questioning of his right to take John Sartoris's silver ("Let God ax John Sartoris who the man name that give me to him. Let the man that buried me in the black dark ax that of the man what dug me free" [U, p. 85]), in the steadfast commitment of the Negroes' pursuit of "Jordan," in the unanalyzed inequities of the relationship of Bayard and Ringo, in the enigmatic character of Ringo, in the aftermath of the march on Jordan and of Loosh's desertion, are unexplored riches of complexity and ambiguity. But these issues are not worked into the major themes of the novel as they so convincingly could be. Unlike *Absalom, Absalom!* where Thomas Sutpen's fall is directly attributable to his denial of his mulatto wife and son, John Sartoris's demise is not precipitated by racial discrimination.

Rather, the Sartorises have a genuine sense of aristocratic *noblesse oblige*. They are dictatorial and proud, but they care for "their" people with generosity and concern. Granny steals mules to benefit the entire community as well as her own extended family. Drusilla feels a responsibility to the swarming deluded Negroes who "are not Yankees." John Sartoris's dream, unlike Thomas Sutpen's, is for the benefit of "this whole country which he is trying to raise by its bootstraps" (U, p. 256). Uncle Buck and Buddy McCaslin implement enlightened views on social relationships. The long insertion of their history can best be explained in terms of the added emphasis given to the depiction of the leading citizens' responsibility to the larger community. In a five-page addition to the original "Retreat" (U, pp. 52–57) are reiterated Buck and Buddy's ingeniously ritualized treatment of slavery (locking the front door while the slaves run out the back), their method whereby slaves buy their freedom, their instillation of successful cooperative farming among poor whites, their insistence—even at their advanced age—on participating in the Confederate cause. The McCaslins are so highly respected in the community that the people look upon them "like Deity Himself."

But where responsibility lies so does pride, privilege, and power that can harden into a disregard for the rights, sanctity, and autonomy of others, no matter how well meaning or altruistic the intention. The Sartorises are particularly susceptible to the sin of pride and the overweaning assumption of privilege. Although Granny is generous to a fault with the people of the community, she assumes the royal prerogative to supervise and to censure their use of the spoils of her enterprise (U, p. 157). She confesses her sins to God in an act of attempted humility but she cannot resist defiant self-vindication. She upbraids God for his failure to help his own creatures and their cause: "I did not sin for gain or for greed . . . I did not sin for revenge. I defy You or anyone to say I did. I sinned first for justice. And after that first time, I sinned for more than justice; I sinned for the sake of food and clothes for Your own creatures who could not help themselves—for children who had given their fathers, for wives who had given their husbands, for old people who had given their sons to a holy cause, even though You have seen fit to make it a lost cause" (U, p. 167). If it is suggested that Granny's pride made her overstep her human limitations, the point is made emphatically by her son, John, and daughter-in-law, Drusilla.

In "Skirmish at Sartoris" John autocratically imposes his will upon the post-war community by killing the Burdens who are attempting to implement Negro voting. In "An Odor of Verbena" his intolerance and pride are more sharply delineated. In fact, minor changes between the manuscript and the published story illustrate Faulkner's intensification of John and Drusilla's blunted humanity.[9] In the manuscript Sartoris is said to have killed one of two men who had tried to rob him, whereas in the printed story the man he killed might have been trying to rob him "because Father had shot too quick." Even worse he had tried to pay off the wife of the dead man who, in turn, "flung the money at Father's face" (U, p. 255). Furthermore, the culpability of Sartoris in creating the enmity between Redmond and himself is intensified. Added is the telling comment on Sartoris's character: "Father and Mr. Redmond were not only still partners, they were still friends, which as George Wyatt said was easily a record for Father" (U, p. 254). Redmond's honorable behavior during the war (U, pp. 258–59) also makes Sartoris's taunting of him all the more reprehensible. Another addition is Wyatt's admission that "maybe you're right, maybe there has been enough killing in your family" (U, p. 289). The exaggerated rigidity and the absurd formality of Drusilla are also emphasized by added description and dialogue. Her desexing is underscored with repeated reminders of her boylike appearance, "the same boy-hard body, the close implacable head with its savagely cropped hair" (U, p. 257). Whereas in the manuscript she is described merely as "tearless, and with two loaded pistols" as she waits for Bayard to avenge his father's death, in the printed story she is

> holding the two loaded pistols (I could see that too, who had had no presentiment; I could see her, in the formal brilliant room arranged formally for obsequy, not tall, not slender as a woman is but as a youth, a boy, is, motionless, in yellow, the face calm, almost bemused, the head simple and severe, the balancing sprig of verbena above each ear, the two arms bent at the elbows, the two hands shoulder high, the two identical duelling pistols lying upon, not clutched in, one to each: the Greek amphora priestess of succinct and formal violence). [U, p. 252]

The inhumanity of her attitude is given emphasis by another addition where she insists that John's arrogant dream is worth more than human life (U, p. 257). Bayard does not agree; his courageous dedication to principle—Thou shalt not kill—stands as a fine counterpart to the ruthless intolerance of his father.

The Unvanquished is much more than the sum of the original magazine stories. The introduction of an older, ruminative narrator successfully qualifies Bayard's view of his father throughout the volume and prepares convincingly for his final repudiation of his father's code. The book is ultimately disappointing, however, because the two major kinds of revisions—the introduction of the retrospective narrator and the heightening of the significance of race—are not more complementary. It is disappointing that our retrospective narrator, who is otherwise so unwilling to accept sentimental distortion, is totally uncritical of the racial inequities in his family and in his society. Faulkner admits having had some difficulty answering all the questions that were raised by the stories as he was writing them: "when I got into the first one [story] I could see two more, but by the time I'd finished the first one I saw that it was going further than that, and then when I'd finished the fourth one, I had postulated too many questions that I had to answer for my own satisfaction. So the others had to be—the other three or two, whichever it was, had to be written then."[10] Although I do not feel that he has been totally successful in answering all the questions that the book raises, *The Unvanquished* is by no means the failure that some readers would make it. The complete volume gives a vivid sense of the effect of the Civil War and Reconstruction upon the moral growth of one individual as no other work of Faulkner does. In fact, it is the only long work concentrating upon this time and the first book in Faulkner's canon postively demonstrating an individual's moral opposition to the self-destructive and antiquated behavioral patterns of the past. It succeeds in those terms but promises much more in its enticingly incomplete and ambiguous treatment of slavery and abolition.

"GO DOWN, MOSES": 3 CONSTRUCTION OF A SHORT STORY COMPOSITE

Go Down, Moses is perhaps the most singular book in Faulkner's canon because, more than any of the others, it is a collage, a pastiche of dissimilar pieces. One might look upon *The Wild Palms* as an audacious intermeshing of two dissimilar stories, but in *Go Down, Moses* Faulkner put together not two but ten separately written stories, and he created a new synthesis through extensive revision and addition. Perhaps because the book straddles the fence between a short story collection and a novel, critics have been troubled about what to call it. It has been described as: "a remarkably unified novel," "a single novelistic structure," "a loosely constructed novel," an "experimental novel," a "hybrid: a loosely jointed but ambitious novel masking as a collection of short stories," "if not exactly a novel, then, at least a narrative which begins, develops, and concludes," "a blend," "a mosaic in which not only the sequence but the very presence of all seven stories is meaningful," "a set of variations upon two major themes," and a "book of related short stories."[1] Critics generally agree that the structuring of *Go Down, Moses* is unusual.

In spite of the uniqueness, perhaps because of it, few studies of the formal structure of the volume have been made. Commentators have readily praised the success of "The Bear," and voluminous critical exegesis has been expended on this story as an isolated entity. While the story (parts 1, 2, 3, and 5) is one of Faulkner's high achievements, part 4 belongs only to the larger volume, not the autonomous story. Although Faulkner suggested that when reading "The Bear" as an isolated story, part 4 should be skipped,[2] critics have not taken him at his word. Part 4 without the context of *Go Down, Moses* is too compact to be other than confusing and incomplete; how anyone can find it otherwise is hard to understand.

In addition to elucidating the complexities of part 4 of "The Bear," critics have traced through thematic correspondences among the stories and have commonly recognized that Ike emerges as the central character, that historical perspective is created by the across-the-generations look at the McCaslins, and that exploitation of the black man and of the wilderness is the common theme.[3] Readers often have been puzzled by "Pantaloon in Black," the only story that is not about the McCaslin descendants. Lionel Trilling and Malcolm Cowley suggest and Stanley Tick insists that the story is not a part of the "six-section narrative." They apparently are not troubled that, ignored or not, the story remains in the volume as Faulkner conceived it. Several commentators seem compelled to insist upon the lack of autonomy of the individual story in order to demonstrate the book's unity. Michael Millgate, for example, suggests that the apparently separable units cohere with "closer reading."[4] Tick claims that "no section is fully autonomous, and the tensions generated in these component parts are resolved only when one understands them in their full contexts."[5] Only recently has a critic, Joseph W. Reed, Jr., argued that the book has a dualistic form; he claims that *Go Down, Moses* is "Faulkner's most successful attempt at a generic middle-ground, the short-story compound, and clearly an attempt to justify this as a self-sufficient genre." Yet he catalogues the book as one of the "uncertainties" in Faulkner's narrative art, partially because he feels that part 4 of "The Bear" (and to a lesser degree part 1 of "Was") is not totally assimilated into the imaginative and structural complex of the "short story compound."[6]

Having closely studied Faulkner's process of revision and composition in *Go Down, Moses,* I am convinced that he was attempting to create a new synthetic form, the short story composite, in which the stories are autonomous units governed by their own principles while they are at the same time integral parts of a larger whole. I do not think that Faulkner was self-consciously establishing a new genre, but that he was attempting to find a form flexible enough to accommodate both the expansive panoramic across-the-generations look at a host of characters and incidents and an intensive examination of the moral consciousness of one individual, Isaac McCaslin. Those critics who have proclaimed its "novelistic" unity have underestimated the unusual development of *Go Down, Moses.* One-half the "novel" and four of the seven stories have very little to do with the central character, Ike. Except for the fragmentary part 1, the incidents of "Was" take place long before he is born. Lucas Beauchamp and Roth Edmonds think in passing about his repudiation in "The Fire and the Hearth," but Ike does not appear in the story. He is not even mentioned in "Pantaloon in Black." Appearing for the first time "in person" as a young boy in "The Old People" and "The Bear," and as a young man in part 4 of "The Bear," Ike reappears as an old man in "Delta Autumn" and is absent in the final story, "Go Down, Moses." Obviously if Faulkner had wanted to portray Isaac McCaslin, he could have done so in a much more efficient and logical way. He has, rather, retained the narrative frame of the original stories, although he has considerably enlarged the characterization, interlinked the characters genealogically, and implanted suggestions that the diverse stories, directly or indirectly, will bear ultimately upon a central moral issue, Ike's repudiation. The stories retain their autonomy, but they also work as coordinate parts of the larger whole. The two fragments, part 1 of "Was" and part 4 of "The Bear," are key unifying devices of the composite; they are the only parts which are not autonomous, a seeming inconsistency which, as I mentioned above, troubles Reed, who is otherwise willing to credit success to the dual structure of the book. But Faulkner can certainly use whatever means he wishes to effect his new form. Suspended in time, these fragments indicate that the narrative stories eventually will lyrically cohere around the sketchy portrait of Ike and his controversial repudiation. The addition of these fragments, although extremely significant, is only a small part of the total process of amalgamation, addition, and revision that went into the construction of this short story composite.

"WAS"

"Was," the first story of *Go Down, Moses,* is surely one of the most hilariously funny stories that Faulkner ever wrote. It has, however, annoyed and puzzled those critics who feel that a comedy is an inappropriate introduction to the seriously rendered characters and issues taken up elsewhere in the text.[7] Faulkner apparently did not agree, since his revisions of unpublished typescripts of the story show a decided inclination both to intensify the humor and to mold the story into an introduction to *Go Down, Moses*. An examination of the kind of changes that he made reveals a great deal about the method and conception of this short story composite and about the careful craftsmanship of William Faulkner.

A complete twenty-two page untitled typescript of "Was" and five fragmentary, unnumbered pages from different drafts have been deposited in the Alderman Library. Several differences between the complete typescript and the published version are for the most part inconspicuous but significant genealogical links to the larger volume. The most conspicuous link, part 1 of the printed story, does not appear in the typescript. This section, a fragment without capitalization and final periods in its three paragraphs, presents a capsule characterization of Isaac McCaslin, a character who is not yet born when the events of the story transpire. This initial section introduces much more material than can be assimilated by even the most patient and painstaking reader, but seasoned readers of Faulkner's fiction will not be troubled by this familiar device of emphasis through suspension and reflexive amplification. Faulkner frequently introduces an important character or scene and holds it in suspension while he circuitously depicts the past that informs the present. Only with the completion of the entire volume is the fragmentary reference to Ike's heritage, marriage, and dispossession fully clarified. The suspended fragment suggests that *Go Down, Moses* is no mere collection of short stories; it instead promises to reveal reflexively this central character.

Part 1 also clarifies the narrative point of view of the tale to follow. While the typescript story is told in the first person by a boy named Bayard, the revised one is told in the third person filtered through the perspective of the boy McCaslin (Cass) Edmonds, cousin to the phantom central character, Ike. Since Bayard mentions his black companion, Ringo, he is probably the same Bayard as in *The Unvanquished,* suggesting that Faulkner did not originally write the story with *Go Down, Moses* in mind. Although some people might be troubled by his grafting of the story on to this context, I think that it is revealing to see how Faulkner discovered the potential of his stories.

What Faulkner obviously discovered was the richly ambiguous perspective that the ritualized hunts of "Was" would take on when complicated by past and future miscegenetic and genealogical interrelationships among the participants, and when seen from the dual perspective of the past and present. Where Tomey's Turl is merely a black slave in the typescript, Hubert Beauchamp refers to him as "white half-McCaslin" and his black hands become "saddle-colored" in the revision.[8] Where Mr. Jason Prim and his sister Sophonsiba are neighbors with no immediate or eventual relationship to the boy-narrator in the original, the reader discovers later in the volume that Miss Sophonsiba did eventually marry Buck and become the mother of Ike McCaslin, and so the Beauchamps too are ultimately drawn into the entangling genealogical framework of *Go Down, Moses*. The name changes, Tomey's Turl's McCaslin blood, and the complex narrative point of view established by part 1 of the revised story, then, underscore the potential importance of genealogy as the transmitter of the past to the present.

Another change that hints at greater complexity is the brief mention that the McCaslins established an unusual living arrangment for their slaves: "Uncle Buck and Uncle Buddy moved all the niggers into the big house which his great-grandfather had not had time to finish" (GDM, p. 6). Only later in *Go Down, Moses* is it mentioned (GDM, pp. 262–63) that they locked the front door and let the slaves run out the back, their way of implementing the letter but not the spirit of slavery. The change from the working title of the story to "Was" also highlights the new perspective Faulkner established for the story. Although the typescript in the Alderman Library is untitled, Russell Roth, who studied "the Brennan papers" (pages of this story and of "Go Down, Moses" that Faulkner rejected during the process of writing), claims that the story was originally entitled "Almost."[9] "Almost" is a fitting name for a tale which depicts only an amusing series of near captures: of Turl by Buck, Buck by Miss Sophonsiba, even the fox by the dogs. But "Was" is a more appropriate title for the distanced, romanticized legend, "the old times, the old days" presented in *Go Down, Moses*. The title implies a duality of focus: this is the way that it "was," but not as it now 'is" assimilated into the consciousness and person of the present descendant, Ike McCaslin. In fact, Faulkner claimed, "There is no such thing really as was because the past is. It is part of every man, every woman, and every moment. All of his and her ancestry, background, is all a part of himself or herself at any moment. And so a man, a character in a story at any moment of action is not just himself as he is then, he is all that made him. . . . [10] Indications of genealogical and miscegenetic complications here make the reader vaguely anticipate that the inheritance that "is" is interlaced with guilt and shame.

Since this linkage is latent rather than overt, unobtrusive rather than obvious, humor is the dominant mode of the story and only reflexively, as the composite develops, does one question the relationships among the characters of the story. What gives the story an air of simplicity and unreality is the codification of life into games, where everything is determined by rules, strategies, and stakes that everyone implicitly accepts. The hunting of Turl is a game; as is the bet between Hubert and Buck and the husband hunt of Miss Sophonsiba; as is the game of poker between Hubert and Buck, which loses Buck his freedom and forces him to buy Tennie for three hundred dollars; as is the poker game between Hubert and Buddy which cancels the results of the previous game; as is, for that matter, the hunt of the fox by the dogs in the house, which are regularly released by Buck, regularly arousing Buddy's anger. The pervasive gamesmanship militates against any serious reading of the issues and people involved.

Certainly from one point of view it would be atrocious to deal with Tomey's Turl and Tennie with so little regard for their humanity. By sheer whim or perversity or turn of the card, their fates are determined. Nevertheless, the story creates no pathos. Turl and Tennie are not suffering under this system, and their feelings are not described and are unimportant to the story. Ironically, but not tragically or pathetically, Turl deals and apparently stacks the cards which decide the ownership of his loved one and himself. In this never-never world of "was," Tomey's Turl does not suffer under slavery and Buck escapes the clutches of Miss Sophonsiba. Nothing mars the idyllic world that was, where the vagaries and complexities of human existence are reduced to rituals, the agonies and indecisions settled by games. Later in *Go Down, Moses* it is revealed that not only has Buck succumbed to the determined husband hunt of Miss Sophonsiba but atrocity and tragedy were also connected with Tomey's Turl's conception. In his ruthless pride and arrogance, Carothers McCaslin fathered a child, Tomey, on his own daughter, Tomasina, an act which caused her mother Eunice to commit suicide in grief. In "Was" Faulkner has abstracted out the serious and presented a very amusing picture of the old times, but the humor is made poignant by subdued reminders that the serious—the tragic and the terrible—is a part of the same picture.

The change from the first person to the third, of course, necessitated changes of diction. For the most part the folksy and ungram-

matical are replaced by more standard diction and grammar, although
enough of the original diction is left to maintain the light colloquial
tone. Indeed, frequently some expressions take on an added dimension of humor when reported from an adult's rather than a boy's
perspective. For example, in both versions the idea of the boy and
Uncle Buck dragging their collective foot is amusing, but the narrator
capitalizes on the humor of the balanced foot while he more fully
renders the complete transparency of Miss Sophonsiba's flirtation.
The original reads: " 'Why Mr Theophilus,' she says. 'What a surprise. Welcome to Primrose.' Me and Uncle Buck drug our foot"
(TS, p. 7). The revised reads:

> "Why, Mister Theophilus," she said. "And McCaslin," she
> said. She had never looked at him and she wasn't talking to him and he
> knew it, although he was prepared and balanced to drag his foot when
> Uncle Buck did. "Welcome to Warwick."
> He and Uncle Buck dragged their foot. [GDM, pp. 10–11]

The narrator creates a sense of vivid immediacy by providing fuller
descriptions and making greater use of direct quotation, as is done in
the rendering of Uncle Buck on the chase: "So Uncle Buck told me
to stay back where Tomey's Turl wouldn't see me and flush, and he
would circle and bay him at the creek ford" (TS, p. 4); "Uncle
Buck flung his arm out and back, reining in, crouched on the big
horse, his little round head and his gnarled neck thrust forward like
a cooter's. 'Stole away!' he whispered. 'You stay back where he
wont see you and flush. I'll circle him through the woods and we
will bay him at the creek ford' " (GDM, p. 8). Later, although
Bayard quotes Buck in part, "We'll cut him off before he can den"
(TS, p. 11), the narrator includes more of Buck's incongruous hunting jargon for his human prey: " 'I godfrey, we've got him,' Buck
said. 'He's going to earth. We'll cut back to the house and head him
before he can den' " (GDM, pp. 17–18). So if anything is lost in
omitting Bayard's folksy diction (a facile way to create atmosphere,
at best), it is more than compensated for by the narrator's greater
story-telling skill. Most of the changes either intensify the humor or
increase the precision of rendering. They display Faulkner's skillful
attention to detail.

Many of the additions to the story are often its most priceless
passages of humor. Miss Sophonsiba, already a comic figure in the
typescript, is even more humorous, partly because Faulkner comi-

cally plays upon the nine-year-old boy's awe of her roan tooth.
Bayard reports "she had a roan-colored tooth" (TS, p. 6), but Cass
is obsessed with it: "and he stood quietly a little behind Uncle
Buck, watching her lips until they opened and he could see the roan
tooth. He had never known anyone before with a roan tooth"
(GDM, p. 10); "and he watched the roan-colored tooth flick and
glint between her lips" (GDM, p. 11); "She stood there, the roan
tooth not flicking now but fixed because she wasn't talking now"
(GDM, p. 12).

Much more of Miss Sophonsiba's conversation is included.
Her ridiculous analogy relating Buck to a bumblebee wasting his
sweetness on Uncle Buddy's desert air is entirely new (GDM, p. 11).
Again the humor is intensified by filtering the absurdity of Miss Sophonsiba's manner through the boy's awed and blurred impression. A
fuller sense of Buck's discomfort and anxiety to verify his firm intention to remain a bachelor is added to the summary of the dinner
conversation that follows. Whereas in the typescript Uncle Buck is
apparently suffering in silence and only capable of one word responses to Miss Sophonsiba's ever-exuding flirtatious monologue
(TS, p. 7), in the revision Uncle Buck even stops eating to defend
politely but firmly his bachelordom; Miss Sophonsiba, in turn, merely
increases the pressure (GDM, pp. 11–12).

A minor change is the alteration of Miss Sophonsiba's name
for their plantation from the tastelessly quaint Primrose (a play on
the family name, Prim) to the pretentious Warwick. That the name
Warwick underscores Miss Sophonsiba's aristocratic pretension is
made clear in the following added explanation: "Miss Sophonsiba . . . was still trying to make people call [the plantation] Warwick after the place in England that she said Mr Hubert was probably the true earl of only he never even had enough pride, not to
mention energy, to take the trouble to establish his just rights"
(GDM, p. 5). This change both adds to the ridiculousness of Miss
Sophonsiba and lays the groundwork for the satire and pathos to
come. As Faulkner has repeatedly emphasized in his conversation as
well as in his fiction, life in antebellum Mississippi was far from the
romanticized South that films such as *Gone with the Wind* have
given us.[11] These were country people with country ways glossed
over with some rudimentary trappings of culture and manners. The
breach between Miss Sophonsiba's pretentious manner and the ram-
shackled state of the plantation (a missing gate, a broken shutter, a

rotted floor board, a lethargic and indifferent Mr. Hubert) is a source of humor in "Was." Later, however, the pretension to aristocratic living is linked to the injustice of slavery. This, too, is part of the serious and the terrible facilely omitted from the picture "of the old times, the old days" in "Was." That the devastation of the Civil War totally destroyed even this paltry gentility is pathetically shown in Miss Sophonsiba's anguish over their diminishing wealth in part 4 of "The Bear."

Some of the improvement in descriptive clarity in the revised "Was" is linked in part to the differing context of the *Go Down, Moses* story. For example, Uncle Buck and Uncle Buddy are of indefinable age in the typescript and their appearance is left unspecified. In the printed version they are sixty years old, a fact made evident in two vivid descriptions that sharply differentiate them. The first depicts the wiry sprightliness of Uncle Buddy mounting a horse;[12] the second describes the formidable stillness of the poker expert, Uncle Buddy.[13]

Most of the other significant changes in "Was" center around the complicated series of bets and poker games exchanged between the twins and Hubert Beauchamp. While Faulkner does a great deal to clarify the terms of these various wagers, all but the most experienced gambler will have some trouble following the evolution of stakes. Be that as it may, Faulkner has added some fortuitous touches to this sequence, the first of which is the emphatic exchange between Hubert and Buck over their initial five-hundred-dollar bet as to the likelihood that Buck would find Tomey's Turl before the night's end. Although they make the same wager in the original, the determined, repeated verification of those terms which climaxes in a series of resounding "dones" does not appear (GDM, pp. 16–17).

After the fiasco where Uncle Buck unwittingly gets into Miss Sophonsiba's bed, the conversation between Buck and Hubert is expanded to include some humorous exchanges, including Buck's eminently reasonable defense: "Be reasonable. Say I did walk into a lady's bedroom, even Miss Sophonsiba's; say, just for the sake of the argument, there wasn't no other lady in the world but her and so I walked into hers and tried to get in bed with her, would I have took a nine-year-old boy with me?" (GDM, p. 22). Mr. Hubert's response is also a new addition. He gleefully equates Buck's experience to that of lying down with a bear in its den and ties Miss Sophonsiba's husband hunt to the story's race motif:

"Reasonable is just what I'm being," Mr Hubert said. You come into bear-country of your own free will and accord. All right; you were a grown man and you knew it was bear-country and you knew the way back out like you knew the way in and you had your chance to take it. But no. You had to crawl into the den and lay down by the bear. And whether you did or didn't know the bear was in it dont make any difference. So if you got back out of that den without even a claw-mark on you, I would not only be unreasonable, I'd be a damned fool. After all, I'd like a little peace and quiet and freedom myself, now I got a chance for it. Yes, sir. She's got you, 'Filus, and you know it. You run a hard race and you run a good one, but you skun the hen-house one time too many." [GDM, pp. 22–23]

The exchanges that follow make for a more satisfactory progression. Originally Buck asks for a chance ("Give me a chance") to extricate himself from Miss Sophonsiba; now he takes it: "He drew his breath in and let it out again, slow and not loud. But you could hear it. 'Well,' he said. 'So I reckon I'll have to take the chance then' " (GDM, p. 23). What he does is hold—on a technicality—Mr. Hubert to the five-hundred-dollar bet. Hubert in turn resorts to poker. In the ensuing poker game is added Buck's attempt to dismiss the alleged obligation to Sophonsiba as foolishness and include only the question of ownership of the slaves in the deal, a dismissal which Hubert, of course, will not even consider (GDM, p. 24).

In both versions the reader might at first be confused about the undertaking of a second poker game between Buddy and Hubert. The only preparation for it is the boy's knowing remark: "Uncle Buck looks like he's settled. But Uncle Buddy aint got here yet" (GDM, p. 25). A couple of lines on the back of page 18 of the typescript, however, indicate that at one time Faulkner clarified more explicitly that the reason Buddy got Mr. Hubert to engage in another poker game was his knowledge that Hubert did not want to pay his sister's dowry. (The lines read: ' "poker with you aint gambling. But never mind. A gamble for what?' 'For Miss Sophonsiba's dowry,' Uncle Buddy says.") Perhaps this more explicit rendering of the psychological gamesmanship would have been better. The uninitiated needs all the help he can get in these poker intrigues.

Uncle Buddy is a super-card shark in the typescript, but telling details are added to the revision that augment that image as well as Mr. Hubert's uneasiness. In the revised story Hubert offers Uncle Buddy a toddy. His response, "I dont drink," causes Hubert to retort sarcastically and nervously: " 'That's right . . . I knew there was

something else besides just woman-weak that makes 'Filus seem human. But no matter.' He batted his eyes twice at Uncle Buddy''
(GDM, p. 26). Buddy's composure is also evident when he waits until
all the cards are dealt before he even looks at his down-card.

While in both accounts the two poker players do not register
the identity of the dealer called in from the outside, only in the revised story is the reader aware of the irony of Turl's dealership
throughout the game. Moreover, in the original the word *waiting*
strongly suggests that the dealership was a prior arrangement between
Buddy and Turl: "So I went to the back door and called. Only he was
waiting right outside . . ." (TS, p. 18). Later that fact remains vague:
"But he didn't have to call because Tomey's Turl was squatting
against the wall just outside the door'' (GDM, p. 27).

A final major addition is Hubert's interruption to review un-
easily the stakes of the game as they have evolved after Uncle
Buddy raises by including the two slaves in the deal. Although
Faulkner was undoubtedly trying to help the reader sort out the
stakes here, some confusion exists either on his part, on Buddy's,
on Hubert's, or on mine.

The only way one can make sense out of the wager is to credit
Uncle Buddy with a super-subtle and crafty manipulation of terms.
As the game has evolved to this point, Buddy is wagering Miss Sophonsiba's dowry against Uncle Buck's freedom. If he wins, Buck is
free. If he loses, Buck is caught, and Hubert does not have to pay any
dowry. Buck and Hubert already settled the "nigger business" in the
first poker game. Since Buck lost, he is obliged to pay Hubert three
hundred dollars for Tennie and to take her to his plantation. The
"nigger business" is not included in the original stakes of the game
between Buddy and Hubert, so the three hundred dollars is still owed
and Tennie presumably belongs to the McCaslins. Although the
slaves are monetary assets, they are looked at by all three white men
as undesirable possessions. It is the loser who get the "niggers." Or
as Hubert politely puts it, it is the low hand that "wins Sibbey" and
takes the "niggers." The question is, then, what does Uncle Buddy
mean when he says, "I'll bet you them two niggers"? Since he now
owns them and, one presumes, still regards their ownership as undesirable, is he thus declaring them as a liability rather than an asset?
Seemingly he is having it both ways. From a monetary point of view,
the slaves are the equivalent of six hundred dollars in cash, certainly
a substantial and legitimate raise in a poker game. Yet by using them

as a raise, he is cornering his opponent. He has turned an actual liability (possession of the slaves) into a seeming asset (the equivalent of six hundred dollars), and he is using this seeming asset to rid himself of the actual liability. As far as the "nigger business" is concerned, he stands to win either way, because the three hundred dollar debt for Tennie will be canceled no matter how it goes. As Hubert sorts out the stakes he says: " 'We'll check up for a minute. If I win, you take Sibbey without dowry and the two niggers, and I dont owe 'Filus anything. If you win—' '—Theophilus is free. And you him the three hundred dollars for Tomey's Turl,' Uncle Buddy said" (GDM, p. 28). In other words, if Buddy wins, he is relieved of possession of the slaves and gets three hundred dollars for Tomey's Turl. If he loses, he gets to keep both slaves for free. Either Faulkner or Hubert or both forgot about the three hundred dollars still owing for Tennie, or I am confused. Admittedly, because Mr. Hubert failed to mention the three hundred dollars does not necessarily mean that he forgot it. Perhaps both men understood that the three hundred dollars for Tennie would be paid if Buddy lost. If that is so, Faulkner could have rendered this scene with more clarity. Of course, the determining factor in Hubert's decision to pass is his belated cognizance of Tomey's Turl's dealership. But even here the situation is not as clear as it could be.

Faulkner's own statements about the story indicate that he wanted us to believe that Turl would have searched the deck for the three Buddy needed to complete his straight and win the game, so Hubert's suspicion of a stacked deck is well-founded. Faulker claimed that Turl's desire to be with his loved one Tennie prompted this action.[14] But since the men had decided "to settle this nigger business once and for all," Turl and Tennie would be together no matter which man won. As a matter of fact, since he was a McCaslin, one would think that Turl would prefer that he and Tennie be owned by Buck and Buddy rather than Hubert Beauchamp. But as the story reads, by helping Buddy to win, Turl is securing his sale to Beauchamp. Even though the poker scene is more carefully rendered in the revised version, the logistics of the stratagem remain annoyingly jumbled. Either Faulkner credits his reader with more acumen than is warranted, or he himself was confused.

For a postscript, it is interesting to observe some plans that Faulkner fortunately decided to forego in both versions. Page 12 of the typescript has the following sentence crossed out: "So Uncle

Buck taken the last drink out of the bottle and throwed it away . . .''
Later Faulkner apparently discovered the comic possibilities of
Uncle Buck falling on the whiskey bottle (when Turl knocked him
over) and fearing that it was blood. Another change is registered in
"the Brennan papers." Roth shows that the "Buchanan motif" un-
dergoes three different forms before it was rejected. Part of the last
version reads:

> He [Tomey's Turl] couldn't do nothing right, and he wouldn't even do
> it wrong unless Uncle Buck was standing right over him. And Uncle
> Buck couldn't sell him not even by taking him all the way to Memphis
> because Uncle Buck said even the folks in Memphis had done already
> heard about Tomey's Turl and he said how he thought once he would
> send him under government frank to President Buchanan only he said
> he didn't even think little enough of President Buchanan to unload
> Tomey's Turl on him without warning.[15]

No such mention of Uncle Buck's opinion of Tomey's Turl's use-
lessness is retained; he is incorrigible and he is slow moving, and
Hubert emphatically does not want him, but he is not the subject of
heavy-handed humorous ridicule by anyone. He should not be noto-
riously stupid in *Go Down, Moses* because he is, after all, the half
brother of Buck and Buddy and the very embodiment of the pride
and arrogance of their mutual father, Carothers McCaslin, who also
happens to be—atrociously enough—Tomey's Turl's grandfather. Of
course, Buck and Buddy could be seen as callous, gambling to rid
themselves of their half brother's ownership, but the serious ramifications of actions are scrupulously ignored in the ritualized world
of "Was." Nevertheless, Tomey's Turl's history will be dealt with
seriously later. For this reason, he must not be portrayed as a no-
account fool who "couldn't do nothing right." Faulkner, as usual, is
his own best critic.

"THE FIRE AND THE HEARTH"

The care that Faulkner lavished on his craft is nowhere more evident
than in the evolution of "The Fire and the Hearth." Three main episodes correspond to its three chapters: the first centered on the stills;

the second, the gold-divining machine; and finally, the proposed divorce. Of course all three episodes are related, since Lucas seeks to expose George Wilkins's still so his own moonshining and gold-divining are not disturbed, and Molly seeks a divorce, since she is convinced that Lucas is immorally violating the land by searching for gold. Each of the three narratives is humorous in tone and intent. The first two chapters were previously published as magazine stories and the third existed in typescript form before the three were revised and amalgamated into "The Fire and the Hearth." But the total effect of the three-chaptered story is very different from that of three related narrative episodes. The story, in fact, is a microcosm of the larger volume. *Go Down, Moses,* like most of Faulkner's fiction, achieves its formal unity from the spatial arrangment of the parts rather than from narrative chronology. *Go Down, Moses* is particularly noteworthy, however, because the different pieces retain their identities as separable short stories while they fit within a larger unified structure. Likewise, each chapter of "The Fire and the Hearth," at first glance, is a narrative tale in the traditional sense in which the unfolding of the action provides the story's development. But the narratives are interspersed with reminiscences of and interpolations from the past, so that character and event are viewed in broad sociological and familial contexts. Here, as in the larger volume, the arrangement of parts, rather than sequential development, becomes the dominant formal element.

The first chapter is based on the simple and not-so-well motivated story "A Point of Law" which exists in two forms, an unpublished twenty-one-page typescript on deposit in the Alderman Library[16] and a published version which appeared in *Collier's.*[17] The original story depicts Luke Beauchamp's foiled attempt to eliminate George Wilkins, a foolish competitor in the moonshine business and a foolish suitor of his daughter's, in one cleverly set-up exposure. The conflict is not between George and Lucas though—even here George is no match—but between Lucas and the white establishment of Roth, the sheriff, and the law. Lucas manages to circumvent the white establishment twice: once by producing miraculously the marriage certificate invalidating Nat and George's court testimony and a second time by again starting up in business with George by using Nat's home improvement money for new equipment. Lucas is a stereotyped black comic character. In fact, the caricatured illustrations by William Meade Prince in *Collier's* invite one to view the story as a kind of

Amos and Andy comedy. This comic dimension, still present in the revision, is moderated by the new perspective from which these events are seen.

The thrust of the revision throughout "The Fire and the Hearth" is to make the central character Lucas a complex multi-faceted person rather than a comic stereotype and to make his confrontations with Roth reverberate with an accumulated history of family and racial tension. This increased emphasis upon Lucas is effected in large part by establishing his perspective as the point of view of chapter one. Added to the original is a new scene—part 1 of chapter one—depicting Lucas's midnight machinations to rid himself of George Wilkins. The perspective is that of Lucas, but as reported by a detached, slightly ironic, effaced narrator.[18] Faulkner is very effective with this kind of paraphrased stream-of-consciousness. Lucas's self-righteous rationalizations become unwittingly a self-portrayal which sets him up in relationship to all the important people and elements in "The Fire and the Hearth": George, Nat, Molly, and Roth; the moonshining, the gold-digging, the land, his heritage, and his race.

Unlike the black man of the *Collier's* story and of the typescript, who is no relation to his white landlord, Lucas of the final text is a mulatto related by blood to Roth Edmonds. The most obsessive element in Lucas's thoughts, as he plots to rid himself of George, is his proud status as "not only the oldest man but the oldest living person on the Edmonds plantation, the oldest McCaslin descendant even though in the world's eyes he descended not from McCaslins but from McCaslin slaves" (GDM, p. 36). Faulkner has not awkwardly attached a complicated genealogy to the volume; genealogy is important in *Go Down, Moses* because the characters themselves are obsessed with it. The time that Lucas and Roth and others live in is colored by the clinging tenacity of the past; their very personalities are shaped and informed by the lives of their ancestors.

Before the particular events of the moonshining fiasco occur, then, Lucas is a man who is proud of his age and lineage, and of his skill and experience as a moonshiner and farmer. Furthermore, this new scene introduces an important new element—the discovery of the gold coin—that serves to tie the three-chaptered story together. The search for buried treasure, although not undertaken in this part, is the basis of chapter two of "The Fire and the Hearth."

The scene depicting Lucas and Molly at the breakfast table

(part 2 of chapter one) is where "A Point of Law" begins. The particulars of this humorous tale remain essentially unchanged, but the manner of presentation is markedly dissimilar. The innumerable differences between the typescript and *Collier's* versions are for the most part minor rather than major alterations and display Faulkner's fastidious attention to the finer points of style. Often the *Collier's* story is expanded from the apparently earlier typescript with fuller descriptive detail, smoother transition, more dialogue, more precise rendering. In the following two quotations, italics indicate wording added to the *Collier's* version; brackets indicate wording found only in the typescript.

> Lucas pushed his chair back from the supper table and got up. He gave *the sullen and watchful face of* his daughter, Nat, a single grim veiled look. "Gwine down the road," he said.
> "Whar you gwine *dis* [this] time *er* [of] night?" his wife demanded. *Messin' around up yon in de bottom all last night; gittin' back just in time to hitch up and be in de field when de sun cotch you!* You needs to be in bed if you gonter [be in the field by sunup tomorrow—] *git done plantin' fo Roth Edmonds—*" [TS, p. 1; PL, p. 20]

Faulkner progressively expands and refines the descriptive phrasing in each retelling:

> He had nothing against George Wilkins personally. If George Wilkins had just stuck to farming, *to working the land which he too share-cropped from Roth Edmonds,* he, Lucas, would just as soon Nat *were* married *to George* [him] as anybody else, sooner than most of the other *buck niggers in that neighborhood* [young men he knew]. [TS, p. 1; PL, p. 20]

> It was not that he had anything against George personally, despite the mental exasperation and the physical travail he was having to undergo when he should have been at home in bed asleep. If George had just stuck to farming the land which Edmonds had allotted him he would just as soon Nat married George as anyone else, sooner than most of the nigger bucks he knew. [GDM, p. 34]

Since the changes made from magazine story to "The Fire and the Hearth" include major alterations of perspective, structure, emphasis, and characterization, many of the stylistic alterations, like those outlining Lucas's exasperation and weariness above, contribute to Lucas's fuller characterization.

Lucas's central role is emphasized in chapter one also by the frequent insertions of italicized passages of his direct thoughts. In the earlier drafts Lucas's feelings about Nat's empty bedroom are summarized: "it was empty. He had expected it to be. George Wilkins was entitled to one more evening of female companionship, because tomorrow he was going to take up residence for a long time where he would not have it" (PL, p. 20). In chapter one the same feelings are directly rendered: "It would be empty too. He had expected that. *I reckon George Wilkins is entitled to one more night of female company,* he thought. *From what I have heard, he wont find none of it where he is going tomorrow"* (GDM, p. 62). Furthermore, Lucas is almost always referred to as "he," "his," and "him" in chapter one rather than by his proper name as is typical in "A Point of Law." Many descriptions that were earlier told through the omniscient narrator's point of view are now filtered through Lucas's eyes. While George's appearance is originally part of the narrative: "His hat was still raked above his right ear, but his sepia face was not full of teeth as it usually was" (PL, p. 30), in the revised story, this description is more appropriately part of Lucas's vindictive feelings toward George: "*Leastways his face aint all full of teeth now like it used to be whenever it found anybody looking at it,* he thought viciously" (GDM, p. 66).

One can observe Faulkner's progressive clarification of intent and reworking of detail to focus more centrally upon Lucas and his control of the situation. For example, although the surprise appearance of Nat and George's marriage license is unexplained in all three accounts, Faulkner alters details from version to version which indicate that he was building grounds for the speculation that the marriage license was valid rather than falsified and that Lucas divined this fact and proceeded accordingly.[19]

Most of chapter one is closer to the *Collier's* story than to the typescript, but Faulkner apparently drew from both when writing the latter part of the chapter, gathering up clues suggesting that Lucas can, without explicit proof and verbalization, both perceive and control his daughter and son-in-law's behavior. Where the *Collier's* story relates the confrontation of Nat and Lucas sparsely with little authorial comment, the final version, like the typescript, elaborates upon the mutual conjecture and challenge that underlie the tense meeting of father and daughter (TS, pp. 11–12; PL, p. 30; GDM, p. 68). On the other hand, Lucas's authoritative command that Nat come to him is drawn from the *Collier's* story. But Faulkner always works to improve a scene; Lucas is even more commanding in "The Fire and the Hearth" because now he does not even look up, so confident is he that Nat has been keenly listening to their conversation and will feel compelled to come when he calls. In the masterfully drawn battle of wills between father and daughter, Lucas's formidable control is again impressively shown.[20]

If passages are rewritten to insure our recognition of Lucas's self-command, impregnability, composure, and dignity, others are altered that detract from that image. One such passage is while they are waiting in the court building for Roth to show the marriage license to Judge Gowan. In the earlier accounts Lucas sits humbly, indistinguishable from Nat and George: "They sat in a small office, on the edge of a hard bench, decorous and in silence, their backs not touching the bench's back, while the deputy marshal chewed a toothpick and read a paper" (PL, p. 30). This aspect of humility is removed and once again our impressions are filtered through Lucas's perspective (GDM, p. 72).

The total effect of the numerous major and minor changes is to prepare convincingly for the central confrontation between Roth and Lucas. His own man, Lucas is incorrigibly independent and a formidable opponent on any matter. With the genealogical perspective that both Roth and Lucas bring to their relationship, however, their encounters become representative of repeated instances of confrontation and misunderstanding within this extended family. While Lucas's original involvement of Roth in the exposure of the stills is related sparsely in "A Point of Law," a greater degree of familiarity and informality is interjected into the encounters of Lucas and Edmonds in the revised text. Importantly, in the revision it is not merely "the big house" that Lucas approaches to talk to Roth, but a particular house with a history he knows and recalls:

> He approached the house—the two log wings which Carothers McCaslin had built and which had sufficed old Buck and Buddy, connected by the open hallway which, as his pride's monument and epitaph, old Cass Edmonds had enclosed and superposed with a second storey of white clapboards and faced with a portico. He didn't go around to the back, the kitchen door. He had done that only one time since the present Edmonds was born; he would never do it again as long as he lived. Neither did he mount the steps. Instead he stopped in the darkness beside the gallery and rapped with his knuckles on the edge of it until the white man came up the hall and peered out the front door. [GDM, pp. 44–45]

Furthermore, this encounter is preceded by a three-page transcription of Lucas's feelings showing a decided inclination on his part to view the present time as inferior to the stronger men and the finer standards of the past. The simplest events and people take on complexity as one is aware of the past that informs them. In "A Point of Law" Roth is just the concerned and exasperated landlord. In "The Fire and the Hearth" he is the landlord who is related by blood to the independent tenant who refuses to grant him any deference whatsoever as landlord and as white man. Several passages depicting Roth's intimidation by Lucas's age and descent from the male rather than female line of Carothers McCaslin are also added. His feeling of inferiority and intimidation colors their every encounter, a feeling that Lucas exploits.

Roth is intimidated by what he sees as Lucas's pure and primitive origins: "He thought, and not for the first time: *I am not only looking at a face older than mine and which has seen and winnowed more, but at a man most of whose blood was pure ten thousand years when my own anonymous beginnings became mixed enough to produce me*" (GDM, p. 71). This sentence finds a close parallel in the typescript but not the *Collier's* story. It is one of the several indications that Faulkner's method of composition was probably an amalgamation, revision, and addition to two or more versions. But, more importantly, it suggests that even in its early, relatively simple form, the seeds for a more complicated relationship were present. Lucas's familial relationship to Roth was apparently not foreseen. The original wording, "*a man whose race was pure*" (TS, p. 15), was changed to read, "*a man most of whose blood was pure.*" Since the *Collier's* story depends for its comic effect on the stereotypical presentation of Lucas, this sentence was omitted. (Of course, one could also cynically conjecture that Faulkner did not want to offend the pedestrian reader of *Collier's* magazine with any outrageous suggestion of Negro superiority.) Similarly, the fire in the hearth, the central symbol of marital fidelity, is mentioned in both versions of "A Point of Law," but it is undeveloped and irrelevant in this story, which is about moonshining not marriage. It remains one of those untapped riches that Faulkner later explores. This exploration not only takes the form of the divorce episode, which evolved through earlier versions to become chapter three of "The Fire and the Hearth," but it is also the most significant revision of "A Point of Law" in its metamorphosis into chapter one, the fourteen-page interpolation (GDM, pp. 45–59) of a past confrontation between Lucas and Zack Edmonds over Lucas's fears that Zack was sexually using his wife.

Lucas remembers this incident as Roth comes out onto the gallery, since it was the birth of Roth and the death of his mother that precipitated the incident forty-three years earlier. Although Marvin Klotz claims that interpolations like these mar the comic effect of the story and incongruously puff Br'er Rabbit-Lucas "into a heroic, a mythic figure in the Odyssey of the Old South,"[21] I hope that I have convincingly demonstrated that Faulkner has made us sufficiently aware of Lucas's stature for such interpolations. This episode is extremely important in both "The Fire and the Hearth" and *Go Down, Moses*. It shows the sanctity of the fire and the hearth for Lucas, a symbol of the inviolability of the marital union that Lucas will preserve with murder if necessary. This interpolation is the serious counterpart to the comic portrayal of Lucas's deference to Molly's wishes in chapter three of "The Fire and the Hearth." Twice he demonstrates that in his priorities marriage comes first; it comes before his landlord's life in the first instance and before his gold-divining in the second. Aside from its thematic importance, the scene contains some of Faulkner's writing at its best. The passage superbly draws Lucas's affronted pride, his exasperation at having both to reclaim first his wife and then his dignity from Zack Edmonds and to answer satisfactorily the agonizing question: "How to God . . . can a black man ask a white man to please not lay down with his black wife? And even if he could ask it, how to God can the white man promise he wont?" (GDM, p. 59). Here is one of those few instances in *Go Down, Moses* where the omnipresent racial tension within this biracial family is the issue rather than the undercurrent. Lucas, who at most times is untroubled by the social stratification which classes him a "nigger" rather than a McCaslin descendant, who takes pride in his descent from his white grandfather, is confronted with what appears to him to be, however wrongly construed, the stealing of his wife, an act of blatant racial privilege and prerogative. For such a personal insult Lucas is ready to deny the McCaslin blood which has been the source of his pride: "And if this is what that McCaslin blood has brought me, I dont want it neither" (GDM, p. 57). But in the misfire of the gun, a fortuitous chance allowing Lucas both to vindicate his pride and to spare his kinsman, he feels reconciled with his white blood: "*So I reckon I aint got old Carothers' blood for nothing, after all. Old Carothers*, he thought. *I needed him and he come and spoke for me*" (GDM, p. 58).

Chapter two is based on a simple story depicting Lucas's outsmarting of the gold-divining machine salesman. This story, entitled "Gold Is Not Always," was published in *Atlantic*[22] and an obviously earlier draft is in the Alderman Library.[23] Although this chapter, unlike the other two, does not contain interpolations of past scenes into the narrative, it illustrates the familiar pattern of revision: stylistic improvement and changed emphasis from plot development to character revelation effected through a careful tailoring of the episode to reflect more directly upon Lucas.[24] Through judicious minor revision, Faulkner thematically enriches and changes a comparatively simple tale about a black outsmarting a white city slicker to one about a mulatto who is carefully balanced against three other men and found to be undoubtedly superior. The conflicts are not merely country and city or black and white but also youth and age, McCaslin male line and McCaslin female line—all substantially improved by minor changes. The specific changes may be minor, but the cumulative effect is enormous.

Here as elsewhere in "The Fire and the Hearth" Lucas's speech is changed from black dialect to "almost" standard English which both distinguishes him from his inferior, George Wilkins, and also places him on an equal footing with the two white men of the story: the salesman and Roth Edmonds. Other minor changes also serve to increase Lucas's dignity and to draw attention to comparisons with the other men, such as when the salesman is described in the second paragraph of chapter two as follows: "He stopped. He recoiled actually; another step and he would have walked full tilt into Lucas" (GDM, p. 78). By sheer physical presence Lucas can direct the salesman at will. The magazine version is less explicit: "Then the salesman stopped. He did not know why" (GA, p. 563). Similarly, returning unsuccessfully from a plea to Roth for money, Lucas glances at the salesman and thinks: "*Hah . . . He mought talk like a city man and he mought even think he is one. But I know now where he was born at*" (GDM, p. 80). In both earlier accounts, this bit of smug self-confidence and obvious cunning is missing altogether, and one might erroneously think that perhaps for once Lucas is not in complete control of the situation. Moreover, "where he was born at" is now Memphis, a demotion from St. Louis; the salesman is merely a regional agent. So, Lucas's confidence that this city slicker is not nearly as slick as he pretends is given more credence in the final text. Lucas's upperhand in his dealings with the salesman is augmented in other changes, most notably in the expansion of the no-nonsense bargaining with the salesman who now wants more information about the location of the alleged second treasure.[25] Lucas's cunning is also played off against George's limited intelligence. Earlier, when Lucas tells George to go to town for fifty silver dollars, and George complains, "I could have rid in and come back with him [the salesman], if you had just said so sooner," Lucas responds, "Hah . . . But I didn't" (GDM, p. 89). This added exchange indicates once again that Lucas, unlike George, is planning ahead and anticipating foul-ups.

Although other revisions are similar, Lucas's obvious superiority to George and the salesman does not need elaboration. More important is the intensification of the conflict between Roth and Lucas. They confront each other in each of the three sections of the chapter. Slight additions suggest a closer degree of interaction between the two men, such as: references to past conversations (" 'Yes,' Edmonds said. 'You told me. And you didn't believe it then either. But now you've changed your mind. Is that it?' " [GDM, p. 80]); Roth's knowledge of Lucas's exact age and the size of his bank account (" 'Fine! You've got over three thousand dollars in the bank. Advance yourself the money. Then you wont even have to pay it back.' Lucas looked at him. He didn't even blink. 'Hah,' Edmonds said. 'And because why? Because you know damn well just like I know damn well that there aint any money buried around here. You've been here sixty-seven years' " [GDM, p. 79]); and a greater informality in their conversations. When Lucas comments upon how he can no longer stand missing sleep, he adds, "You wont neither when you are my age" (GDM, p. 96), a remark missing from the earlier versions. And when Edmonds comments in the *Atlantic* story, "So you've found that out at last, have you?" (GA, p. 569), in chapter two he says, "And I've got better sense at half your age than to try it. And maybe when you get twice mine, you'll have too" (GDM, p. 96). Finally, rather than calling Lucas's mate "your wife" (GA, p. 570), he calls her Aunt Molly.

Faulkner carefully augments Roth's exasperation during the midnight search for his missing mule.[26] Three fragmentary typescript pages show his repeated attempt to find a satisfactory presentation of Edmonds's belated cognizance that what happened to his mule was both known by his black servants and initiated by Lucas. Of course, that Roth is so utterly outraged at Lucas's actions heightens the tension of the final conversation between the two men in part 3 of the chapter. To this final scene are added two passages that describe Lucas's appearance and manner, additions that serve to intensify his composure, dignity, and supreme control. As he tells the exasperated Roth how the salesman is now renting the gold-divining machine from him, he pauses, and this description follows:

> He let himself go easily back against the edge of the counter. He took from his vest pocket a small tin of snuff and uncapped it and filled the cap carefully and exactly with snuff and drew his lower lip outward between thumb and finger and tilted the snuff into it and capped the tin and put it back in his vest pocket. [GDM, pp. 96–97]

Not only is he making Roth wait and not only is he telling his story with complete placidity but he is also casually preparing his snuff in Roth's presence, granting him no deference whatsoever as white man and landlord. Furthermore, the description of Lucas differs in the two published versions. The magazine story reads:

> Edmonds stared at him as he leaned against the counter with only the slight shrinkage of the jaw to show that he was an old man, in his clean, faded overalls and shirt and open vest looped across by a heavy gold watch chain, and the thirty-dollar handmade beaver hat which Edmonds's father had given him forty years ago above the face which was not sober and not grave but wore no expression whatever. [GA, pp. 569–70]

"The Fire and the Hearth" versions reads:

> Edmonds put his hands on the chair arms, but he didn't move yet. He sat perfectly still, leaning forward a little, staring at the negro leaning against the counter, in whom only the slight shrinkage of the jaws revealed the old man, in the threadbare mohair trousers such as Grover Cleveland or President Taft might have worn in the summertime, a white stiff-bosomed collarless shirt beneath a pique vest yellow with age and looped across by a heavy gold watchchain, and with the sixty-dollar handmade beaver hat which Edmonds' grandfather had given him fifty years ago above the face which was not sober and not grave but wore no expression at all. [GDM, p. 97]

No homey clean faded overalls for the later Lucas of greater stature, who is dressed in gear befitting a President of the United States, a fitting match for his prized and now older and more expensive heirloom, the beaver hat of Edmonds's grandfather. No indication of the relatedness of the two men is given in the *Atlantic* story. Since chapter two of "The Fire and the Hearth" must inevitably follow chapter one, however, the reader is aware of the context of the McCaslin genealogy, an awareness that makes him much more cognizant of the strained tension between these two men. Placing these three narrative stories in juxtaposition has the effect of making their relationship the prime focus of the complex story, "The Fire and the Hearth." Faulkner is taking full advantage of the spatial arrangement to enrich the middle episode.

If the spatial arrangement of the narrative pieces is such in chapter one that it creates a portrait of Lucas Beauchamp, chapter three does the same for Roth Edmonds. Although several passages earlier in the story suggest Roth's frustration with his cardboard authority when confronting Lucas, chapter three fully portrays Roth's consciousness. The two chapters are structurally parallel and carefully balanced. Now the "he" of the story is Roth; the long part 1 contains Roth's reminiscences, and the interpolated events are Roth's memories. Like Lucas, Roth does not see the "present as a pure or separate time; it is infused with the past, it has meaning only in terms of it, and its complex nature results from a fusion of the two."[27]

Like "A Point of Law," the narrative frame story was originally a relatively simple tale about Molly's request for a "voce," although it was never published. Two versions of the story ("An Absolution" and "The Fire on the Hearth") are in the Alderman Library.[28] Most noteworthy is the evolution of the special relationship between Roth and Molly and Roth and Lucas. In "An Absolution" Molly is merely the wife of Lucas whom Roth has rarely seen for ten years "and that only from a distance when he would chance pass Lucas' house on his mare" (TS, p. 1). A penciled-in addition, however, shows the beginnings of further complexity in this now long-standing tenant-landlord relationship: "the wife of Lucas Beauchamp his eldest tenant who had been on the place in his father's time long before he was born" (TS, p. 1).[29] In "The Fire on the Hearth" typescript she is much more than the wife of his oldest tenant: "Because she had not only been his wet nurse in his infancy, she had delivered him at birth." When his mother died in childbirth she "moved into the house, leaving Lucas to take care of their older children. She lived in the house until he was weaned; she was never out of it very long at any time afterward until he went off to school at twelve years of age" (TS, pp. 1–2). He now no longer merely rides past, but stops, brings her gifts of tobacco and candy, and visits for five or ten min-

utes. In the final draft Roth finds burdensome and frustrating his complicated relationship and obligation to this woman and her inscrutable
husband, who is now, of course, his own blood relative. Now he
spends more time, a half hour regularly once a month, with Molly and
he does it out of a sense of obligation, guilt, and ambivalence toward
her: "He called it a libation to his luck, as the centurion spilled first a
little of the wine he drank, though actually it was to his ancestors and
to the conscience which he would have probably affirmed he did not
possess, in the form, the person, of the negro woman who had been
the only mother he ever knew . . ." (GDM, pp. 99–100). The hered-
itary obligation of the McCaslins and Edmondses to this family—with
its far-reaching reverberations of wrong and shame—is indirectly referred to later as well when Edmonds mentions that his father had
"fixed it in his will to take care of you for the rest of your life"
(GDM, p. 101). But to make the bond even more personal between
Roth and Molly, now not only did she deliver and wean Roth, but she
suckled him together with her own child until they were weaned. It no
longer is Molly who has spent most of her time in his house—Lucas
had demanded that she come back—but Roth who found the two
houses interchangeable as a child, "actually preferring the negro
house, the hearth on which even in summer a little fire always
burned, centering the life in it, to his own" (GDM, p. 110). Out of the
childhood companionship of Roth and their child, Henry, grows the
irrevocable altercation between the two when Roth forbid Henry to
sleep with him and thus broke forever the equality of their relationship. This painful childhood experience, compounding Roth's obliga-
tory relationship to this family, is related as part of a long newly written
addition to "The Fire and the Hearth" (GDM, pp. 104–18). Like the
interpolated Zack Edmonds episode of chapter one, this scene is one
of those rare and important instances where the racial tension that
underlies the narrative events is openly faced by a character.

The fifteen-page addition, occasioned by the exasperated rage
Roth feels towards Lucas after his discussion with Molly, is a record
of "an accumulation of floutings and outrages covering not only his
span but his father's lifetime too, back into the time of his grandfather
McCaslin Edmonds" (GDM, p. 104). Now Roth obsessively dwells
on Lucas's position as "the oldest person living on the place," on his
descent from the male rather than the female line of old Carothers
McCaslin, and on his seeming indifference and imperviousness to his
dual heredity:

It was as if he were not only impervious to that blood, he was indifferent to it. He didn't even need to strive with it. He didn't even have to bother to defy it. He resisted it simply by being the composite of the two races which made him, simply by possessing it. Instead of being at once the battleground and victim of the two strains, he was a vessel, durable, ancestryless, nonconductive, in which the toxin and its anti stalemated one another, seetheless, unrumored in the outside air. [GDM, p. 104]

The narrator summarizes rhetorically rather than directly rendering Roth's thoughts. This narrative voice—ruminating above character, events, and time—reiterates information and events from the past which are not bounded exclusively by what Roth is consciously and immediately thinking, but nonetheless color his relationship with Lucas. The history of the three children of Tomey's Turl and Tennie—James, Fonsiba, and Lucas—is capsulized and includes a conversation between Ike McCaslin and Lucas on the latter's twenty-first birthday. Obviously Roth could not know the particulars of this scene, but he knows very well the ramifications of that meeting and, in fact, feels them when he faces Lucas. The narrator brings the historical review up to Roth's own childhood and then, described dramatically, is the incident when Roth destroyed his boyhood friendship with Henry, when "the old curse of his fathers, the old haughty ancestral pride based not on any value but on an accident of geography, stemmed not from courage and honor but from wrong and shame, descended to him" (GDM, p. 111). The review continues with him puzzling over many aspects of his relationships with his black relatives. As an adolescent Roth asks his father why Lucas did not treat him with the respect befitting a white landlord. With bitter sarcasm his father responds: "You think that because Lucas is older than I am, old enough even to remember Uncle Buck and Uncle Buddy a little, and is a descendant of the people who lived on this place where we Edmonds are usurpers, yesterday's mushrooms, is not reason enough for him not to want to say mister to me?" (GDM, p. 114). Roth divines that within the strained relationship of his father and Lucas lies an important confrontation over a woman that Lucas won. That confrontation is the interpolated scene in the first chapter, where Lucas demands and wins his wife and his integrity from Zack Edmonds.

The final section of this long addition returns to the present with a summary of Roth's frustrated relations with Lucas and his undeniable debt to Molly, "who had surrounded him always with care for his physical body and for his spirit too, teaching him his manners, behavior—to be gentle with his inferiors, honorable with his equals, generous to the weak and considerate of the aged, courteous, truthful and brave to all—who had given him, the motherless, without stint or expectation of reward that constant and abiding devotion and love which existed nowhere else in this world for him'' (GDM, p. 117). Molly has indeed changed from the single-dimensional character she was in the original story. The section ends with Roth's thoughts as he sits over his solitary supper and ponders Lucas's freedom from any limitation and any definition:

> . . . and he thought with amazement and something very like horror: *He's more like old Carothers than all the rest of us put together, including old Carothers. He is both heir and prototype simultaneously of all the geography and climate and biology which sired Old Carothers and all the rest of us and our kind, myriad, countless, faceless, even nameless now except himself who fathered himself, intact and complete, contemptuous, as old Carothers must have been, of all blood black white yellow or red, including his own.* [GDM, p. 118]

Roth's preoccupation with the past and the narrator's amplification of it serve to concentrate the related themes of the story in the relationship of Roth and Lucas as representative of an entire history of such relationships. The stills, the gold-divining, and the divorce recede as the reader, like the characters, sees these incidents as frameworks for the interaction of the descendants of Carothers McCaslin. Although each of the chapters has a narrative frame, "The Fire and the Hearth" lyrically converges upon a portrayal of this representative relationship.

Except for these major additions to part 1 of chapter three, the frame story remains essentially unchanged. As always, however, the story has undergone extensive stylistic revision, occasioned in large part by the highly charged and highly complicated interactions of Roth and Lucas. Interestingly, the mentor-mentee aspect is dropped in the final version: "It was Lucas who had gone with him when he first began to ride a horse, after his father had taught him how to sit and how to use his hands; it was Lucas who had walked slightly behind him when he took a man-sized gun afield" ("An Absolution" TS, p. 5). Faulkner erases all traces of intimacy and affection between the two men. Roth's frustration with Lucas, compounded by his obligations to Molly, exacerbates his feelings in the final story.

The more informal conversations of Roth and Lucas in the final text also augment Roth's poorly disguised rage. Similarly, the court clerk's exasperation with Lucas's interruption of the proceedings is a further reinforcement of Lucas's mulish insistence and success at having his own way. Another addition is Edmonds's protest against Lucas's command to "Wait a minute" after the court proceedings, a protest which as usual has no effect whatsoever on Lucas. Here the tension between the two men is heightened and the latent seeds for the eventual blood relationship are sown. Although no familial bond between Lucas and Roth exists in "An Absolution," Faulkner has nonetheless suggested in this early story that Lucas's bearing was modeled on Roth's father: "walking with something of the unswerving and dignified deliberation which every now and then, Edmonds recognised as having come from his own father" (TS, p. 16). What was apparently little more than an imitation in "An Absolution," becomes a disturbing similarity for Roth in the next typescript, "The Fire on the Hearth"—"and with something sharp at his heart, Edmonds recognised as having come from his own father as the hat had come" (TS, p. 18). In the final version, however, it is painful evidence of the genealogical bond, since Lucas's bearing and his hat come from his *McCaslin* ancestry not from Zack Edmonds who was, after all, merely a descendant of the female side of their mutual family. Roth as always feels impotent and frustrated by Lucas's confident selfhood.

Although in "An Absolution" Lucas confuses Roth with Zack and mistakenly calls him "master" ("and suddenly Edmonds knew that Lucas also was speaking not to him but to his father, because he could not remember when Lucas had even said 'sir' to him and he knew that Lucas even called him 'Roth' behind his back: 'No, master, get rid of hit . . . ' " [TS, p. 17]), in the two later versions Faulkner wisely omits this detail. Lucas as he has finally evolved would no more call Zack Edmonds master than he would Roth. In fact, it is mentioned earlier that "Lucas referred to his father as Mr Edmonds, never as Mister Zack; he watched him avoid having to address the white man directly by any name at all with a calculation so coldly and constantly alert, a finesse so deliberate and unflagging, that for a time, he could not tell if even his father knew that the negro was refusing to call him mister" (GDM, p. 114).

The one-dimensional Lucas of the short stories evolves into one of the most brilliantly realized and most positive characters in Faulkner's fiction. What started out as a comic story—the frustrating attempt of a landlord to patch up a marital quarrel between his childlike and obstinate tenants—becomes a richly suggestive and representative episode in the lives of this interracial family.

Whereas the separate narrative pieces of "The Fire and the Hearth" are spatially arranged so as to complement and enrich each other by their placement within the larger structural composite of the three-chaptered story, so does this story, in turn, expand in richness when placed within the yet larger structural context of *Go Down, Moses*. As such, "The Fire and the Hearth" is microcosmic of Faulkner's technique in *Go Down, Moses*. The concentric circles of reference become larger and larger as more and more of the past which informs the present is revealed.

Within "The Fire and the Hearth," a few brief references to Ike McCaslin are made. Lucas is fond of comparing his age and lineage to that of Ike, and he thinks at one point that old Cass Edmonds "beat" Ike out of his patrimony (GDM, p. 36). At another point, he rather inconsistently concludes that Ike "had turned apostate to his name and lineage by weakly relinquishing the land which was rightfully his" (GDM, pp. 39–40). In a passage of chapter three mentioned above, the omniscient narrator shows that Roth's frustrated dealings with Lucas are historically preceded by Ike's. Nonetheless, "The Fire and the Hearth," as an isolated story, has very little to do with Ike McCaslin who makes no appearance "in person" in it. When the story is placed within the context of *Go Down, Moses*, however, the history of racial tension, capsulized in the relationship of Roth and Lucas, becomes part of Ike McCaslin's complex heritage. Moreover, Lucas, who accepts his legacy, who is "free," and who preserves "the fire and the hearth," emerges as an important foil to Ike, who denies his legacy and is not "set free," and who fails to remember anything he "ever knew or felt or even heard about love" (GDM, p. 363). In fact, parallel love relationships across the volume implement its converging lyrical unity. Repeatedly the black love relationship shows strong emotional bonds and a sense of familial roots that pales the white counterpart, whereas loveless interracial relationships create an entire history of "wrong and shame" that brings tragedy and anguish to both sides of this interracial family.

The lyrical unity of "The Fire and the Hearth" parallels the structure of *Go Down, Moses*. The revisions of the original stories demonstrate Faulkner's masterful assimilation of the narrative events of the simple stories into the complex portrayal of the representative relationship of Lucas and Roth; the stylistics as well as the structure of the revised story are also vastly superior to the originals. That every page gives evidence of more precision in detail, more care with transition, smoother diction, and more logical development suggests that far from a Procrustes, Faulkner is a skillful craftsman of fiction.

"PANTALOON IN BLACK"

Critics have argued that the third story, "Pantaloon in Black," is not integrated into *Go Down, Moses,* since it is the only story not about McCaslin descendants. Genealogical links, however, are not the only unifying devices in *Go Down, Moses.* The story contributes to a sharpened focus on race relations and to a more somber tone in the volume, while it in turn is enriched by its placement within the larger context of the short story composite.

The story, comprehensible and powerful in isolation, is a poignant expression of the grief and self-destruction of a black man following the death of his young wife. Its two-part presentation is relatively straightforward. The first part depicts Rider immediately after his wife's death: his actions at the funeral, his return to their house, his brief encounter with her ghost, his peculiar behavior at work, his confrontation with the moonshine dealer, his drunkenness, and finally his encounter with and killing of the shady white gambler, Birdsong. The much shorter second part takes place after Birdsong's men have lynched Rider and relates the sheriff's uncomprehending account of Rider's behavior after his wife's death, at his arrest, and in jail. At the end Rider rips off the bars, flings one black prisoner set upon him after another, saying, "It's awright. It's awright. Ah aint trying to git away" (GDM, p. 158), and finally sits laughing and crying, saying "Hit look lack Ah just cant quit thinking. Look lack Ah just cant quit" (GDM, p. 159). The sheriff's repeated comment about blacks contrasts ironically with the incredible intensity of Rider's grief:

> Because they aint human. They look like a man, and they walk on their hind legs like a man, and they can talk and you can understand them and you think they are understanding you, at least now and then. But when it comes to the normal human feelings and sentiments of human beings, they might just as well be a damn herd of wild buffaloes. [GDM, p. 154]

"Pantaloon in Black" of necessity has a certain completeness; it is not only a characterization but a complete history of a man. Its position amid the McCaslin history and Faulkner's inferential links to the rest of the volume work against this closure, however. The story was only very slightly revised from the account published in *Harper's* in 1940.[30] Both versions include two details that serve to link the story tangentially to the larger volume: Rider's landlord is "Carothers Edmonds" and Rider's lighting of a fire in the hearth on his wedding night is explicitly compared to a similar act by Lucas Beauchamp: "as the tale told of Uncle Lucas Beauchamp, Edmonds' oldest tenant, had done on his forty-five years ago and which had burned ever since" (GDM, p. 138). By such tangential links, Faulkner is deliberately inviting the reader to draw parallels and to look for interrelationships. The expansion is through counterpoint rather than explicitly developed parallel, or even necessarily planned parallel. Although the story is not as essential as the others in the volume because it deals with peripheral characters and adds no new vital information to the developing composite, yet it contributes to a changed tone; the humor is lessened through repeated instances of confrontation and misunderstanding between the races. The black man emerges as a complex human being in relationship to his white counterpart and to his love partner. Turl conforms to the rules and ritual of the hunt of Uncle Buck and Buddy in order to get what he wants, Tennie. The tone is light and distanced and comic. Lucas exasperates Roth and ignores his dictates about giving up gold-divining only to give it up finally to keep Molly from getting a "voce." Lucas's antics are humorous, but Roth sees the threats to his masculinity and mastery as deadly serious, and Lucas views the inviolability of marriage—symbolized in the fire in the hearth—as sacred. Rider succumbs to his white captors eventually, but his whole tragedy is generated by the unbearable grief for his wife, grief that his white counterpart, the sheriff, can not possibly understand. While the sheriff's obtuseness generates some humor, Rider's suffering does not. The natural and emotional strength and vitality of the black man is reflected by the shallowness of the white perceiver.

Just as the story contributes to the composite, the composite thematically enriches the story. Rider's grief is not an isolated incident of intense emotion experienced by the blacks in this volume. The sheriff's misunderstanding is not just a humorous account of an unperceptive, simple man, but is an instance of repeated misunderstanding and underestimation of the humanity of the black by a white man who could never approach such a degree of pure and unreasoning feeling. Repeatedly, the games, enjoyments, and deceptions of the white man—liquor, gambling, money, possession—trip up the black man who, in this case, wants only to forget, who in Turl's case wants only to be free and with his mistress, who in Lucas Beauchamp's case wants to be rich like the two white men who found the gold, and who in his grandson's case (in the final story of the volume) wanted to become rich and did too fast.

Because the effect of the first three stories is to highlight the significance of race relations, the reader expects a continuation of this theme. Instead, he is transported by the next three stories, "The Old People," "The Bear," and "Delta Autumn," into the realm of hunting and hunters. The elevated tone and language with which "The Old People" is told contrast sharply with the relatively straightforward telling of the first three stories. Again, Faulkner is taking full advantage of the looseness of the short story composite form. Each story conforms to its own formal requirements and does not need to be consistent with the tone, style, point of view, and time of the other stories. Some links of the hunting trilogy to the rest of the volume are soon apparent. Sam Fathers's tripartite racial composition, Indian-Negro-Caucasian, brings the theme of racial injustice into the seemingly pristine world of huntsmanship. The shadowy central character, eighty-year-old-repudiating Ike McCaslin, takes flesh and blood as a young boy. But the most fruitful way to look at the shape of *Go Down, Moses* is again to see the kind of revisions and additions that Faulkner made when incorporating self-contained stories into the volume.

"THE OLD PEOPLE"

Three versions of "The Old People" are extant, the earliest an unpublished seventeen-page typescript on deposit in the Alderman Library,[31] then a revised text published in *Harper's* magazine,[32] and a final account yet further revised for publication in *Go Down, Moses*.[33] While not extensive, the revisions are indicative of the emphasis that Faulkner was working toward in the short story composite. The most obvious change, the alteration of names of characters, shows that the story was initially conceived in another context. Like "Lion," another early hunting story, the protagonist in the typescript of "The Old People" is probably Quentin Compson, and the mentor who comments upon the significance of his experience is his father (only Mr. Compson is explicitly named in the story). In *Harper's,* the boy and his father are unnamed. In *Go Down, Moses,* the boy becomes Ike McCaslin, and old Ike McCaslin, an incidental character in the earlier versions, is dropped. Conversely, General Compson, added to the cast of peripheral characters, replaces the old man. The boy's father becomes his cousin, McCaslin Edmonds, reinforcing that special tutorial relationship that Cass has with the fatherless Ike. Jimbo becomes Tennie's Jim and is thus tied into the McCaslin genealogy. This link is seemingly casual until one is aware of the past and the future that informs it. Faulkner unobtrusively prepares the way both for Ike's discovery at age sixteen that his legacy is shamefully tied up with the lineage of Tennie's Jim, and for his confrontation in the distant future with the granddaughter of Tennie's Jim who comes looking for Roth at the hunting camp in "Delta Autumn."[34]

Another way that the story is assimilated into the composite is the change of point of view from first person to third. The almost incantatory voice of this all-knowing narrator occurs frequently in *Go Down Moses,* and serves as an important unifying device. Unrestricted by temporal progression, it reaches forward and backward in time and catches the full significance of events across the expanse of Ike's long life. While the boy's reaction to the shooting of his first deer is related sparsely in the *Harper's* story: "I don't remember that shot at all. I don't even remember what I did with the gun afterward" (OP, p. 418), the narrator places this event within the entire compass of Ike's life:

> The boy did not remember that shot at all. He would live to be eighty, as his father and his father's twin brother and their father in his turn had lived to be, but he would never hear that shot nor remember even the shock of the gun-butt. He didn't even remember what he did with the gun afterward. [GDM, pp. 163–64]

The narrator's elevated diction amplifies the moral and ritualistic aspects of the boy's initiation:

They were the white boy, marked forever, and the old dark man sired on both sides by savage kings, who had marked him, whose bloody hands had merely formally consecrated him to that which, under the man's tutelage, he had already accepted, humbly and joyfully, with abnegation and with pride too; the hands, the touch, the first worthy blood which he had been found at last worthy to draw, joining him and the man forever, so that the man would continue to live past the boy's seventy years and then eighty years, long after the man had entered the earth as chiefs and kings entered it. [GDM, p. 165]

In a later addition, the high ethical code is again reiterated: "—had not Sam Fathers already consecrated and absolved him from weakness and regret too?—not from love and pity for all which lived and ran and then ceased to live in a second in the very midst of splendor and speed, but from weakness and regret" (GDM, p. 182). By changing the point of view Faulkner also has removed the awkward pomposity of the boy recording the significance of his own initiation: "So the instant came; I pulled the trigger and ceased to be a child forever and became a hunter and a man" (OP, p. 421). The ritual is accentuated in the revision of this passage, as is Sam Fathers's role in Ike's initiation: "So the instant came. He pulled trigger and Sam Fathers marked his face with the hot blood which he had spilled and he ceased to be a child and became a hunter and a man" (GDM, pp. 177–78).

Sam Fathers assumes a more prominent role through both the addition of new passages and a significant change in his lineage. In both the typescript and *Harper's,* Sam's grandfather is Ikkemotubbe and his grandmother and mother are presumably all-black slaves, while in the final story, Sam's father is Ikkemotubbe and his mother a quadroon. In the final story Sam's name is derived from the fact that he has two fathers, his actual father, Ikkemotubbe, and his legal father, a black slave. In the original it is Sam's father, not Sam, who has two fathers, making Sam one-quarter Indian and three-quarters black; in *Go Down, Moses* he is one-half Indian, three-eighths white, and one-eighth black. That Sam's Indian rather than Negro lineage is the dominant one and that he is the son of an Indian chief underlie the special position of dignity and aloofness from the Negroes that Sam occupies in the composite. That he also has white blood prepares for the theme of bondage that figures so prominently in the hunting trilogy and ties Sam in with so many other characters in the volume who are burdened by a complicated interracial heritage.

In a three-page addition to the final text ("That was seventy years ago. . . . sons after him" [GDM, pp. 166–69]), emphasis on Sam's racial bondage is ironically complemented by his increased dignity and independence. After McCaslin claims that Sam is "like an old lion or a bear in a cage," Ike passionately requests that McCaslin "let him go," introducing the important analogy of Sam's bondage to that of Moses'. McCaslin replies that Sam's cage "aint us" but rather that Sam is imprisoned by the little bit of white blood he possesses: "himself his own battleground, the scene of his own vanquishment and the mausoleum of his defeat." With a humorous reference to Sam's special status as a man who instinctively enlists respect—and autonomy—from white, black, and red men alike, McCaslin asks, "Did you ever know anybody yet, even your father and Uncle Buddy, that ever told him to do or not to do anything that he ever paid any attention to?" (GDM, p. 168). The addition ends with an expository summary of Sam's solitary and independent life.

Also changed is the conversation between Sam and McCaslin when Sam requests that he go to the Big Bottom to live. Since the conversation is moved from the office of the boy's father in the original to the kitchen in the final text, the boy thinks of how rarely the inscrutable Sam approaches the house (GDM, pp. 172–73). Sam's abstracted look ("looking at something over their heads or at something not even in the room") and his paradoxical bondage-and-independence are now emphasized. Although he now insistently repeats his request (" 'I want to go,' he said. 'Let me go' "), when McCaslin asks him "You want to go soon?" Sam replies with total independence: "I'm going now." Augmenting the closeness of Sam and Ike is the addition of McCaslin's questions: "What about Isaac here? . . . How will you get away from him? Are you going to take him with you?" Two additional passages, summarizing the boy's thoughts about Sam and his own forthcoming initiation into huntsmanship, are inserted into the following narration ("he could understand that Sam . . . six months before the moon for hunting" [GDM, pp. 173–74]; "But that was all right. . . . and the hunts to come as hunters talked" [GDM, pp. 174–75]). The additions show that the intuitive understanding the boy has of his special relationship with his tutor leaves him untroubled by Sam's exit into the woods. A third addition is inserted into the final text after Ike has had his first November at the hunting camp ("Because he did not come back

with them. . . . Then November, and they would come back''
[GDM, pp. 175-76]). Again the boy's separation from Sam is emphasized, but now he carries with him "an unforgettable sense of
the big woods" in which he is, "until he has drawn honorably blood
worthy of being drawn, alien." In other words, the passage helps to
highlight the important initiation rite to come in which he will be
reunited with Sam. Other additions to parts one and two are comparatively minor, including an occasional phrase or sentence expound-
ing upon the profound solitude or size of the wilderness. Sam's
leadership role during the hunts is made more dominant by both
expanded description ("Sam led them on foot . . . still walking"
[GDM, pp. 179-80]) and dialogue. For example, responding to Boon
and Walter's argument over the size of the deer Boon allegedly saw,
Sam says, "Aint nobody going to shoot him standing here." The
addition of this argument (GDM, pp. 180-81) also prepares for Ike's
sight of this extraordinary deer later in the story.[35]

Finally, in part three the dialogue between the boy and his
father in the first two accounts and between Ike and Cass in the final
version has been significantly altered. In all three the father-cousin
explains the eternal life cycle to the boy and discloses that he too was
taken by Sam to see the old deer, the very embodiment of this eternality, after he had killed his first deer. But this father figure gets
increasingly philosophical. Perhaps Faulkner was attempting to suggest that Ike's hunting experience as a boy laid the groundwork for
his later examination of the ethical principles of his own ownership of
the land. Added to the *Harper's* story is the father's comment upon
the preciousness of life: "even suffering and grieving is better than
nothing; there is nothing worse than not being alive" (OP, p. 424).
But in the final text, which now takes place more vividly and more
intimately in bed rather than outdoors, Cass states that the ethical
quality of life is more important than life itself: "there is only one
thing worse than not being alive, and that's shame" (GDM, p. 186).
This change prepares smoothly, of course, for Ike's repudiation of the
"wrong and the shame" in his legacy in "The Bear." The emphasis is
on the high code—how to shoot honorably and how to live honorably—that Ike learns from *both* his mentors.

The effect of the altered names of some of the characters, of
the third person narration and heightened diction, of the expanded
religious and ritualistic dimension to Ike's initiation, of the enriched
characterization of Sam as a caged man of increased stature, of the

intensified significance of the relationship of Sam and Ike, and of the changed philosophy of McCaslin is to make "The Old People" an integral piece of a larger context, which is elaborated more fully with the other two stories of the hunting group, and elaborated yet further in *Go Down, Moses.* The theme of racial bondage and injustice, the effect of this sacred initiation into huntsmanship upon Ike's later life, and the brief mention of other members of his family and the hunting party create expectations of meaning greater than the individual story can fulfill. The more one learns, the more that information coheres to produce a portrait of Ike McCaslin.

"THE BEAR"

The central story in that portrait of Ike McCaslin, "The Bear," incorporates two stories, the *Post* version of "The Bear" and "Lion,"[36] and much newly written material, including the long part 4 which, except for the fyce-Grecian Urn sequence (GDM, pp. 295–97), is entirely new.[37] Of those critics who have compared the short stories with the five-part story, William Van O'Connor and Marvin Klotz are critical of the success of the revisions; Edward M. Holmes refrains from making judgment upon the relative merit of the stories, and James Early perceives the final story as superior to the two short stories.[38] Agreeing with Early, I think that the five-part story is not only remarkably different from the two short stories but that it is undoubtedly superior.

The introductory paragraph of part 1 of the revised "The Bear," appearing in no other story, cryptically sets before us the four important actors in the ensuing drama—Old Ben, Lion, Sam, and Boon—and suggests that a special kinship of incorruptible blood exists among the first three. In the next paragraph the use of the pronoun *he* emphasizes Ike's central role and establishes the present time of the story as December when "he was sixteen. For six years now he had been a man's hunter" (GDM, p. 191). The following evocation of the wilderness and of "the ancient and unremitting contest according to the ancient and immitigable rules" (GDM, p. 192) is an expanded version of a passage less effectively placed (shortly before the reading of "Ode on a Grecian Urn") in the *Post* version of

"The Bear." The important elements of the story are set forth with economy, beauty, and deliberate obscurity, while the third paragraph initiates a retrospective look at the past that informs the present: "He realised later that it had begun long before that. It had already begun on that day when he first wrote his age in two ciphers . . ." (GDM, p. 192). The *Post* story, in contrast, starts at this point. Although the past is briefly alluded to here, the development is chronological, whereas the development of the five-part story is retrospective: a look back from age sixteen to age ten rather than the perspective at age ten.

The two versions of "The Bear" differ in scope as well as perspective. The *Post* story is limited to Ike's initiation into the spirit of the wilderness through his experience tracking, sighting, and finally saving Old Ben. With additions and alterations, part 1 and three pages of part 2 parallel the *Post* story. A better proportioned unit, part 1 ends climactically with the sight of Old Ben by the boy who has relinquished his gun, watch, and compass; but in the *Post* story this scene is unfortunately muted by a second climax—the fyce-bear confrontation. Moreover, the reverential attitude of the boy toward the wilderness is given much fuller amplification in the composite, when repeated reminders of the boy's tedious wait for the important day to come when he can enter the big woods are included: "Still a child, with three years then two years then one year before he too could make one of them" (GDM, p. 194). Repeatedly mentioned also is Ike's awareness of the need to prove himself worthy of the status of hunter: "to earn for himself from the wilderness the name and state of hunter provided he in his turn were humble and enduring enough" (GDM, p. 192). "But it was not for him, not yet. The humility was there; he had learned that. And he could learn the patience" (GDM, p. 196). While the boy's first entry into the wilderness is not heralded with any special attention in the *Post* story, a page and a half description ("His day came at last . . . . that he would even hear the running dogs this first time" [GDM, pp. 194–196]) elaborates the profound effect of this event for the boy who feels "that at the age of ten he was witnessing his own birth. It was not even strange to him. He had experienced it all before, and not merely in dreams." This passage also underscores Ike's prescience. In the *Post* story he dreamt about his experiences before they happened; in *Go Down, Moses* he feels that he has actually experienced them before. His prescience intensifies the quality of timeless eternality the wilderness takes on in the composite. Similarly, the narrator again is unrestricted by time as when, describing Ike's new gun, he says: "he would own and shoot it for almost seventy years, through two new pairs of barrels and locks and one new stock, until all that remained of the original gun was the silver-inlaid trigger-guard with his and McCaslin's engraved names and the date in 1878" (GDM, p. 205). Other significant passages in part 1 which do not appear in the *Post* story serve to augment Sam's role as Ike's tutor and as the undisputed seer of huntsmanship. The total effect of these differences makes Ike's initiation, culminating with the sight of Old Ben, the single uncluttered focus of part 1.

But the two versions of "The Bear" differ in meaning as well, a difference that hinges in large part upon the treatment of the fyce-bear confrontation that climaxes the *Post* story and is relegated to an episode in part 2 of the *Go Down, Moses* version. In both stories, the fyce's bravery inspires the boy's courageous rescue, and the perfect matching of the bear's strength and freedom with Sam and the boy's humble, honorable, proud, and pitying refusal to destroy the bear constitute the "truth" that the boy empirically experiences. But in the *Post* story, this scene is immediately followed by the father's explanatory reading of "Ode on a Grecian Urn." Like the bride on the urn, the bear is at the height, the perfect fruition of its nature. To destroy the virginity of the bride or to destroy the "furious immortality" of the bear would be to subject these timeless embodiments of perfection to the ravages of time. Instead, the boy chooses to relinquish his role as destroyer. This, along with his earlier relinquishment of "the three lifeless mechanicals" with which "he had fended the wilderness off" (B, p. 158), is the central point of the *Post* story.

In *Go Down, Moses,* in contrast, relinquishment is not a final answer in man's relationship to the wilderness. The wilderness and the bear that is its apotheosis are inevitably doomed and all that the properly initiated hunter can do is to insure that their end is befitting their life. The lesson learned from the fyce is that the end will come "some day," and therefore it must be in a confrontation worthy of the old bear and "when even he dont want it to last any longer" (GDM, p. 212). In the *Post* version, the boy equates the fyce with "the right dog, a dog in which the size would mean less than nothing" (B, p. 160). In the other version Sam says: "You's almost the one we wants . . . You just aint big enough. We aint got that one yet. He will need to be just a little bigger than smart, and a little braver than

either'' (GDM, p. 212). The inappropriate size of the six-pound dog
and the premature time of the conflict are emphasized. This mismatch
is reduced to an episode which signals the way for the greater dog,
Lion. Ike feels:

> He should have hated and feared Lion. Yet he did not. It seemed to him
> that there was a fatality in it. It seemed to him that something, he didn't
> know what, was beginning; had already begun. It was like the last act
> on a set stage. It was the beginning of the end of something, he didn't
> know what except that he would not grieve. He would be humble and
> proud that he had been found worthy to be a part of it too or even just
> to see it too. [GDM, p. 226]

William Van O'Connor sees this passage as ''a plant, suggesting, but
without explaining, to the reader that the apotheosis of Lion is not
contradicting the apotheosis of Old Ben. But as a matter of fact, it
does contradict it. If Ike is the voice of the wisdom to be learned from
the wilderness, then indeed he should have been opposed to the spirit
represented by Lion.''[39] In a similar vein, Marvin Klotz expresses his
consternation over Sam Fathers's embarrassing illogic about dogs:
''If he was so determined to kill the bear, why didn't he shoot when
the fyce gave him the opportunity?''[40] The answer is obvious; the
little fyce was an inappropriate match for the grand old bear. Both
Klotz and O'Connor confuse their interpretations by simplistically
applying the meaning of the *Post* story. According ''to the ancient
and immitigable rules which voided all regrets and brooked no
quarter,'' Sam prepares the right dog for the right time. Sam's symbolic identity with the wilderness neither conflicts with his part in the
death of Old Ben nor is his death a ''sort of suicide.'' Death is an
intrinsic and inevitable part of life; only irreverence for life is wantonly destructive. To kill the ambushed bear when the foolhardy fyce
held him at bay, then, *would* be wanton destruction. Furthermore, it
is neither contradictory, as O'Connor implies, both to have reverence
for the hunted and to kill it, nor is it being unduly sentimental to
respect bears even though they ''wantonly would crush one's head or
rip off one's limbs.''[41] O'Connor was writing before the ecology
movement made us so aware of how wantonly man is destroying
wildlife. (As a matter of fact, O'Connor badly misinterprets an important point in the revised ''The Bear.'' He claims that Old Ben has
broken the rules by wantonly killing the colt, whereas clearly it was
the untamed Lion who killed the colt.)

The Grecian Urn sequel to the fyce-bear confrontation is not presented in the final story until part 4. Respect for the bear and the wilderness is recalled as one reason for Ike's repudiation of his tainted heritage. As a child he humbly and reverentially relinquished his role as a destroyer; now as a man he wants to relinquish his family's history of destructive injustice. He wants to remove himself from the consequences of time as he has temporarily stayed the bear's "furious immortality." But he has forgotten the whole truth of the fyce episode. The truth that Sam Fathers's two acts—his refusal to shoot Old Ben and his preparation of Lion—demonstrated was that one must play his proper role. Relinquishment is no permanent solution to man's complex involvement with the processes of life and death. The differing placement and treatment of the fyce-bear confrontation in the final story, then, indicate an important difference of meaning.

If part 1 of "The Bear" coheres to produce a single effect, so does part 2. The refrain, "So he should have hated and feared Lion," which begins, ends, and interlaces the section, effects a beautifully conceived single focus capsulizing Lion's role in the drama, signaling the inevitability of the end, and maintaining the "he" as Ike McCaslin, the central perceiving agent. Again the time of the story is measured by the boy's age: "He was thirteen then" (GDM, p. 209), but this section of the story provides another retrospective look at the past that informs the present: December when Ike is sixteen. Except for the fyce-bear confrontation and some details, like Boon's fascination for Lion (which occurs in different form in "Lion"), part 2 depicting Sam's training of Lion is newly written for this version of the story. Obviously a parallel is being drawn between Sam Fathers, the "caged Lion," and the caged dog, Lion, who will submit to only the peripheral trappings of civilized behavior.

Parts 3 and 5 of "The Bear" follow in rough outline the *Harper's* story, "Lion," but with major differences in meaning, execution, and structure. "Lion" is changed more extensively than the other three magazine stories incorporated into the hunting trilogy; the bulk of parts 3 and 5 is newly written for "The Bear." Both stories extend in time from the trip to Memphis for whiskey by the sixteen-year-old boy and Boon to their trip back to the camp the year after the deaths of Old Ben and Lion. But in the revision, the first person narration is changed to third; Quentin becomes Ike; the father becomes cousin McCaslin; Ad becomes Ash; Uncle Ike McCaslin is dropped from the story (along with his grandson, Theophilus McCaslin); Sam Fathers is added; and the dog, Lion, that was owned by Major de Spain becomes the wild dog trained by Sam Fathers. Whereas "Lion" is primarily a story about a courageous dog and his effect upon those who loved him, the dog is just one component of the drama in "The Bear." Old Ben, little more than a tough old bear in "Lion," becomes the very embodiment of the wilderness in "The Bear."

Many passages that appear in "Lion" are expanded, or rewritten, or slightly altered, or interlaced with new dialogue. The longest expansion of dialogue is the humorous and touching altercation of Boon and Ike over the dollar for whiskey ("They passed the first saloon. . . . 'and get the hell out of here' " [GDM, pp. 231–34]). Undoubtedly, the revised story is more complex, more profound, and more vividly told, especially in the treatment of the climactic meeting of dog and bear. Curiously, this scene occurs off-stage in the *Harper's* story, and all of the immediacy is lost through the filtered perspective of second-hand narration. Much superior is the vividly realized chase across the water and the life and death struggle of bear-dog-man seen as a tableau by the stunned boy and related by the effaced narrator: "For an instant they almost resembled a piece of statuary: the clinging dog, the bear, the man stride its back, working and probing the buried blade" (GDM, p. 241). Furthermore, in "Lion" Quentin is a fearful, inexperienced hunter cut off from the action of the story, much different from the initiate, Ike, who registers the climactic events. The revised story, of course, records the simultaneous collapse of Sam Fathers who is not a character in "Lion," an event which necessitates much newly written material and which entirely alters the meaning of the story. In both versions, Boon insists upon getting a doctor for Lion before having his own wounds seen to, but in the revised story Boon apparently later effects the mercy killing that Sam requested. At the end of part 3 he furiously guards Sam's body as McCaslin questions him and Ike cries "Leave him alone! . . . Goddamn it! Leave him alone!" (GDM, p. 254).

Part 3 functions as a dramatic and powerful climax to the hunt story. Faulkner interrupts this story with a long digression, part 4, which depicts Ike's decision at age twenty-one to repudiate his heritage. This section is, as Faulkner clearly understood, not part of "The

Bear" as a detached story, but it is the key unifying device of the
short story composite. In fact, except for the fyce-Grecian Urn sequence, part 4 is newly written for the composite. Both "The Bear"
(in four parts) and *Go Down, Moses* are carefully structured, unified
wholes. Faulkner creates different "truths" by altering the perspective and expanding the context. Without part 4, *Go Down, Moses*
would be a collection of short stories loosely related by theme, character, and setting, but without a very meaningful shape. With it, the
volume becomes a spatially ordered composite of what Ike McCaslin
is and why, filling out both in particular and in general the sketchy
portrait of Ike which prefaces the first story, "Was." In fact, *Go
Down, Moses* is so structured that its various pieces, while comprehensible and diverse stories, come cumulatively and reflexively to
bear upon the central moral issue of the volume, Ike's repudiation.
Part 4 brings together the various factors which have caused Ike to
repudiate his heritage and shows the effect of that decision upon his
relationship with his wife. The reasons for Ike's decision are embedded within his cultural heritage as a Southerner after the Civil War,
within the atrocities in his family's history recorded in the ledgers,
and within his unique experiences—particularly his experiences with
Sam Fathers and the wilderness. Ike's life, then, particularizes that of
his family and of the South. The spatial arrangement is such that the
reader's full appreciation of Ike's guilty heritage (the conflict) and of
his repudiation (the climax) is achieved in part 4 of "The Bear." Our
putting together of the truth corresponds with Ike's. The reader, like
Ike, has been introduced to some of the characters and has heard of
some of the specific incidents. He too is forced to sort out genealogy
and truth finally and climactically in the sparse ledger accounts.

Part 4 is the most concentrated section of "idea" in the volume. The controlling formal element is again the incantatory Faulknerian voice that ranges over events past and future, reiterating
genealogy, action, and idea, most of which have been dramatized
elsewhere. Not limited to what Ike is immediately thinking, this voice
operates both as a summary and as a commentary upon Ike's recording consciousness. The dialogue of Ike and his cousin in the commissary grounds the scene within a particular locale and time, Ike's
twenty-first year. Thus, part 4 is the most important bridge between
the boy-hunter and the man without his heritage. Dialogue, a conve-
nient device to dramatize conflicting opinions, is a fitting form for
amplification of Ike's controversial repudiation.

Although part 4 is in the nature of an extended addition rather than a revision, it is an essential part of this study which seeks to gain insight into the structural design of *Go Down, Moses*. Because it is so dense and wide-ranging, a summary of its major sections, with a brief commentary upon them, follows.

Part 4: Descriptive Summary

Narrative summary, pp. 254–56:

Like the first section of "Was," also a new addition to the revised volume, part 4 is a fragment suspended, as it were, amid Ike's hunting experiences in order to augment the significance of those experiences in the wilderness upon his later decision to repudiate the tamed land. In fact, the two kinds of land and their two differing heritages are set in opposition by the omniscient narrator from the beginning of part 4: "then he was twenty-one. He could say it, himself and his cousin juxtaposed not against the wilderness but against the tamed land which was to have been his heritage." The human bondage and the disrespect for the land mentioned here in the beginning, which were concomitant with the taming of the land by old Carothers McCaslin and others, are to become dominant themes in the section.

Dialogue, pp. 256–61:

The dialogue between McCaslin and Ike interlacing the section begins here with McCaslin's exasperated response to Ike's apparent declaration to relinquish the land. It is transcribed directly without authorial comment beyond the identification of speakers. Of course, Ike's central role continues to be indicated by the unspecified *he* used to refer to him. McCaslin's position in the argument is that no matter how the land was acquired, Ike's responsibility, as direct male descendant, is to accept it. Ike claims that he can not repudiate the land because "it was never mine to repudiate." He claims that the attempted possession of the land violated God's desire that the earth be held "mutual and intact in the communal anonymity of brotherhood." McCaslin responds that nevertheless old Carothers and others did own it "else why do you stand here relinquishing and repudiating." And besides, was God "perverse, impotent, or blind: which?" while this was happening? Ike claims God was "dispossessed of Eden." But he gave man a second chance with the new world. He let Grandfather and people like him own the land "because He ordered and watched it." And the new world too was corrupted by Ikkemotubbe and his descendants. So, "maybe He saw that only by voiding the land for a time of Ikkemotubbe's blood and substituting for it another blood could He accomplish His purpose." "He used the blood which had brought in the evil to destroy the evil as doctors use fever to burn up fever, poison to slay poison." In other words, God used the white man who brought in an evil, slavery, to destroy the curse on the land the Indian had created. Ike then believes in a divine providence which shapes man's actions and which specifically shapes his own family's destiny and his own unique role as a latter-day Moses. He speculates that possibly God had foreseen that within the descendants of old Carothers would be the impulse "to set at least some of His lowly people free." McCaslin's blunt response, "the sons of Ham," is apparently his weak argument that God biblically sanctioned slavery. Ike retorts that the men who wrote the scriptures were fallible human beings who could not always know the truth like "the heart knows the truth, the infallible and unerring heart." McCaslin apparently concedes the point and argues that Ike is only two generations (not three as he had said) from old Carothers and there were thousands of others beside Buck and Buddy who tried to effect this freedom, "not to mention 1865."

Narrative summary, interspersed with some directly rendered thoughts of Ike and some embedded dramatic scenes, pp. 261–82:
Although little if any time lapses in the on-going discussion, the omniscient narrator interrupts the dialogue to expound rhetorically upon the history recorded in the ledgers which has been assimilated into Ike's consciousness: "To him it was as though the ledgers in their scarred cracked leather bindings were being lifted down one by one in their fading sequence and spread open on the desk." Although what is recorded in the ledgers is not necessarily what Ike is *immediately* thinking, this knowledge has shaped his current frame of mind. The narrator tells of Buck and Buddy's attempt to cope with the heritage of guilt. They ritualized slavery, moving the slaves into the big plantation house, routinely locking the front door knowing full well that the slaves ran out the back. They built with their own hands their living quarters, a log cabin, and they recorded the history of the family cryptically in the ledgers, which Ike puzzled over as a boy.
Some of the ledger entries are humorous like those having to

do with Percival Brownlee, but others are not like those of Thucydus, Eunice, Tomasina, and Tomey's Turl. Surely the emotional center of the book is the narrator's reconstruction of Ike's puzzlings at age sixteen over the suicide of Eunice. That he is sixteen is important because he is also sixteen when Sam, Ben, and Lion die, and his initiation into his other heritage, the wilderness, has been effected. What Ike discovers at age sixteen is not only that Turl is Carothers's son but that the old man also fathered him on his own daughter Tomasina, an outrageous act that caused Eunice, Tomasina's mother who loved Carothers, to commit suicide "in formal and succinct repudiation of grief and despair who had already had to repudiate belief and hope." With this knowledge the events of the volume retrospectively take on deeper significance. One can no longer avoid the serious undercurrents in the old times that are so scrupulously avoided in "Was." The cryptically recorded genealogy in the ledgers serves to pull the volume together as does the following reiteration of the history of the black descendants of the family told in narrative summary. James disappears (and his granddaughter will appear significantly in "Delta Autumn"), and Ike tries unsuccessfully to find him in 1886 in order to give him his thousand-dollar legacy. Included in this summary are specific scenes before and after Fonsiba's marriage. At age nineteen Ike searches out Fonsiba to give her the thousand-dollar legacy. He is appalled at the "imbecile delusion" of her husband who thinks he has achieved "freedom, liberty, and equality for all." Ike's claim that the black people must be patient and wait for the curse of the land to be lifted ("Then your peoples' turn will come because we have forfeited ours. But not now. Not yet. Dont you see?") is an ironic prelude to a similar claim for patience he will make in "Delta Autumn." Similarly, Fonsiba's insistence that she is "free" is ironic foreshadowing of the mock freedom Ike is to attain. The entire scene is one of the many instances in part 4 where the illusory nature of freedom is examined. In fact, at the end of this narrative section, the narrator briefly reviews the significant dates in Ike's life, even jumping ahead to the time after the repudiation and marriage when he discovers his bogus freedom: "and that was all: 1874 the boy, 1888 the man, repudiated denied and free; 1895 and husband but no father, unwidowered but without a wife, and found long since that no man is ever free and probably could not bear it if he were." The decided emphasis on dates in part 4 forces the reader into the role of historian, participating in the reconstruction of the truth dominant in geneaolgy and chronology. Finally, a brief scene records Lucas's demand for his share of his legacy at age twenty-one from Ike. The repeated "that was all" which interlaces the section acts as ironic commentary upon how it is *not* all for Ike. Although he desires to be free from the burden of his heritage, he is still called upon to play the role of head of the family.

Dialogue, pp. 282–89:
McCaslin continues the uninterrupted dialogue referring to the Civil War and stating that there were "more men than that one Buck and Buddy to fumble-heed that truth so mazed for them." Ike claims that nonetheless there were "not enough." God could foresee not only Buck and Buddy but also himself, "an Isaac born into a later life than Abraham's and repudiating immolation: fatherless and therefore safe declining the altar because maybe this time the exasperated Hand might not supply the kid." McCaslin's single-word response to this explanation, "Escape," implies that Ike is evading responsibility, not achieving freedom. The correctness of Ike's decision is perhaps the most important single issue of the volume; McCaslin's strong argument here and elsewhere certainly casts some doubts on Ike's decision, which are confirmed in the latter-day view of Ike provided in "Delta Autumn." Ike stipulates that his escape is the equivalent of God saying, *"This is enough,"* because the South that God had so favored in natural resources was defiled by the slavers and their descendants. Ike implies that his action has its parallel in John Brown's similar stand against slavery. The actions of individuals like Brown caused God to turn back "once more to this land which He still intended to save because He had done so much for it." Ike then sees divine providence acting through the good intentions of individual human beings. McCaslin, however, is sardonic about God's favor to the South: "His face to us?" The implication is how can the devastating Civil War and its aftermath be construed as God's smiling benevolence toward the South. Ike claims that God observed the shred of humanity in Southerners like the women who cared for sick slaves although "that was not enough." He had to condone the Civil War as an act of purgation: *"Apparently they can learn nothing save through suffering, remember nothing save when underlined in blood—"* Citing examples of disorganized stupidity and reckless bravado on the part of Confederate soldiers, McCaslin is puzzled by Ike's interpretation: "His face to us? His face to us?" But Ike insists that the very impulse

to fight such an obviously larger, better-equipped, and trained army was God-inspired. These men were moved by a "love of land and courage." McCaslin's cynical down-playing of these men is clear in his inclusion of two other qualities which they possessed: "And an unblemished and gallant ancestry and the ability to ride a horse." The only conclusion McCaslin can reach about the Civil War is, "Well, maybe that's what He wanted. At least, that's what He got." To be sure, how Ike sees God on the side of the losers who were trying to preserve the evil, slavery, is rather difficult to understand. Although this discussion of the Civil War serves to place Ike's action within a broad historical context, it is unnecessarily digressive and confusing.

Narrative summary, pp. 289–94:

The narrator reviews the terrible Reconstruction period which McCaslin remembers from his adolescent years and about which Ike has been told: "that dark corrupt and bloody time while three separate peoples had tried to adjust not only to one another but to the new land." Continuing the evaluation of freedom and bondage is a reflection upon the misuse of freedom by those who have been so long in bondage: "*Apparently there is a wisdom beyond even that learned through suffering necessary for a man to distinguish between liberty and license.*" The narrator brings his general picture of the Reconstruction down to the specific history of the McCaslin black descendants after the war recorded daily now by McCaslin in the ledgers, "that chronicle which was a whole land in miniature, which multiplied and compounded was the entire South." Of the black descendants, "only Lucas was left, the baby, the last save himself of Old Carothers' doomed and fatal blood which in the male derivation seemed to destroy all it touched, and even he was repudiating or at least hoping to escape it."

Dialogue and authorial comment, pp. 294–95:

Ike, responding to the gesture McCaslin made toward the ledgers, says that the blacks are in bondage "for a while yet," but "not always, because they will endure. They will outlast us because they are—." In this pause, as the narrator points out, is Ike's sharing in his grandfather's evil ("so that even in escaping he was taking with him more of that evil and unregenerate old man . . . than even he had feared"), the denial of the equal humanity of the black man. But Ike gets it out: " 'Yes.' He didn't want to. He had to. 'Because they will endure. They are better than we are. Stronger than we are.' '' Ike's faltering assertion shows both the difficulty and the determination of this high-minded young man to act upon principle and to deny tradition. McCaslin does not share Ike's views of Negro superiority and caustically underplays ("so have dogs") the qualities of endurance "and pity and tolerance and forbearance and fidelity and love of children" that Ike praises. Ike insists that they got these qualities "from the old free fathers a longer time free than us because we have never been free."

Narrative summary with an embedded dramatic scene, pp. 295–98:

This discussion of "old free fathers" occasions Ike and McCaslin's shared reminiscence of Sam Fathers and in particular of the moment when Ike had learned under Sam and McCaslin's tutelage, bravery and, concomitant with it, respect for the freedom exemplified in Old Ben. The specific incident is the one of the six-pound fyce ambushing Old Ben and holding the old bear at bay until Ike rushed in and rescued the dog. The italicized scene included within this summary also appeared as the final scene in the *Saturday Evening Post* "The Bear," where the father (now McCaslin) read "Ode on a Grecian Urn" to the boy to explain why he did not shoot the bear and how the heart knows the truth. Ike has learned to respect freedom but, as suggested above, he has forgotten that Old Ben, unlike the bride on the urn, was a mortal being. Similarly, the illusory freedom Ike is pursuing is also transient. Nevertheless, the inclusion of this incident is another way to emphasize the importance of Ike's hunting experiences in the wilderness in shaping his decision to repudiate the tamed land.

Dialogue and authorial comment, pp. 298–300:

Returning to the thread of the dialogue, McCaslin attempts to summarize Ike's position: "So this land is, indubitably, of and by itself cursed." He vaguely gestures toward the ledgers and the narrator expounds rhetorically upon the injustice and ruthless rapacity that went into the building and the solvency and efficiency of the running of the McCaslin plantation. But Ike insists that it is "not the land, but us" who are cursed. Then Ike proclaims, "I am free." Sardonically commenting upon how long and how much it took to produce Ike, McCaslin echoes the biblically enriched question, "How long then? How long?" In other words, when will the curse be lifted and the

South be purged and free? Ike claims that it will be long, but the blacks will endure. McCaslin, in perhaps the most telling remark of the entire section says, "And anyway, you will be free.—No, not now nor ever, we from them nor they from us." Repudiate as he will, Ike will never free himself from the inextricably intermingled fates of blacks and whites in the South. Practical and tough-minded, McCaslin accepts himself as an imperfect product of tradition: "I am what I am; I will be always what I was born and have always been." The differences between the two men are sharply drawn here. Ike, the Christian existentialist, insists that he has defined himself both in accordance with his principles and with God's dictates. Through his experiences, particularly through his hunting experiences, he has become what he is. McCaslin, the traditionalist, accepts the character and the role unquestioningly that his family, history, and circumstance have given him, recognizing within his legacy wrongs and injustices, but refusing to play the role of redeemer. He makes a strong final argument by granting Ike's premise that Ikkemotubbe lost the land the moment he tried to sell it, and claiming that therefore the land belonged to Sam Fathers: "And who inherited from Sam Fathers, if not you?" In other words, Ike through Sam, if not through his blood heritage, is the rightful owner of the land. Ike insists that Sam gave him freedom, not responsibility, an interpretation that is shrouded in doubt throughout part 4. In the final words of the discussion, he says simply, "Yes. Sam Fathers set me free." At the close of the discussion, then, both men remain entrenched in the positions that they had at the beginning.

Narrative summary with some partially dramatized scenes, pp. 300–9:

Sketching Ike's life after the repudiation ("And Isacc McCaslin, not yet Uncle Ike, a long time yet before he would be uncle to half a country and still father to none . . ."), the narrator mentions the "fireless rented room"—which contrasts detrimentally with the fire in the hearth of Lucas Beauchamp's house—the carpenter trade he adopts, and the ownership of a "bright tin coffee-pot." The last item occasions the inclusion of the history of Ike's maternal legacy embodied in the pot.

It is appropriate that included in part 4, in which all the various factors that occasioned Ike's repudiation are brought together, his maternal heritage be also included. This heritage too is one of debt. It is tied up with the coffeepot which Ike inherits at age twenty-one from his uncle Hubert Beauchamp. The narrator records the history of the legacy up to the point where Ike himself can remember; then the narrative summary has the flavor of a reminiscence. The narrator records how the legacy was originally a gold cup filled with gold coins, but Ike remembers how the sound of the coins progressively deadened and how the bundle changed shape mysteriously. The disclosure of the pathetic substitution of I.O.U.'s for gold and finally the coffeepot for the gold cup is humorously told, but it depicts a serious subject, the diminishing wealth of the South after the war. Depleted is not only the stock of gold but also the furnishings of the plantation house; eventually the house itself accidentally burns. The world of "Was" is destroyed forever. Only in the never-never world of "Was" did Buck escape forever the husband-hunting clutches of Miss Sophonsiba. Here she is Ike's mother. Moreover, the fateful attraction of the races is depicted in the scene with Hubert's black mistress whose appearance in Miss Sophonsiba's house and dress is a torment and defilement to her.

Ike apparently opened this bundle in the presence of his cousin shortly after the scene in the commissary. The next day McCaslin's disapproval of Ike is apparent in his gruff refusal to call the money he brings to Ike's rented room a "loan," in his refusal to deliver in person the next installment, and in his refusal to stay overnight when Ike asks him to; "Why should I sleep here in my house when you wont sleep yonder in yours?"

Narrative summary with an embedded dramatic scene, pp. 309–15:

The narrator continues to summarize the nature of Ike's existence after the repudiation: his christlike occupation ("because if the Nazarene had found carpentering good for the life and ends He had assumed and elected to serve, it would be all right too for Isaac McCaslin"), his unsuccessful attempt to pay off the account McCaslin established in his name in the bank (and thereby his failure symbolically to cancel all debt to the past), and his marriage.

Part 4 ends with a description of Ike's married life and a dramatic scene in which his wife, acting the Jezebel, succeeds in seducing Ike into a temporary acceptance of his ancestral farm. Although the behavior of Mrs. Ike McCaslin here is rather shoddy—she would compromise her husband's principles for her material comfort—Ike's limitations have been obvious throughout. He has failed to provide a proper house for his wife who is driven to the extreme expedient she takes, just as he has failed to assume responsibility for the tainted tamed land. He has attempted to find freedom and peace, but clearly he has found neither.

Part 5 of "The Bear" functions as a denouement to the climactic deaths of Old Ben, Lion, and Sam in the hunting story. The denouement to Ike's repudiation, in contrast, occurs later in "Delta Autumn." In other words, the short story and the composite maintain their separate structures in Faulkner's masterful craftsmanship. In part 5 Ike returns to the camp a year and a half later for the last time.

A similar return to camp is rather awkwardly attached to the story "Lion" by the phrase: "This is how Lion's death affected the two people who loved him most" (L, p. 146). Although in part 5 the reaction of these two people, Major de Spain and Boon, resembles that in "Lion," the episode is now expanded with a detailed account of Ike's feelings. In "Lion" the boy-narrator is peripheral to the story, whereas Ike remains the central character of "The Bear" upon whose consciousness the events of the story are registered. He responds with "shocked and grieved amazement" at the omnipresent signs of change: the planing mill, the steel rails, the men and mules ready to invade the wilderness. While the train had once seemed harmless, it now seems to signal the impending doom of the wilderness. In fact, by the very sight of the mill he feels himself to be a carrier of "the shadow and portent of the new mill not even finished yet" (GDM, p. 321). He "would return no more." Yet, after he gets off the train and its sound recedes into the distance, he recovers a sense of the timeless and immortal wilderness: "The wilderness soared, musing, inattentive, myriad, eternal, green; older than any mill-shed, longer than any spur-line" (GDM, p. 322). The grumpy and careless Ash also portents the change that has occurred in the camp, but as Ike goes off into the timeless woods, he recovers a sense of nostalgia and peace. He affectionately recalls the killing of his first deer and Ash's bogus hunting attempt that followed. Acknowledging the formative nature of his experiences here, he thinks of the wilderness as "the mother who had shaped him" and Sam Fathers as "his spirit's father." Of course, in part 4 he quite literally substitutes this mother and this father for his blood parentage. Faulkner sows the seeds for that substitution here when he is seventeen. Returning to the gravesite of Lion and Sam he feels that it "was no abode of the dead because there was no death." Lion and Sam and Old Ben are "not held fast in earth but free in earth and not in earth but of earth" (GDM, p. 328). But "the ancient and accursed above the earth . . . evocative of all knowledge and an old weariness and of pariah-hood and of death" (GDM, p. 329) crawls through the wilderness. Although Ike repeats the salutation, "Grandfather," that Sam Fathers gave to the eternal deer in "The Old People," undoubtedly Ike, preoccupied with the seemingly edenic and eternal wilderness, misses the associations of evil and death conjured up by the snake. This oversight suggests some blindness to "all knowledge" in this seventeen-year-old initiate, blindness more fully amplified in part 4 and in "Delta Autumn."

I cannot agree with James Early's claim that

> by saluting the snake, Isaac shows that he understands what his cousin, McCaslin, had been trying to tell him when he said that he could be only what he was born and what he had always been. He now realizes that no man can ever be wholly free. Having shed his youthful illusions of redeeming the South from evil through personal renunciation, and being still unencumbered by the bitterness which was to sour his old age in "Delta Autumn," Isaac McCaslin has attained a wise and tragic understanding that to be fully human is to be contaminated with evil and, ultimately, to die.[42]

Although part 4 spatially precedes part 5, chronologically it will be three years before Ike has that discussion with McCaslin. Here Ike is an idealistic seventeen-year-old who does not differentiate between the eternal deer and the eternal snake. Ike has already peered into the ledgers at age sixteen and discovered his grandfather's atrocious behavior, but he has not yet decided to act on that knowledge. When he is twenty-one he will express his "youthful illusions of redeeming the South from evil through personal renunciation." It is the omniscient narrator, not Ike, who comments upon the "pariah-hood" and "death" associated with the snake. And it is the reader, not Ike, who sees the snake in Eden, who recalls the snake-like train which is signaling the destruction of the wilderness and the snake-like grandfather Carothers McCaslin who contaminates his grandson's legacy.

That the sight of the snake is a prelude to Ike's discovery of Boon at the gum tree invites us to see this frenzied desire to possess ("Get out of here! Dont touch them! Dont touch one of them! They're mine!" [GDM, p. 331]) as the tainted heritage of modern man, severed now from the regenerative code of the old people. In "Lion" Boon's madness is explicitly explained: "He was living, as always, in the moment; nothing on earth—not Lion, not anything in the past—mattered to him except his helpless fury with his broken gun" (L, p. 149). In "The Bear" his actions take on a new significance. Without the mentors, Sam and Lion, who inspired in this loyal, childlike man two acts of courage, Boon is only capable of this inglorious and pathetic response. An anomaly in the civilized world, Boon is yet unable—by himself—to carry on the hunting life. The implication is that the dying wilderness is now in the hands of bogus hunters like Boon, who unmaliciously yet irreverently try to "own" wildlife. Ike knows better, yet by "dispossessing" the tamed land which the wilderness is becoming, he insures his ineffectuality and puts responsibility into irresponsible hands.

"DELTA AUTUMN"

If part 4 of "The Bear" serves to focus all the related themes of the volume upon a portrait of Ike McCaslin, further alteration of that portrait is effected with "Delta Autumn" which has been fashioned—through revision—into a denouement to his repudiation. An unpublished typescript and the magazine version of "Delta Autumn" depict a modern-day hunting expedition during which Don Boyd, an irreverent lover and hunter, pays off his mulatto mistress and shoots a doe for camp food.[43] Ike, an old man who acts as an intermediary in the payoff, comments upon the action and nostalgically reminisces on the past. When the story was incorporated with *Go Down, Moses,* several important differences significantly alter its meaning; the differences between the typescript and the magazine accounts are mostly minor stylistic alterations, although they too are illuminating, particularly of the way that the characterization evolved. Don Boyd, who is no relation to Ike in the earlier versions, becomes his fourth cousin Roth Edmonds in the composite and ten years are added to the old man's life (near eighty rather than near seventy). The age difference and the kinship are repeatedly emphasized in the way the men are introduced, and the importance of this link between the two generations becomes increasingly significant as the story progresses. A much fuller sense of the antithetical philosophies of the two men is interjected into the narrative by expanding two conversations, one as they drive to camp and another as they have dinner (more than five pages are added to the latter: "he said grace . . . and less warm enough" [GDM, pp. 344–49]). Ike is shown to be a rather pompous, complacent, sentimental old man who believes in the divine purpose of creation ("I reckon He created the kind of world He would have wanted to live in if He had been a man" [GDM, p. 348]), in the essential goodness of human nature ("most men are a little better than circumstances give them a chance to be" [GDM, p. 345]), and in the divinity of sexual union ("I think that every man and woman, at the instant when it dont even matter whether they marry or not, I think that whether they marry then or afterward or dont never, at that instant the two of them together were God" [GDM, p. 348]).

Roth's response to the latter point, "Then there are some Gods in this world I wouldn't want to touch, and with a damn long stick . . . And that includes myself," is indicative of his caustically cynical view of human nature, including his own. He counters Ike's view of essential human goodness with vindictive sarcasm. Contrary to Ike, he is convinced that only policing authorities ("A man in a blue coat, with a badge on it") can make man behave at all. Other additions to his coversation show Roth's preoccupation with conditions of twentieth-century life, such as unemployment and governmental ineptitude and interference, that diminish human dignity and individuality. In the following quotation, italics indicate passages added to the revised text. Brackets indicate wording not incorporated into the final text.

> Half the people without jobs and half the factories closed by strikes. *Half the people on public dole that wont work and half that couldn't work even if they would.* Too much cotton and corn and hogs, and not enough for [all the] people to [wear and eat] *eat and wear. The country full of people to tell a man how he cant raise his own cotton whether he will or wont, and Sally Rand with a sergeant's stripes and not even the fan couldn't fill the army rolls.* Too much not-butter and not even the guns—[DA, p. 48; GDM, p. 339]

As a matter of fact, Roth is more self-critical, more thoughtful, and more troubled than Boyd. Boyd is described as a ruthless, possessive, and aggressive man who "owned, or at least did the driving of, any-thing—animal, machine or human—which he happened to be using."

Even though he feels the war will put an end to the hunting expeditions, he is still determined this last time "to get mine too" (DA, p. 47). These passages are omitted in the revision. Instead, some of Roth's cynicism can be traced to his frustration over the ignominy of his relationship with his mistress. The expanded description of the skidding halt of the car attests to his emotional agitation upon sighting her on the road. Later, he is more reluctant than Boyd to face Ike with the sordidness of his behavior. Where Boyd says bluntly, "There will be a woman here sometime this morning" (DA, p. 52), Roth says, "There will be a message" (GDM, p. 355). Of course Roth, like Boyd, is an irreverent hunter and lover, but in the revision his torment is more sympathetically portrayed. Later, one sees that Roth's failure can be partially attributed to his elderly kinsman whose complacent satisfaction with his life is vividly contrasted with Roth's almost pathetic self-hate. Originally, Boyd had one redeeming quality: he served bravely in World War I. Crossed out on the back of page 4A of the "Delta Autumn" typescript is a page which includes the following:

> "I'm going on it," Boyd said harshly. He had been too young for the draft of 1917 but he had seen service anyway by lying about his age and had been demobilised a trained air officer. For that reason the old man, McCaslin, himself son of a Confederate soldier and bred up in the hard aftermath of that war, even found excuses constantly for the rudeness of his speech and the inconsiderateness of his actions such as the abruot stopping of the car.

This passage is omitted, but in the magazine version Ike briefly mentions the medals Boyd brought home from the war (DA, p. 47). Roth is stripped of Boyd's war heroics (although he did serve in the war) on the one hand, but on the other he is made a more sensitive and tormented human being.

Ike has a more clearly central role in the revised story. An anachronism of the past, he is "insulated by his years and time from the corruption of steel and oiled moving parts which tainted the others" (GDM, p. 342). Through more detailed reminiscence, his past experiences are brought to bear upon the present. While he recalls his initiation into the high code of Sam Fathers in earlier versions, now he also thinks of his repudiation. He repudiated "the wrong and shame, at least in principle, and at least the land itself in fact" (GDM, p. 351). While he makes reference to his dead wife, only in the revision does he sentimentalize her: she was lost "because she loved him. But women hope for so much. They never live too long to still believe that anything within the scope of their passionate wanting is likewise within the range of their passionate hope" (GDM, p. 352). As a matter of fact, this sentimental view of his wife coupled with his prior opinion of the "divinity" of sexual union form an ironic prelude to his meeting with Roth's mistress, which indicates just how shallow Ike's high-minded views of love and women are. Furthermore, in the earlier versions reference is made to "children" he had had once, "though no more" (TS, p. 10; DA, p. 51), whereas the revised story makes reference only to a lost son (GDM, p. 351), who may be either the son he wanted to have or an actual son that died. In all accounts, the hunting companions are described as being like Ike's kin, but the final version elaborates the point: "and not one of whom even bore any name he used to know . . . were more his kin than any" (GDM, p. 352). Indeed, his blood kin, Roth Edmonds, is the equivalent of another "lost" son. The climactic meeting with Roth's mistress also points out Ike's failure to be the father to Roth that Sam Fathers was to him.

Several key changes alter dramatically the scene between Ike and the woman, and here it is particularly interesting to trace the evolution of scene and character. In the two earlier versions, little authorial commentary upon the way the two participants look or feel is included. Not so in the final account where Ike's emotional agitation is more graphically depicted and the woman's cool intelligent dignity is heightened, as in this added passage:

> "Here." He fumbled at the envelope. It was not to pick it up, because it was still in his hand; he had never put it down. It was as if he had to fumble somehow to co-ordinate physically his heretofore obedient hand with what his brain was commanding of it, as if he had never performed such an action before, extending the envelope at last, saying again, "Here. Take it. Take it!" until he became aware of her eyes, or not the eyes so much as the look, the regard fixed now on his fact with that immersed contemplation, that bottomless and intent candor, of a child. If she had ever seen either the envelope or his movements to extend it, she did not show it.
> "You're Uncle Isaac," she said.
> "Yes," he said. "But never mind that. Here. Take it." [GDM, pp. 357–58]

Ike does not pick up her familiarity with the family here, or later when she elaborates upon her knowledge. The insertion of these comments serves to bind the volume together genealogically, preparing for the revelation of her kinship later in the story (italics indicate wording added to the typescript for the magazine story. The rest of the passage was newly added to the final version):

> *"Yes,"* she said. And while [H] *he glared at her, his white hair awry from the pillow* [,] and *his eyes, lacking the spectacles to focus them, blurred and irisless and apparently pupilless,* [.] he saw again that grave, intent, speculative and detached fixity like a child watching him. "His great great—Wait a minute.—great great *great* grandfather was your grandfather. McCaslin. Only it got to be Edmonds. Only it got to be more than that. Your cousin McCaslin was there that day when your father and Uncle Buddy won Tennie from Mr Beauchamp for the one that had no name but Terrel so you called him Tomey's Terrel, to marry. But after that it got to be Edmonds." She regarded him, almost peacefully, with that unwinking and heatless fixity—the dark wide bottomless eyes in the face's dead and toneless pallor which to the old man looked anything but dead, but young and incredibly and even ineradicably alive—as though she were not only not looking at anything, she was not even speaking to anyone but herself. "I would have made a man of him. He's not a man yet. You spoiled him. You, and Uncle Lucas and Aunt Mollie. But mostly you."
>
> "Me?" he said. "Me?"
>
> "Yes. When you gave to his grandfather that land which didn't belong to him, not even half of it by will or even law."
>
> "And never mind that too," he said. "Never mind that too. You," he said. "You sound like you have been to college even. You sound almost like a Northerner even, not like the draggle-tailed women of these Delta peckerwoods. [DA, p. 53; GDM, pp. 359–60]

Notice how Faulkner has through revision sharply contrasted the two figures in the above passage: he has the enfeebling blindness of old age; she is "young and incredibly and even ineradicably alive." And the implication is, of course, that Ike's blindness is more than physical. Not only does Ike observe her more cultured manner but the woman also gives a fuller, more evaluative explanation of the evolution of her relationship with Roth, revealing perceptive insight into both herself and Roth. Added is her observation that despite her rational agreement with Roth about their terminal relationship, emotionally she has long been impervious to reason and logic: "I wasn't even listening to him anymore by then because by that time it had been a long time since he had had anything else to tell me for me to have to hear. By then I wasn't even listening enough to ask him to please stop talking" (GDM, p. 359). Roth is now more generous with money, and her perception of his sense of honor and code is more ironical (italics indicate wording added to the final revised version): "He gave money last winter. *Besides the money he sent to Vicksburg. Provided. Honor and code too*" (DA, p. 54; GDM, p. 361). "I knew what I was doing. I knew that to begin with, *long before honor I imagine he called it told him the time had come to tell me in so many words what his code I suppose he would call it would forbid him forever to do*" (DA, p. 53; GDM, p. 358).

The climax takes place when she mentions that her aunt took in washing, and Ike blurts out with "amazement, pity, and outrage," "You're a nigger." The typescript, however, includes no elaboration of his response. In the magazine story, Ike's response includes sympathy for the plight of this woman, and by implication of her people: "the lips and skin pallid and colorless yet not ill, the tragic and foreknowing eyes. *Maybe in a thousand or two thousand years it will have blended in America and we will have forgotten it,* he thought. *But God pity these*" (DA, p. 54). In the final text, the racial outrage is stronger and the pity less as Ike responds with spontaneous racial prejudice: "*Maybe in a thousand or two thousand years in America,* he thought. *But not now! Not now!*" (GDM, p. 361). She goes on in this version to identify herself as the granddaughter of Tennie's Jim, and thus Ike and the reader perceive what she has intimated earlier: she is part of the family.

The volume has come full circle; her child is doubly the product of incest and miscegenation, symbolically a latter-day replica of Tomey's Turl. Although the particular atrocity in the ledgers which caused Ike to recoil at the "wrong and shame" was a similar instance of miscegenation, incest, and payoff (the callous sexual exploitation by Carothers McCaslin of his half-black daughter, Tomasina, and the consequent thousand-dollar legacy), Ike's inadequate response is to advise his distant kinswoman to take the money, go North, and marry a black man. To be sure, his reluctance even to touch the woman in the typescript ("for an instant their fingers touched before he jerked his own hand back" [TS, p. 16]) and his refusal to do so in the magazine story ("He picked up the sheaf of bank notes and laid it on the blanket at the foot of the cot and drew his hand back beneath the blanket. 'Here' " [DA, p. 54]) are replaced in the composite by his deliberate reaching out to the woman:

> She came back to the cot and took up the money; whereupon once more he said, "Wait:" although she had not turned, still stooping, and

he put out his hand. But, sitting, he could not complete the reach until she moved her hand, the single hand which held the money, until he touched it. He didn't grasp it, he merely touched it—the gnarled, blood-less, bone-light bone-dry old man's fingers touching for a second the smooth young flesh where the strong old blood ran after its long journey back to home. "Tennie's Jim," he said. "Tennie's Jim." [GDM, p. 362]

His nostalgic response capsulizes the paradox of his tender memories of his mulatto relatives together with his feelings of horror at this modern repetition of the miscegenetic union. That he now gives her the hunting horn seems to evidence his recognition that this child is the inheritor of the traditions of the family, but since the woman is being paid-off just as her predecessors were, the gesture is shallow indeed, especially in the context of the following italicized transcrip-tion of Ike's thoughts in which he demonstrates just how entrenched is his horror of racial blending. Although the color-blind hierarchy of hunters had taught him the equal humanity of all men and although reverence and respect for all of life were concomitant with his initia-tion into the wilderness, he reverts to automatic racial prejudice and irreverent categorical blame for the "ruined woods" upon people who do not know their place or race:

> *This land which man has deswamped and denuded and derivered in two generations so that white men can own plantations and commute every night to Memphis and black men own plantations and ride in jim crow cars to Chicago to live in millionaires' mansions on Lakeshore Drive, where white men rent farms and live like niggers and niggers crop on shares and live like animals . . . Chinese and African and Aryan and Jew, all breed and spawn together until no man has time to say which one is which nor cares. . . .* No wonder the ruined woods I used to know dont cry for retribution! he thought: The people who have de-stroyed it will accomplish its revenge. [GDM, p. 364]

Indeed, he earlier urged the woman to accept *her* place and race. But his feeling of flustered embarrassment when his unrestrain-able bigotry is met by the woman's penetrating wisdom is under-scored in the revision: " . . . *he knew that his voice was running away with him and he had neither intended it nor could stop it:* 'That's right [he said]. Go back North. Marry: a man of your own race' " (GDM, p. 363; italics indicate passages newly added to the revised test.) Moreover, the intensification of Ike's callous advice, added to the magazine story, is retained in the final text: "you could find a black man who would see in you whatever it was you saw in him, and who would ask nothing from you and expect less and get even still less if it's revenge you want'' (DA, p. 54). Her response is a stinging indictment of the old man in all three versions, but it is an especially damning assessment of the well meaning old man in *Go Down, Moses* who has tried to imitate Christ's life but who has failed to embrace his love: "Old man . . . have you lived so long and forgotten so much that you dont remember anything you ever knew or felt or even heard about love?" In this context his platitudes on the divinity of sexual union have an even more hollow ring. The impotence of this manqué Christ is underscored at the end of the story in the addition of descriptive detail. When Ike sadly states to himself his conviction that Roth killed a doe, he lay back down, "the blanket once more drawn to his chin, his crossed hands once more weightless on his breast in the empty tent" (GDM, p. 365). Isaac can only creep back sadly into his solitary retreat from responsibility and involvement in the human community, his crossed hands a "weightless" and mocking gesture of christlikeness.

The belated testing of Ike's high-minded principles exposes them as fraudulent. The snake he salutes as "Grandfather" at age seventeen has indeed become his grandfather; the eighty-year-old repeats the sin of his grandfather. Neither relinquishment nor repudiation is a final answer to man's complex role in life. Ike is partially to blame for the history of "wrong and shame" he repudiates, the "ruined woods" he laments, and the callous Roth he condemns. Indeed, in a passage quoted above, the woman insists that Ike "spoiled" Roth "when you gave to his grandfather that land which didn't belong to him, not even half of it by will or even law" (GDM, p. 360). The failure of Ike to live without "wrong and shame" is a revealing denouement to his well-intentioned repudiation. Faulkner has skillfully revised and integrated the magazine story into the complex portraiture of Ike McCaslin in *Go Down, Moses*.[44]

Faulkner's revisions show his ability to manipulate the components of the short story to alter its effect, emphasis, and meaning. The hunting trilogy evidences the careful craftsmanship that built larger unified structures from comparatively simple and one-dimensional stories. Each revised magazine story both contributes to and is enlarged by the composite structure of *Go Down, Moses*. Knowledge of the genealogical history that lies behind Ike's meeting with Roth's mistress, for example, vastly alters the implications of this meeting, while Ike's response, in turn, vastly alters the portrait of him in *Go Down, Moses*. Rather than a thorough and chronological history, Faulkner sets in mutually illuminating juxtaposition the important moments in Ike's life: the killing of his first deer; the sight of Old Ben; the deaths of Ben, Sam, and Lion; the repudiation of his heritage; the returns to camp as a boy and as an old man. The omissions (for example, of sixty years of Ike's adult life) are as important as the inclusions. Ike's relinquishment makes his life a blank page until he is met with a belated test of his principles. His conspicuous absence in the final story, "Go Down, Moses," highlights his failure. Since he has absolved himself of family and communal responsibility, others must care for the burial of the distant relative, Samuel Worsham Beauchamp.

"GO DOWN, MOSES"

"Go Down, Moses" was published in *Collier's* in 1941[45] and slightly revised for inclusion in *Go Down, Moses*. The innumerable minor changes in wording are for the most part stylistic improvement or stylistic tinkering. More revealing is a crossed-out section on page 1 of an early typescript which shows that Faulkner at one time intended the executed young man to be Henry Coldfield Sutpen, apparently a descendant of the Sutpen blacks of *Absalom, Absalom!*[46] Since both *Absalom, Absalom!* and *Go Down, Moses* deal with the descendants of miscegenetic unions, it is not surprising that Faulkner was thinking of the story as a sequel to that volume. But this abortive linkage of the Sutpens to the volume indicates again just how loose and wide-ranging were the materials that Faulkner welded together in *Go Down, Moses*. Stories that were at one time conceived in terms of other great Faulknerian families—the Sartorises ("Was"), the Compsons ("The Old People," "Lion"), and the Sutpens ("Go Down, Moses")—are refashioned into McCaslin-Edmonds episodes. The black Beauchamps are tied into the entangling genealogy of the McCaslins, profoundly altering the characterization and meaning of the original one-dimensional stories like "A Point of Law" and "Gold Is Not Always." *Go Down, Moses* is a unique package of amalgamation and revision.

This story serves as an epilogue to the short story composite. As suggested above, appropriately Isaac McCaslin does not appear in this projection into the modern Southern community, because he has absolved himself of communal responsibility. The heritage of guilt must be carried by others, the new men such as Gavin Stevens who imperfectly recognize it for what it is. No white McCaslin assists in the burial of their black brother, Samuel Worsham Beauchamp. Mollie[47] insists that Roth Edmonds was responsible for her grandson's corruption ("Roth Edmonds sold my Benjamin. Sold him in Egypt. Pharaoh got him—" [GDM, p. 371]), since he sent the boy away from home for breaking into his commissary and forbade him to return. But to say that Roth is immediately responsible for Samuel's corruption would be simplistic; it is suggested rather that the boy was doomed to a bad end by his very nature ("a youth not yet twenty-one, with something in him from the father who begot and deserted him and who was now in the State Penitentiary for manslaughter—some seed not only violent but dangerous and bad" [GDM, p. 372]). That the McCaslins and the Edmondses and by implication white society are responsible generally for the fate of Samuel is true. Samuel Worsham Beauchamp was not *sold,* but his great-grandfather, Tomey's Turl, and his great-grandmother, Tennie Beauchamp, were. His grandfather, Lucas Beauchamp, was *paid off* as was his cousin, Roth's mulatto mistress. Failure to recognize the black man as a brother within the community at large, and particularly within the McCaslin family, undoubtedly created the situation that was Samuel Worsham Beauchamp's ruin. His ruin was the acquisition of white man's vice, "getting rich too fast" (GDM, p. 370). Ike's comment about blacks in part 4 of "The Bear" is apt: "Their vices are vices aped from white men or that white men and bondage have taught them" (GDM, p. 294).

The bondage that Mollie speaks and sings of is real: the volume records the infamous history of servitude, payoff, abuse, exploitation, and injustice, and Moses has "gone down"—not to the promised land but to defeat. Sam Fathers is Isaac's Moses who he claims "set me free" by leading him to the promised land, the wilderness—away from Egypt, the tamed land. But Sam, caged by his own mixed blood, was himself incapable of freedom. Similarly, Isaac, who idealistically saw himself as the savior of the South, the Moses who would remove the curse from the promised land, saves no one, not even himself, because he mistook retreat for freedom, abnegation for amelioration, principle for practice. Finally, in this story a third manqué Moses, Gavin Stevens, goes down in defeat when he discovers with embarrassment that he can neither participate in nor understand the grief of Mollie nor can he successfully defend Roth Edmonds and by implication all white men from her indictment. All he can do is accommodate the wishes of this simple-minded, intractable, illiterate, and religious old woman and give her grandson the public and proper burial she believes he must have.[48] This is not deliverance to the promised land. The forces that led to Butch's "badness" are still present; the gulf of communication between Stevens and Mollie is enormous and disturbing, but Steven's efforts do show some redemptive promise, and do suggest that people of humane instincts will keep trying to fulfill their obligations to all members of the community. James Early finds the too-kindly behavior of Stevens and the editor unrealistically sentimentalized: "the whites in 'Go Down, Moses' are implausibly charming and indulgent of the vagaries of the 'darkies.' "[49] But while Gavin Stevens is annoyingly ubiquitous in Faulkner's fiction, often as an inept bungler and an obtuse windbag, he is nonetheless the vehicle for Faulkner's belief in the redemptive potential, floundering as it may be, of education and idealism in man. "Phi Beta Kappa, Harvard, Ph.D., Heidelburg," Gavin is acquainted intellectually with some of mankind's best attempts to deal with human experience creatively, analytically, and morally, and out of that knowledge he is a well-intentioned do-gooder who like other Faulknerian idealists is frequently unable to bridge the chasm between words and deeds. But the Miss Worshams (or the Miss Habershams, as the character is later called in *Intruder in the Dust*), who respond with the "heart" not the "mind," who feel instinctively "it's our grief," turn good intentions into deeds. It is a hopeful view of man; the same view that caused Faulkner to say: "I believe that man will not merely endure: he will prevail. He is immortal, not because he alone among creatures has an inexhaustible voice, but because he has a soul, a spirit capable of compassion and sacrifice and endurance."[50] I do not believe that it is an unduly unrealistic or sentimental view. Only the out-and-out cynic would deny the existence of a tenacious shred of humanity in mankind, and Faulkner is not that cynic.

CONCLUSION

Faulkner's use of preexistent short stories demonstrates his considerable talent as a craftsman of fiction. Since so much of his Yoknapatawpha County world seems to have "preexisted" in his mind, his reuse of short stories is neither surprising nor untypical of his craftsmanship in general. One advantage of following the evolution of a discrete story as it becomes refashioned into a part of a larger whole, however, is that it reveals the control that Faulkner exercises over the diffuseness of his Yoknapatawpha material. The story is the raw material shaped into differing constructs with differing meanings through Faulkner's skillful revision. In each of the five longer works I have discussed, a unique structure governs the revision of the stories incorporated into it. The reworking of each story, moreover, makes different demands on Faulkner's skills; nothing is formulaic about Faulkner's craft of revision. The Snopes Trilogy demonstrates his preservation of the integrity of self-contained novelistic structures, even though the Snopes saga spilled over the boundaries of a single work.

In some ways *The Hamlet* is a rich amplification of the unfinished story "Father Abraham." That Faulkner duplicates the distanced perspective on the antics of the Snopeses and the buoyant, comic tone—tinged with moral disapproval—contribute immeasurably to the success of the novel. The barn-burning episode had to be rewritten because the short story violates this perspective and tone. Faulkner successfully refashions the episode into the first stage of the Snopeses' invasion of Frenchman's Bend; establishes a pattern to be repeated with subtle variation throughout the trilogy—the Snopeses' advance is built on the moral vulnerability of others; and ties the episode integrally into the prevalent context of barter and trade in the novel. Reinforcing the association of Snopes with this trading contest,

Faulkner drew into Snopes-lore the Pat Stamper story, "Fool About a Horse." Originally about V. K. Suratt's father, it is now V. K. Ratliff's illustrative tale of how Ab Snopes "soured." But despite Ratliff's glib explanation, I think that the episode still jars somewhat with the design of *The Hamlet* by presenting the "unsoured" Ab as a sympathetic human being rather than as a recognizable member of that sub-species, Snopes. The episode does serve to reinforce Ratliff's role as Snopes-watcher and prepare for his confrontations with Flem which give shape to the trilogy. The opposition of Suratt and the Snopeses was part of Faulkner's original inspiration for the saga, but the metamorphosis of this shrewd trader into Ratliff, the intellectual and moral opponent of Snopesism, and the increased emphasis on the opposition of Flem and Ratliff are among the most significant and effective of Faulkner's alterations of the original stories. Furthermore, by strategically placing the two incidents of "Lizards in Jamshyd's Courtyard" in Book One and Book Four of *The Hamlet,* these two confrontations between Ratliff and Flem over goats and over the alleged buried treasure at Old Frenchman place contribute to the encompassing framework of the novel. Flem not only dupes the Frenchman's Bend residents—and that duping reaches its climactic finale in the spotted-horses episode reworked into Book Four—but he also triumphs over V. K. Ratliff.

By weaving another non-Snopes story "The Hound" into *The Hamlet,* Faulkner prepares for Mink Snopes's eventual role as murderer of Flem. Unlike Ernest Cotton, Mink is not merely a man who has murdered Jack Houston and who is plagued by his hound but he is also disturbed by the failure of his kinsman to come to his aid. The concern grows into the life-long plot of revenge portrayed in *The Mansion.* Mink's story is a significant part both of the overall design of the saga and of the unique structure of *The Hamlet.* Appearing in Book Three, "The Long Summer," of *The Hamlet,* Mink is one of several individuals driven by the forces of passion rather than of profits; his compelling and tortuous relationship with his wife—newly written for the volume—is paralleled by that of Houston and his wife and, on another plane, Ike and his cow. These episodes contribute to an aspect of *The Hamlet* not sketched in early Snopes stories. For although the Snopes saga grew out of a single inspiration and although a number of early Snopes stories are colorful and comic variations of a common theme—the mercenary opportunism of Snopes—the material drawn from early stories forms only a part of the three novels of the trilogy, a decreasing part, as Faulkner gradually moves away from the original bolt-of-lightning inspiration. That movement begins in *The Hamlet* with Faulkner's use of Eula as the counterpoint to Flem. This dual center allowed Faulkner to play off his Snopesian stories of barter and trade against the newly interjected tales of love and passion, laying the groundwork for a moral confrontation between the two which grows in prominence as the trilogy proceeds. In *The Hamlet,* Mink's story is skillfully tied into this opposing thematic center.

Much of *The Town,* centering on Gavin Steven's inept vigilance to protect Eula and her daughter Linda from Flem, is not drawn from Faulkner's early design for the saga. Here, as elsewhere in his canon, he perhaps too readily presses that faint-hearted do-gooder Gavin Stevens into service and weakens the vitality of his materials. In this novel with the forces of love and passion falling victim to those of greed and with Eula sacrificed and turned into a tombstone monument ("A Virtuous Wife is a Crown to Her Husband") in her husband's drive to respectability, it was perhaps inevitable that Eula be demythologized. The tone is more somber than in *The Hamlet,* the threat of Snopesism more clearly perceived in moral terms. Unlike the flexible omniscient voice of *The Hamlet,* the point of view in *The Town* is restricted to the voices of Gavin Stevens, V. K. Ratliff, and Charles Mallison. Unlike *The Hamlet's* structure both of counterpoint where Flem and Eula form dual symbolic centers for the themes of greed and passion and of opposition where Flem and Ratliff are matched as traders and as men, *The Town* is cast in the form of an extended conversation among the three narrators and with the reader. Although this method encourages a lamentable garrulousness and repetitiveness in the telling of Snopes tales, it also greatly enhances the reader's stock of Snopes-lore.

In incorporating three preexistent short stories into *The Town,* Faulkner took care with point of view, accommodating these tales to the conversation format of the novel. He also made each tale function as an important step in Flem's incorrigible drive to the bank presidency. "Centaur in Brass" is reworked into Chapter One of the novel where Flem's defeat in brass stealing becomes his first footprint into Jefferson. By interjecting Flem into the story of I. O.'s fight over mules with Mrs. Hait when refashioning "Mule in the Yard" as an episode in *The Town,* Faulkner signals an important change in Flem's tactics. As Ratliff observes, Flem has discovered that he has got to have respectability and so must jettison his unsavory relatives out of

Jefferson. The final episode of the novel, paralleling "The Waifs," shows him again doing just that, ridding the town of Byron Snopes's Indian children, by paying for the pedigreed dog they ate.

Finally, in *The Mansion* the moral drama entirely usurps the economic stage as Mink, Linda, Gavin, and Ratliff along with "fate, and destiny, and luck, and hope" conspire to put down Flem; the life-affirming forces of love and passion ultimately triumph over the life-denying greed of Flem, and in the process the dominant movement of the Snopes saga is completed. Although sectioned into parts, the novel is for the most part a sustained narrative, and Faulkner is again at the height of his narrative skill in his paraphrase of Mink's stream-of-consciousness. Mink's grievance against Flem and his dogged determination to kill him shape both his life and the structure of the novel. Book One is Faulkner's third telling of the Jack Houston killing and its aftermath. Told from Mink's perspective by a sympathetic, effaced narrator, the emphasis now is on the economic deprivation of Mink and on his simple-minded pursuit of justice from his arrogant neighbor, Houston; from the representative of Law in the county, Will Varner; and from his cousin, Flem, who he erroneously expects will be bound to him by the "simple laws of blood kinship." The Houston killing, of course, is only the germinal core of Mink's grievance against Flem which is developed with such detail in the novel. The original incident produced an extremely powerful short story. It became an integral part of *The Hamlet*. Expanded and enriched, it is part of the extended treatment of Mink in *The Mansion*. This successful reuse of a situation illustrates once again Faulkner's skillful molding of his "raw material" into different contexts with different shapes and meanings.

Faulkner's inclusion of two extraneous comic stories in *The Mansion,* however, is not particularly successful because the demise of these lesser Snopeses, Clarence in the reworked story "By the People" and Orestes in "Hog Pawn," seems digressive in a novel which centers on the destruction of the quintessence of Snopesism, Flem; the economic threat of Snopesism is incidental to the moral one. Moreover, the episodic form and the tall-tale quality jar with the sustained narration and the realistic mode of the novel as a whole.

Even though the Snopes novels are distinct and separate constructs governed by different artistic principles and achieving different degrees of success, the trilogy is richer than any one novel, for it completes the saga and creates a sense of the comic variety and the alarming danger of Snopesism as no single novel can. While each novel is autonomous, it is enlarged by its placement within the larger context of the trilogy. The part contributes to the developing whole; the whole informs the part. In fact, this relationship between the parts and the whole resembles the functioning of the stories within the short story composites, *The Unvanquished* and *Go Down, Moses*. Crafted as detachable stories they yet expand in implication when they become part of the structural design of the composite. Since the individual episodes within each of the Snopes novels, however, are not designed to stand alone, these three works are properly called novels.

The Unvanquished is a relatively simple example of the short story composite. The stories were from the start conceived as a long series. Yet Faulkner created a composite out of what could have been merely a collection by his revisions of the original stories and by the addition of the final story, "An Odor of Verbena." He both altered the perspective and diction of the narrator and heightened the issue of race. An adolescent narrates the original magazine stories, while in the composite an adult looks back on childhood experiences. This change in point of view also contributes to fuller characterization and greater descriptive detail. But because this retrospective narrator is disappointingly uncritical of the racial inequities in his family and in society, the volume is not totally successful; the significance of race is increased without receiving the depth of treatment it deserves.

Go Down, Moses is a much more intricately structured short story composite which more successfully examines racial interrelationships. This work pulls together ten widely varying, separately written stories and much new material. Its boldly experimental structure presents both an expansive across-the-generations dramatization of a host of characters and incidents and an intensive examination of the moral consciousness of Isaac McCaslin. Because of the dual nature of the stories as autonomous units and coordinate parts, the volume achieves simultaneous particularity and generalization, simplicity and complexity, comedy and tragedy. The addition of two fragments, part 1 of "Was" and part 4 of "The Bear," helps to unify the volume, but Faulkner also extensively reworked the various stories brought together into a new synthesis.

The ritualized hunts of "Was" are, through revision, complicated by past and future miscegenetic and genealogical interrelationships among the participants. In the reworking of three comic stories incorporated into "The Fire and the Hearth," the sequential development of the narrative is interrupted by reminiscences of and interpolations from the past so that the characters and events are placed in broad sociological and familial context. The thrust of the considerable revision is to enlarge the characterization of Lucas and to make his confrontation with Roth reverberate with an accumulated history of family and racial tension. When "The Fire and the Hearth" is placed in the context of *Go Down, Moses*, its suggestiveness expands yet further. The latent racial tension between Roth and Lucas is seen as part of Ike McCaslin's unsettling, tainted heritage. Lucas becomes an important foil to Ike. He stays on the land; Ike leaves. He is free; Ike, despite his efforts, is not. He places the sanctity of marriage above his personal obsessions; Ike sacrifices his marriage to his principles. Indeed, throughout the volume the black love relationship—that of Tomey's Turl and Tennie, Lucas and Molly, Rider and his wife— displays a stronger emotional bond than its white counterpart. Meanwhile, the central cause of tragedy and anguish for generation after generation of McCaslins is the fatal attraction between the races. "Pantaloon in Black," although having only minor revision and although outside the volume's genealogical framework, contributes to the increasingly somber tone of the composite by adding yet another example of the gulf between the feelings and needs of the black man and the inability of the white perceiver to comprehend them. Here the obtuse white sheriff totally misconstrues the unbearable grief of the bereaved black man, Rider.

With the next three stories, "The Old People," "The Bear," and "Delta Autumn," the boldness of Faulkner's design for the composite is especially apparent. His revisions and incorporation of four stories into this hunting trilogy display the spatially ordered form he creates to give shape and meaning to his portrayal of the representative life of Isaac McCaslin. Stories about the killing of a deer ("The Old People"), a courageous dog ("Lion"), and a grand old bear (*Post* "The Bear") are revised and reordered and added to in such a way that they are seen to be the formative experiences of Ike McCaslin's rearing. His experience with the Indian Sam Fathers and the wilderness causes him to reject the heritage of his white father and the tamed land. Through enriched characterization, heightened thematic significance, interlinked genealogy, and altered points of view, diction, structure, emphasis, and meaning, Faulkner refashions comparatively simple and one-dimensional stories into an integrated whole. Each revised story contributes to the composite structure of *Go Down, Moses* while its meaning is amplified or altered by the larger context. Through a somewhat circuitous route, the diverse stories come cumulatively and reflexively to bear upon the central moral issue, Ike's repudiation, which is intensively examined in part 4 of "The Bear," an almost entirely new addition to the larger volume. Faulkner's control of the separate structures of the story and the composite is nowhere more evident than in "The Bear." The detachable four-part story achieves its climax in part 3. But the short story composite, operating according to differing structural principles, climaxes in part 4. The structural integrity of both the short story and the composite is maintained.

"Delta Autumn" has been molded through revision into a denouement to Ike's repudiation.[1] Most significantly, Roth's mistress is tied into the genealogical pattern of the whole so that their child is a replica of Tomey's Turl, a product of incest, miscegenation, and payoff. Ike's fumbling response to her reveals his failure to live by his well-intentioned principles. By acting as an intermediary in the payoff, by being shocked that she is a "nigger," and by urging her to go North and marry a black man, he is, at eighty years of age, repeating the sin of his grandfather. Because he has repudiated his role in family and community affairs, Ike does not appear in the final story of "Go Down, Moses," depicting the community's assumption of responsibility for the burial of another McCaslin descendant. This story, like so many of the others, developed out of a different context; Samuel Worsham Beauchamp was at one time Henry Coldfield Sutpen. While only slightly revised, the story serves as an effective epilogue to the volume. Complete with conflict, climax, denouement, and epilogue, *Go Down, Moses* has a clearly discernible structural design, yet it also preserves the autonomy and completeness of its various stories. Faulkner's skill in creating this short story composite can only be fully appreciated by following its evolution from its short story origins.

Although I think that the value of this study lies in the insights it offers into the ideas and structures Faulkner was seeking to implement in specific contexts, I will hazard a formulation of four general observations about Faulkner's craft of revision. First, perhaps the most impressive facet of Faulkner's method of composition and revision is its flexibility. He can begin with a bolt-of-lightning conception—like that of the Snopeses—which informs the various self-contained stories and guides the process of revision, or he can effect bold transformations of character, theme, and tone, as he does in *Go Down, Moses,* so that the unsuspecting reader of the original stories sees little or nothing that would suggest the direction the final work will take. In other words, although Faulkner seems to have held much of his little postage stamp world in his mind so that he could "pull out" what he needed for a particular effect, yet he continued to add to and alter that little world; nothing was sacred about it. He used a preexistent character to do the job, or he created a new one, or he irreverently changed an old one. So in the process of putting together *Go Down, Moses,* Quentin (Compson) of "Lion" becomes Ike McCaslin, and old Ike McCaslin is dropped and his grandson, Theophilus, is exterminated (for the new Ike McCaslin is childless). Faulkner can effect these transformations and exterminations without any apparent regret even though as a result we have a Yoknapatawpha County world peopled with dangling anomalies like Theophilus McCaslin and inconsistencies like Quentin Compson, who is revived from the dead (he died in 1910 according to the appendix of *The Sound and the Fury*) to appear in "Lion" which takes place around 1935 and then returned to the grave when his role in that story is replaced by Ike McCaslin. Yet, as I asserted at the start, the world of Yoknapatawpha County exists above and beyond each individual work informing and enriching it, in spite of Faulkner's lack of reverence for its absolute consistency. Faulkner refused to be limited by his own invention just as he refused to be limited by others' ideas about what constitutes unity.

Second, regardless of conception, these works almost always illustrate Faulkner working from the part to the whole, from simplicity to complexity, and from the comic to the serious rather than vice versa. Although he had a fairly comprehensive idea of the Snopeses, he began by writing stories about them which were simple in characterization, light in tone, and comic in intent. But as he worked with the idea of them over the years, he introduced more and more complexity into the characters, more and more moral seriousness into the evaluation of them, and more and more novelistic elements into the episodic materials. Similarly, the stories of *The Unvanquished* were originally nostalgic, humorous, and simplistic tales of adventure about a young boy growing up during the Civil War, but through revision, the humor and nostalgia are moderated by the retrospective narrator's insistent, thoughtful evaluations. Likewise, the simplicity and the humor of "Was," a tale of ritualized slave-chasing and ludicrous husband-baiting, are moderated by the interjection of details like Tomey's Turl's blood kinship to his masters and by the context into which the story is placed. The humor is lessened as the characterization is developed and the past and future are brought to bear upon the incidents. The same process is at work when the one-dimensional Luke Beauchamp of the simple and comic stories "Gold Is Not Always" and "A Point of Law" becomes the complicated character of "The Fire and the Hearth" who retains his penchant for moonshining and gold-divining but who takes on added stature, dignity, and willfullness from his linkage to the McCaslins and from his repeated demonstration of superiority to individuals from the white half of this family. In his revision and incorporation of preexistent stories into larger constructs, then, Faulkner demonstrates his obsessive exploration and examination of the potential complexity and seriousness of the simplest characters and situations. He takes the Jamesian idea of the *donnée* further than James would have dreamed because the *donnée* grows in magnitude as information from the past, from the future, and from other contexts is brought to bear upon it.

Third, Faulkner characteristically retains the narrative frame into which the original stories were cast. By doing so, he retains the humor and simplicity of the originals, but by interjecting more information about the character and events, and by fitting the part into a developing and reflexive whole, the simple, comic view becomes part of a more complex, serious whole. Sometimes Faulkner's revisions were so minor as in "Pantaloon in Black" that the changes between the independent story and the linked episode are unimportant; sometimes as in "Barn Burning" the story has undergone extensive revision so that the tone, point of view, style, and meaning of the original episode are drastically altered. The kind of revision that is the most common and most interesting is when Faulkner retains the narrative frame of the original story but expands the characterization and links the story to the formal, thematic, or genealogical patterns of the larger whole. Not only does he usually allow the story to retain its identity as a part, but he also frequently augments the single effect of the part in the revision, so that the parts in the larger work are linked spatially rather than chronologically. The tendency to spatialize, that is to arrange formally rather than chronologically blocks of material, is prevalent throughout Faulkner's major fiction. Indeed, Faulkner said in reference to *Light in August,* "Unless a book follows a simple direct line such as a story of adventure, it becomes a series of pieces. It's a good deal like dressing a showcase window. It takes a certain amount of judgment and taste to arrange the different pieces in the most effective place in juxtaposition to one another.''[2] Most critics would say, however, that novels like *Light in August, The Sound and the Fury, As I Lay Dying,* and *Absalom, Absalom!* are of greater synthesis and thus greater magnitude than the more loosely structured *Go Down, Moses, The Unvanquished, The Hamlet, The Town,* and *The Mansion.* But Faulkner was not striving for the same degree or kind of synthesis in each of his works. Often, in fact, he was experimenting with forms quite different from the conventional novel. In *Go Down, Moses* and *The Unvanquished* the ''detachableness'' of the short story component is clearly maintained; these short story composites function differently but not necessarily less successfully than well wrought novels. William Faulkner's craft of revision shows him continually striving to create forms flexible enough to express his particular concerns. If it meant violating the new critical premises about what constitutes unity, and if he went beyond the bounds of what can be called a novel, so be it.

Fourth, just as the characters grow in complexity and the tone grows in seriousness, so too the descriptive details grow in profusion and vividness and the style grows in precision. Faulkner usually cannot resist reworking and adding to his work, and his critical sense was indeed excellent. Although an undeniable element of tinkering precipitated some of his word changes, each reworking of each story is almost invariably better. The care that he lavished on word choice and syntax alone in ''The Fire and the Hearth'' should convincingly demonstrate that he was a scrupulous stylist. This story is not an unusual case, only a well-documented one. Faulkner did occasionally work the other way, from the whole to the part, from the complex to the simple, when he was tailoring a story for a magazine publication. ''Spotted Horses'' is the published story which resulted from Faulkner's several efforts to cut a short story from the long and unfinished ''Father Abraham'' manuscript, and the story is undoubtedly weakened in vividness of characterization and detail. Faulkner, then, was not above counting words, not above cutting and condensing to meet an editor's requirements, but these instances are rare and untypical of his method in general. Indeed, with no other evidence to substantiate the order in which manuscripts were written, one could with some assurance of accuracy place them in the order of increasing complexity and exactness. This method of expansion of detail, enlargement of characterization, heightening of seriousness, and precision of language is so characteristic of that masterful revisionist, William Faulkner.

NOTES

Introduction

1. I exclude here those published excerpts which are identical or nearly identical to sections of novels. The short story collections, *These 13* (New York: Cape and Smith, 1931) and *Doctor Martino and Other Stories* (New York: Smith and Haas, 1934), contain some stories that were slightly revised from earlier magazine publication. *Knight's Gambit* (New York: Random House, 1949) is made up of five reprinted but not revised stories and one newly published story, "Knight's Gambit." *Notes on a Horsethief* (Greenville, Miss.: Levee Press, 1950) was slightly revised when incorporated into *A Fable* (New York: Random House, 1954), pp. 151–89. "A Name for the City," *Harper's* 201 (October 1950): 200–14, was revised to become the narrative prologue, "The Courthouse," of Act 1 of *Requiem for a Nun* (New York: Random House, 1951). *Big Woods* (New York: Random House, 1955) is made up of revised parts of pre-published material. "Hell Creek Crossing," *Saturday Evening Post* 235 (March 31, 1962) was reprinted in *The Reivers* (New York: Random House, 1962) in chapter 4, untitled and without the two and one-half page introduction Faulkner wrote for the story. "Wash," *Harper's* 168 (February 1934): 258–66, reprinted in *Doctor Martino* and *Collected Stories of William Faulkner* (New York: Random House, 1950), pp. 535–50, was extensively revised and incorporated into *Absalom, Absalom!* (New York: Random House, 1936). "Wash" will be discussed below.
2. "Wash," *Collected Stories,* p. 535. Hereafter cited as W in the text.
3. *Absalom, Absalom!* (1936; reprint ed., New York: Modern Library, 1951), pp. 181–87, 277–92. Hereafter cited as AA in the text.
4. *Faulkner in the University: Class Conferences at the University of Virginia, 1957–1958,* ed. Frederick L. Gwynn and Joseph L. Blotner (Charlottesville: University of Virginia Press, 1959), p. 90.
5. Faulkner affixed this date to the final page of the manuscript.
6. *Faulkner in the University,* p. 252.
7. The first is the intention of James Early, *The Making of "Go Down, Moses"* (Dallas: Southern Methodist University Press, 1972), p. ix; the second the method of Edward M. Holmes, *Faulkner's Twice-Told Tales* (The Hague: Mouton, 1966). Although I am grateful to these critics for the unspoken dialogues their studies have provoked, I do not find their methodologies fruitful approaches to Faulkner's craft of revision.

8. Uncle Ike McCaslin first appeared as an old man in "A Bear Hunt," *Saturday Evening Post* 206 (February 10, 1934): 8–9, 74, 76. Reprinted in *Collected Stories*; revised for *Big Woods*.

Chapter 1

1. "Spotted Horses," *Scribner's* 89 (June 1931): 585–97; "Centaur in Brass," *American Mercury* 25 (February 1932): 200–10; "Lizards in Jamshyd's Courtyard," *Saturday Evening Post* 204 (February 27, 1932): 12–13, 52, 57; "Mule in the Yard," *Scribner's* 96 (August 1934): 65–70; and "Barn Burning," *Harper's* 179 (June 1939): 86–96.

2. *Faulkner in the University,* p. 90.

3. "THE HAMLET was incepted as a novel. When I began it, it produced Spotted Horses, went no further. About two years later suddenly I had The HOUND, then JAMSHYD'S COURTYARD, mainly because SPOTTED HORSES had created a character I fell in love with: the itinerant sewing-maching agent named Suratt. Later a man of that name turned up at home, so I changed my man to Ratliff for the reason that my whole town spent much of its time trying to decide just what living man I was writing about, the one literary criticism of the town being 'How in the hell did he remember all that, and when did that happen anyway?'

"Meanwhile, my book had created Snopes and his clan, who produced stories in their saga which are to fall in a later volume: MULE IN THE YARD, BRASS, etc. This over about ten years, until one day I decided I had better start on the first volume or I'd never get any of it down. So I wrote an induction toward the spotted horse story, which included BARN BURNING, and WASH, which I discovered had no place in that book at all. Spotted horses became a longer story, picked up the HOUND (rewritten and much longer and with the character's name changed from Cotton to Snopes), and went on with JAMSHYD'S COURT-YARD." *The Faulkner-Cowley File: Letters and Memories, 1944–1962,* ed. Malcolm Cowley (New York: The Viking Press, 1966), pp. 25–26.

4. Both James B. Meriwether, "Sartoris and Snopes: An Early Notice," *Library Chronicle of the University of Texas* 7 (Summer 1962): 36–39, and Joseph Blotner, *William Faulkner: A Biography* (New York: Random House, 1974), 1: 527–31, date the MS at approximately this time. Faulkner's prefatory note to *The Mansion* would date the inception of the Snopes story even earlier: "This book is the final chapter of, and the summation of, a work conceived and begun in 1925." A 25-page incomplete MS of "Father Abraham" is on deposit in the Arents Collection of the New York Public Library. Two incomplete carbon TSS (54 pages and 51 pages), apparently written later than the MS, are deposited under Item 6074, Box 8, in the Alderman Library, The University of Virginia. This item also includes a 1-page TS (page 29) of a draft of "Father Abraham" and 2-page carbon TS headed "Abraham's Children," the title of a subsequent version of the story. Additionally, several incomplete groups of TS pages of the story, and drafts and partial drafts of several subsequent versions of the story were added to the Alderman Library collection under Item 9817-a, March 22, 1974. See note 6.

5. *Flags in the Dust,* ed. Douglas Day (New York: Random House, 1973), pp. 154–55; *Sartoris* (New York: Harcourt, Brace, & Co., 1929), pp. 172–74.

6. In addition to the Faulkner-Ober correspondence, Item 8969, in the Alderman Library, the following Snopes materials were deposited by Mrs. Jill Summers through Mr. Linton R. Massey under Item 9817-a, March 22, 1974:

"Father Abraham," 54-page titled, incomplete TS (pages 1–54). Pages 17–19 and 21–25 are inserted from a different typing draft, and some of these pages have holograph revisions which were incorporated into the draft of "Father Abraham" represented by the 54-page and 51-page carbon TSS. See note 4.

"Father Abraham," 6-page titled, incomplete TS (pages 1–6), with holograph revisions.

"Father Abraham," 3-page TS (pages 8–10) with holograph revisions; 1-page TS (page 16); 4-page carbon TS; all three groups identified incorrectly as "Abraham's Children" by Linton Massey.

"Abraham's Children," 48-page titled, complete TS (pages 1–48), headed "Abraham's Children" on the top of each page.

"Abraham's Children," 9-page TS (pages 8, 8, 9–15); 13-page carbon TS (pages 10, 37–48); both groups headed "Abraham's Children" on the top of each page.

"The Peasants," 59-page titled, complete, carbon TS (pages 1–16, 16–58).

"As I Lay Dying," 17-page titled, complete, carbon TS (pages 204–220).

"As I Lay Dying," 22-page titled, complete, carbon TS (pages 1–14, 14B, 15–21).

"Aria Con Amore," 16-page titled, complete TS and corresponding carbon TS (pages 1–16 respectively).

"Hog Pawn," 26-page titled, complete, carbon TS (pages 1–4, 4A, 5, 5A, 6–14, 14A, 15–18, 18A, 19–21, 21); some versos.

The Mansion, 13-page TS, including on versos 4-page TS of "By the People" (pages 1, 28, 30, 31) and scattered pages from drafts of "Hog Pawn"; 1-page revised TS.

7. The best textual study of *The Hamlet* to date is James Everett Kibler, Jr., "A Study of the Text of William Faulkner's *The Hamlet,*" Ph.D. diss., University of South Carolina, 1970. His study offers suggested corrections of the text but no critical interpretations of the textual data. *The Town* and *The Mansion* materials—which are abundant and intertwined because Faulkner typed on the versos of earlier drafts—have yet to receive exhaustive textual analysis. Eileen Gregory, "Faulkner's Typescripts of *The Town,*" *A Faulkner Miscellany* (Jackson: University Press of Mississippi, 1974), pp. 113–38, provides a helpful description of *The Town* TSS, including a cataloguing of those pages on versos of *The Mansion* TS, and a brief listing of some of the changes between an early TS of *The Town* and the published text.

8. As mentioned in note 4, two incomplete carbon TSS (54 pp. and 51 pp.) are on deposit in the Alderman Library. My references are to the longer TS throughout, but the copies are identical except in length. Nancy Norris and Edward Gallafent have attached the following note to these materials:

Note to the two carbon typescripts of "Father Abraham":
On July 14, 1971 we collated the two carbon typescripts of "Father Abraham" by reading the entire text of each copy to each other, even

checking, periodically, that misspelled and blurred words matched. In every respect, the two copies were identical (except, of course, for stains, generally restricted to the longer typescript—pp. 1–39, 41–55).

Although the longer typescript seemed to represent the *first* carbon copy, occasionally the papers from the two copies seem to have been switched.

Because the earliest existent version of the story, the incomplete MS of "Father Abraham," is located in the Arents Collection of the New York Public Library, it was impossible for me to collate it with the TSS in the Alderman Library. But Emily Izsak, who has compared a photocopy of the MS with the TSS, has included with the typescripts a note dated March 30, 1968. In addition to noting extensive minor differences in wording throughout the MS and TSS, she makes the following observation:

> Although Mrs. Littlejohn figures in the MS, her role as observer was enlarged in the TS by the addition of her washing and looking on at the auction. One of Buck's speeches is also longer in the TS, and a paragraph in which Henry Armstid waits with a plow-line to catch his horse, while others find ropes, has also been added in the TS.

9. "With this foothold and like Abraham of old, he led his family piece by piece into town." *Flags in the Dust,* p. 154. "With this foothold and like Abraham of old, he brought his blood and legal kin household by household, individual by individual, into town, and established them where they could gain money." *Sartoris,* p. 172.

10. *The Hamlet* (1940: reprint ed., New York: Vintage, 1956), p. 3. Hereafter cited as H in the text.

11. A 17-page incomplete MS of "Barn Burning," dated 7 November 1938, in the Alderman Library has the title "Barn Burning" crossed out and BOOK ONE, Chapter 1 written in. A 32-page untitled, complete TS and a corresponding 32-page carbon TS of the story are headed CHAPTER ONE, indicating that Faulkner at one time intended the story as the first chapter of the longer work. Perhaps he retained this plan until a fairly late date in the process of composition, even as late as the compilation of the TS setting copy, for 33 pages are deleted from this TS, nearly the exact length of the "Barn Burning" TS. One can find evidence of other abortive plans, however, in the wealth of unpublished materials. For example, two fragmentary pages of a rejected carbon TS headed CHAPTER ONE indicate that another rejected plan was to begin the novel directly with the initial meeting of Joby Varner and Ab Snopes in Varner's store. Similarly, pp. 33–42, headed CHAPTER TWO, of what appears to be the same carbon TS begins with the description of the region and its inhabitants that initiates the volume in its final form. These changes are but a small sampling of the extensive rearranging of chapters and sections evidenced in the unpublished materials. Furthermore, Faulkner's plan for the trilogy in late 1938, while closely sketching the eventual shape of the first two books, projected a radically different conclusion to the saga for the final volume. See Blotner, *William Faulkner: A Biography,* 2: 1006–08, for a copy of the plan Faulkner sent to Bob Haas.

12. See note 3. It is interesting to see that Faulkner associates the two poor white short stories, "Barn Burning" and "Wash," with the same genesis. If they did indeed develop out of the same genesis, then the amalgamation of "Wash" into

the totally different context of *Absalom, Absalom!* shows again the flexibility with which Faulkner reworked and reused his stories.

13. Michael Millgate, *The Achievement of William Faulkner* (London: Constable, 1966), p. 185.

14. *Faulkner in the University,* p. 39.

15. On deposit in the Alderman Library are a 10-page complete MS of "Fool About a Horse," a 21-page incomplete, revised TS, and a 33-page complete, revised, carbon TS, a product of the same typing process as the incomplete TS, but bearing different holograph corrections.

16. "Fool About a Horse," *Scribner's* 100 (August 1936): 80–86.

17. Pen changes on pp. 23–28 of the carbon TS from "Pap" to "Ab" and on p. 27 from "Mammy's" to "Mrs Snopes' " seem to indicate that Faulkner used these pages as a preliminary draft for the version of the story that appears in the novel.

18. "Lizards in Jamshyd's Courtyard," *Saturday Evening Post* 204 (February 27, 1932): 13. Hereafter cited as L in the text.

19. Faulkner's spoof: Ernest V. Trueblood (psuedo), "Afternoon of the Cow," *Furioso* 2 (Summer 1947): 5–17, first published in a French translation by Maurice Edgar Coindreau, 'L'Après-midi d'une Vache," *Fontaine* 27–28 (June–July 1943): 66–81, contains some problems with a cow and a fire which are similar to those faced by Ike in Book Three of *The Hamlet,* but the central character, "William Faulkner," is most decidedly dissimilar to the idiot Ike; in fact, the two versions are so radically different that I do not consider a comparison fruitful for the purposes of this study.

20. "The Hound," *Harper's* 163 (August 1931): 266–74. Hereafter cited as TH in the text. Reprinted in *Doctor Martino.*

21. *The Town* (1957; reprint ed., New York: Vintage, 1961), p. 79. Hereafter cited as T in the text.

22. "Father Abraham," "Abraham's Children," "As I Lay Dying," "Aria Con Amore," "The Peasants," and "Spotted Horses."

23. See note 6.

24. Eight of the 9 pages of an incomplete TS, headed "Abraham's Children" on the top of each page (Item 9817-a in the Alderman Library), are from a draft of "Father Abraham." The eight pages are identical to the carbon typescripts of that story (Item 6074) except that Faulkner added the headings, erased the page numbers, renumbered the pages, and made holograph revisions on them. These pages help to substantiate my assumption that "Father Abraham" preceded "Abraham's Children."

25. Linton R. Massey apparently did not realize this fact when labeling the materials in the Alderman Library, and a number of "Father Abraham" TS pages are incorrectly labeled "Abraham's Children." See note 6 for a regrouping of these materials. In addition to the deletion of the Henry Armstid story, Faulkner established the habit of typing "Abraham's Children" on the top of each typescript page—apparently as a help to keep them distinguished from "Father Abraham" pages.

26. Faulkner apparently submitted the story to *Scribner's* for publication in November 1928. See *Blotner, Faulkner: A Biography* 1: 597. *As I Lay Dying* was published October 6, 1930.

27. Ibid., pp. 634–35.
28. A student, Richard Nash, who is interested in verb tenses in the novel, insists that it is Cash who is dying; Addie is already dead.
29. "William Faulkner: The Short Stories," *Contemporaries* (Boston: Little, Brown, 1962), pp. 154–58.
30. "Spotted Horses," *Scribner's* 89 (June 1931): 586. Hereafter cited as SH in the text.
31. See note 6.
32. "The Peasants" begins like the similarly titled section of *The Hamlet*—the arrival of the spotted horses in Frenchman's Bend—although the latter is considerably expanded. The version, which recapitulates briefly some of same background as "Father Abraham" and which maintains some of the descriptive passages, is toned down; the characters are more realistically drawn; the style is less breezy. Not only is Buck the harsher character who appears in *The Hamlet*, but Flem in this version is no longer Father Abraham. Uncle Bill Varner, who in "Father Abraham" is "the big man of the Frenchman's Bend neightborhood. Beat supervisor, farmer, usurer, veterinarian; present owner of the old Frenchman's original homestead and proprietor of his legend. A tall reddishcolored man with little bright blue eyes: he looked like a methodist elder, and is; and a milder mannered man never bled a mule or carried a voting precinct" (TS, p. 4) is now nondescript: "He was a tall thin man. He carried a small worn satchel; he was a licensed veterinary" (TS, p. 37). Faulkner in the last instance obviously preferred the more colorful version of Uncle Billy that was sketched in "Father Abraham," and, in fact, he augmented it in *The Hamlet* where he wrote: "a milder-mannered man never bled a mule or stuffed a ballot box" (H, p. 5).
33. Floyd C. Watkins and Thomas Daniel Young, "Revision of Style in Faulkner's *The Hamlet*," *Modern Fiction Studies* 5 (Winter 1959–60): 330 ff.
34. See note 3.
35. *Faulkner in the University*, p. 108.
36. *The Mansion* (1959; reprint ed., New York: Vintage, 1965), pp. 373–74. Hereafter cited as M in the text.
37. "Centaur in Brass," *Collected Stories*, pp. 149–68. Hereafter cited as CB in the text. Reprinted without revision from *American Mercury* 25 (February 1932): 200–10.
38. In "Centaur in Brass" Faulkner again couples the two traders, Flem Snopes and V. K. Suratt. But little qualitative difference is apparent between Flem's reputation for "shrewd and secret dealing" and Suratt's "technically unassailable opportunism which passes with country folks—and town folks, too—for honest shrewdness" (CB, p. 149). In the story Suratt, who evades exposing the full circumstances of his duping by Flem with the buried money on Old Frenchman place, reluctantly acknowledges Flem's superior trading skill (CB, p. 150). But in *The Town*, Ratliff is less reluctant to reveal his gullibility with the planted money and less ready to express his admiration for Flem's methods.
39. The first two paragraphs of the book explain this complicated narration:

> I wasn't born yet so it was Cousin Gowan who was there and big enough to see and remember and tell me afterward when I was big enough

for it to make sense. That is, it was Cousin Gowan plus Uncle Gavin or maybe Uncle Gavin rather plus Cousin Gowan. He—Cousin Gowan—was thirteen. . . . "Us" was Grandfather and Mother and Father and Uncle Gavin then. So this is what Gowan knew about it until I got born and big enough to know about it too. So when I say "we" and "we thought" what I mean is Jefferson and what Jefferson thought. [T, p. 3]

40. In fact, the energy that Faulkner expended upon finding the right phrases to describe the symbolic importance of this tower can be seen on the rejected page 1 of an earlier version of *The Town*. Here he experiments with various phrases to foreshadow the moral threat of Flem, an indication of the serious dimension that is being interjected into the comic short story. For example, one rejected sentence reads: "And it took us twenty years, when it was exactly twenty-one years too late, to realise it wasn't even just a track; it was a portent, and—as far as Jefferson was concerned—a doom." Although Faulkner eventually rejected this kind of explicit initial statement for the more subtle, "It was a footprint," many other direct and indirect signals of the dangers of Flem remain. One explicit example is: "It was not because we were against Mr Snopes; we had not yet read the signs and portents which should have warned, alerted, sprung us into frantic concord to defend our town from him" (T, p. 15).

41. "Mule in the Yard," *Collected Stories*, pp. 249–64. Hereafter cited as MY in the text. Reprinted without revision from *Scribner's* 96 (August 1934): 65–70.

42. The nature of the complete 10-page MS and of an incomplete 10-page revised TS of the story in the Alderman Library suggests that, as was frequently characteristic of his writing habits, Faulkner wrote a first draft in script and then wrote a second revised version in typescript. Faulkner appears to have returned to the earlier unpublished TS rather than to the published story for a model when writing the novelistic account.

43. "The Waifs," *Saturday Evening Post* 229 (May 4, 1957): 27, 116, 118, 120.

44. William Faulkner, "Address upon Receiving the Nobel Prize for Literature," *Portable Faulkner*, ed. Malcolm Cowley (New York: The Viking Press, 1946), pp. 723–24.

45. A complete carbon TS of the story is included in the Alderman Library collection: see note 6. An incomplete version exists on versos of a TS of *The Mansion*. Faulkner's agent, Harold Ober, received a copy of the story January 10, 1955, and circulated it for publication without success.

46. "By the People," *Mademoiselle* 41 (October 1955): 86–89, 130–39. Hereafter cited as B in the text.

Chapter 2

1. The first five stories appeared in *Saturday Evening Post*: "Ambuscade" 207 (September 29, 1934): 12–13, 80, 81; "Retreat" 207 (October 13, 1934): 16–17, 82, 84, 85, 87, 89; "Raid" 207 (November 3, 1934): 18–19, 72, 73, 75, 77, 78; "The Unvanquished" 209 (November 14, 1936): 12–13, 121, 122, 124, 126, 128, 130, later titled "Riposte in Tertio"; and "Vendé" 209 (December 5, 1936): 16–17, 86, 87, 90, 92, 93, 94. The sixth story, "Skirmish at Sartoris," appeared in *Scribner's* 97 (April 1935): 193–200.

2. Holmes, *Faulkner's Twice-Told Tales,* pp. 46–57. Saying that it would be "an extreme and I believe indefensible position" to claim that the revisions are essential to a depiction of the book's "present themes" and "present measure of significance," Holmes shows how the interpretations of Waggoner and Lyle depend in large part on added or revised passages. Hyatt H. Waggoner, *William Faulkner: From Jefferson to the World* (Lexington: University of Kentucky, 1959), and Andrew Nelson Lytle, "The Son of Man: He Will Prevail," *Sewanee Review* 63 (Winter 1955): 114–37, do not themselves compare versions of the stories, but they do offer perceptive readings of the final text. James B. Meriwether, "The Place of *The Unvanquished* in William Faulkner's Yoknapatawpha Series," Ph.D. diss., Princeton University, 1958, although not systematically comparing the preexistent stories and the revised text, does occasionally mention that the revisions help bind the volume together thematically. Michael Millgate, pp. 165–70, disagrees. He conjectures that Faulkner may have been trying to develop thematic links among the stories, but "the attempt, if such it was, cannot be said to have been very thoroughly pursued." Melvin Backman, *Faulkner: The Major Years* (Bloomington: Indiana University Press, 1966), pp. 113–14, agrees essentially with Millgate, claiming that most of the changes were additions of new blocks of material and that "in their final form the stories remain basically unchanged in plot, theme, and character." Edmond Volpe, *The Reader's Guide to William Faulkner* (New York: Noonday, 1964), p. 76, is the most critically outspoken. He claims that "Faulkner's revisions did little to improve the slick plots, the grating sentimentality, the stereotyped characters and the stock situations."

3. *Faulkner in the University,* p. 252.

4. Some commentators have also noted a duality of vision in this first story, but they have not observed that it was interjected into the revised version and was totally absent in the magazine story. Moreover, I cannot agree with Joseph F. Trimmer, "*The Unvanquished* : The Teller and the Tale," *Ball State University Forum* 10 (Winter 1969): 35–42, who claims that the components of that duality are the teller, Bayard, who even as a man is evasive and romantic, and Faulkner, the implied author, who is realistic. He claims that Bayard scrupulously represses the complexity of emotional responses throughout the volume, and Faulkner makes us aware of this evasion. Rather, the two views in the story are that of the boy Bayard and the man Bayard. Nor can I totally agree with Hyatt H. Waggoner when he claims that "*The Unvanquished* begins as a record, taking the form of objective memory, a reliving without criticism or interpretation, with only a sense of urgency, of poignance, imparted by the fact that all this is *remembered,* a reliving of a boy's experiences as he grows up during and just after the Civil War. What he discovers when he is grown up . . . is not read back into the memories of earlier, boyhood experiences," (p. 171). I agree that the man is attempting to recreate his boyhood experiences, but I do not agree that he interjects no adult awareness into the picture.

5. "Ambuscade," p. 12.

6. *The Unvanquished* (1938; reprint ed., New York: Vintage, 1966), pp. 3–4. Hereafter cited as U in the text.

7. Waggoner also comments upon Bayard's later recognition of his father's small stature and the dependency of his authority on the "caste system," calling it "the uneasy relation between fact and value in our memories of the past," a theme that

is introduced in the first story and carried through the volume. His astute observations here seem to contradict his earlier claim that the volume begins as "a record . . . a reliving without criticism or interpretation . . . of a boy's experiences" pp. 177, 171.

8. Millgate, p. 165.

9. A MS (23 pp.) and a revised TS (54 pp.) of "An Odor of Verbena" are on deposit in the Alderman Library. The TS, except for occasional very minor changes in wording, is similar to the published story.

10. *Faulkner in the University*, p. 252.

Chapter 3

1. Volpe, p. 232; Millgate, p. 201; Olga W. Vickery, *The Novels of William Faulkner* (Baton Rouge: Louisiana State University Press, 1964), p. 124; Lawrance Thompson, *William Faulkner: An Introduction and Interpretation* (1963; reprint ed., New York: Holt, Rinehart, & Winston, 1967), p. 81; Malcolm Cowley, *New Republic* 106 (June 29, 1942): 90; Lionel Trilling, *The Nation* 154 (May 30, 1942): 632; Stanley Tick, "The Unity of *Go Down, Moses*," *Twentieth Century Literature* 8 (July 1962): 69; Stanley Sultan, "Call Me Ishmael: The Hagiography of Isaac McCaslin," *Texas Studies in Literature and Language* 3 (Spring 1961): 51; dust jacket of *Go Down, Moses* (New York: Modern Library, 1955); William Van O'Connor, *The Tangled Fire of William Faulkner* (Minneapolis: University of Minnesota Press, 1954), p. 125.

2. "That story was part of a novel. It was—the pursuit of the bear was simply what you might call a dangling clause in the description of that man when he was a young boy. When it was taken from the book and printed as a short story, the publisher, who is very considerate, has a great respect for all work and for mine in particular, he would not have altered one word of that without asking me, and he didn't ask me. If he had told me he was going to print it separately, I would have said, Take this [part 4] out, this doesn't belong in this as a short story, it's part of the novel but not part of the story. But rather than to go ahead and do that without asking me—and I wasn't available at that time—he printed it as it was. It doesn't belong with the short story. The way to read that is to skip that when you come to it." *Faulkner in the University*, p. 273.

3. Establishing a debatable thesis, Olga Vickery sees each of the stories as a ritual hunt where "the hunt illuminates some facet of the relationship between whites and Negroes, whether personal or social" (p. 125). Lawrance Thompson suggests quite correctly that the volume is "built around different concepts of 'freedom' and 'bondage' " (p. 81). Michael Millgate, along with a number of others, notices that the major themes "centre upon white-Negro relationships and upon the destruction of wilderness," themes that are supplemented by minor ones, "of which the most fundamental is that of love" (p. 204). Edmond L. Volpe emphasizes in particular the history of race relations developed in the volume "and the impact of that history upon the life of the novel's protagonist, Isaac McCaslin" (pp. 230–32).

4. Millgate, p. 204.

5. Tick, p. 73.

6. *Faulkner's Narrative* (New Haven and London: Yale University Press, 1973), pp. 176, 185–200.

7. See, in particular, Jane Millgate, "Short Stories into Novels: A Textual and Critical Study of Some Aspects of Faulkner's Literary Method," Master's thesis, Unversity of Leeds, 1962, pp. 292–93.

8. *Go Down, Moses* (New York: Modern Library, 1955), pp. 6, 27. Hereafter cited as GDM in the text. The volume was published in 1942 under the title *Go Down, Moses and Other Stories.* Although James B. Meriwether, *The Literary Career of William Faulkner* (Princeton: Princeton University Library, 1961), p. 30, suggests that the change was made to emphasize the unity, Millgate, p. 328, n3, mentions that Albert Erskine of Random House claims that Faulkner told him that the words "and Other Stories" should never have appeared.

9. Russell Roth, "The Brennan Papers: Faulkner in Manuscript," *Perspective* 2 (Summer 1949): 219–24. The "Brennan papers" also help to fix the date—summer 1940—of the writing of the first version of this story and also perhaps of "Go Down, Moses," since portions of the latter story appear on the reverse side of these rejected pages of the "Almost" TS.

10. *Faulkner in the University,* p. 84.

11. Faulkner makes this point explicitly about "Was." Ibid., pp. 37–38, 131.

12. "Jonas had the two horses saddled and waiting. Uncle Buck didn't mount a horse like he was any sixty years old either, lean and active as a cat, with his round, close cropped white head and his hard little gray eyes and his white-stubbled jaw, his foot in the iron and the horse already moving, already running at the open gate when Uncle Buck came into the seat" (GDM, p. 7).

13. "Uncle Buddy . . . was sitting at his end of the table with his hands in his lap, all one gray color, like an old gray rock or a stump with gray moss on it, that still, with his round white head like Uncle Buck's but he didn't blink like Uncle Buck and he was a little thicker than Uncle Buck, as if from sitting down so much watching food cook, as if the things he cooked had made him a little thicker than he would have been and the things he cooked with the flour and such, had made him all one same quiet color" (GDM, p. 26).

14. *Faulkner in the University,* p. 40.

15. Roth, p. 222.

16. In addition to the complete TS of "A Point of Law," 25 miscellaneous pages of various drafts of chapter one are on deposit in the Alderman Library. These materials—along with one miscellaneous page from chapter two—are incorrectly listed under "The Fire on the Hearth" which was an early title for chapter three of "The Fire and the Hearth." Another TS page was added with the materials in Item 9817-a.

17. "A Point of Law," *Collier's* 105 (June 22, 1940): 20–21, 30, 32. Hereafter cited as PL in the text.

18. The four rejected versions of this passage which are on deposit in the Alderman Library evidence the care that Faulkner expended on the order, arrangement, diction, and syntax of this passage. Observe the evolution of the first few sentences through four versions, the last being identical (in these opening sentences) to the printed version:

1. "First he had to remove his own still—dismantle it singlehanded and in the dark and load it onto his wagon and remove it."

2. "First, he had to dismantle his own still, transport it singlehanded to the creek bottom a mile away and hide it, doing it all without help since he had never had a partner even in running the still. It was this that enraged him."

3. "First, he had to dismantle his own still and transport it singlehanded to the creek bottom a mile further away and hide it. It was the prospect of this which had enraged him, compounding in advance the physical weariness and exhaustion which would be the night's aftermath."

4. "First, in order to take care of George Wilkins once and for all, he had to hide his own still. And not only that, he had to do it singlehanded—dismantle it in the dark and transport it without help to some place far enough away and secret enough for it to escape the subsequent uproar and excitement and there conceal it. It was the prospect of this which had enraged him, compounding in advance the physical weariness and exhaustion which would be the night's aftermath."

The decision to name George Wilkins explicitly in the beginning clarifies the action; there is no point in keeping the reader in the dark here. Although Faulkner attempted the same effect and had the same perspective in all four versions, the diction and the polished and expanded syntax of the last clearly extablishes the tone of the narrator.

19. In the TS, George explains that he and Nat planted the stills on Lucas's porch because they wanted to blackmail Lucas into allowing them to get married: "She say ifn we tuck and fotch that kettle from whar you and Mister Roth told the shurf hit was and sot it on your back porch, you would have to let us get married to help you get shet of it fo the shurf got here" (TS, p. 10). In the *Collier's* version, he makes a slip that gives Lucas the opportunity to suspect the *fait accompli* of the marriage: " 'She say maybe ifn we took and fotch dat kettle from whar you and Mister Roth told de shurf hit was and you would find it settin' on yo' back porch maybe when we offered to help you git shet of hit 'fo' de shurf got here, yo' mind might change about loanin' us de money to—I mean to leffin' us be married. . . . ' Lucas looked at George. He didn't blink" (PL, p. 30). Furthermore, after the license has already freed them from court action, Lucas implies in the *Collier's* version that the license was indeed authentic. Chiding George about his foolish plan to place his new still where his old one used to be, he says, "When they catch you this time, you ain't gonter have no witness you done already been married to since last fall" (PL, p. 32). Lucas's comments in the TS in contrast reinforce the implication that the license was falsified: "When they catch you this time, you aint gonter have no witness you can marry" (TS, p. 20).

20. Faulkner again drew from the TS for this scene. In fact the only major change that is made from the TS to novel here is to intensify the conflict between Lucas and Nat. She is no longer indirectly speaking to George; it is her father alone who is the formidable opponent. The magazine version, in contrast, is considerably abbreviated.

21. "Procrustean Revision in Faulkner's *Go Down, Moses*," *American Literature* 37 (March 1965): 12.

22. "Gold Is Not Always," *Atlantic* 166 (November 1940): 563–70. Hereafter cited as GA in the text.

23. The collection includes both a complete, revised 19-page TS of "Gold Is Not Always" and 6 pages of another incomplete TS. One page is incorrectly filed under "The Fire on the Hearth."

24. Also see Jane Millgate, "Short Story into Novel: Faulkner's Reworking of 'Gold Is Not Always,' " *English Studies* 45 (August 1964): 310–17, for another discussion of the revisions highlighting the new conception of Lucas's role. Millgate discusses neither the formal structure of the story nor the other chapters and revisions, but she observes and demonstrates the care and judgment that Faulkner brings to the task of revision.

25. Compare, for example, the TS with the final version of the text. The TS:

"Hit was my letter," Lucas said. The salesman looked from one to another of them. They seemed to feel even the still summer air moving to the fierce hot trembling of his body. "I wants half. And the finding machine is mine."

"How much did you say them other fellows found?"

"Twenty-two thousand dollars," Lucas said.

"Hit mought a been more," george said. "Hit was a big—"

"All right," the salesman said suddenly. "Where's the other place?"

"Let's fix up the papers first," Lucas said. They went back to the car. [TS, p. 16]

Final version:

"It was my letter," Lucas said. "That aint enough."

"Twenty," the salesman said. "And that's all."

"I want half," Lucas said.

"Half?"

"And that mule paper back, and another paper saying that that machine is mine."

"Ha, ha," the salesman said. "And ha ha ha. You say that letter said in the orchard. The orchard aint very big. And most of the night left, not to mention tomor—"

"I said it said some of it was in the orchard," Lucas said. They faced one another in the darkness.

"Tomorrow," the salesman said.

"Now," Lucas said.

"Tomorrow."

"Now," Lucas said. The invisible face stared at his own invisible face. Both he and George seemed to feel the windless summer air moving to the white man's trembling.

"Jack," the salesman said, "how much did you say them other fellows found?" But Lucas answered before George could speak.

"Twenty-two thousand dollars."

"Hit mought er been more than twenty-two thousand," George said. "Hit was a big—"

"All right," the salesman said. "I'll give you a bill of sale for it as soon as we finish."

"I want it now," Lucas said. They returned to the car. [GDM, pp. 94–95]

26. Added to the magazine version is the following sentence: "They would not have told him who made the tracks even if he demanded to know, but the realization that they knew would have enabled him to leap to the correct divination and so save himself the four or five hours of mental turmoil and physical effort which he was about to enter" (GA, p. 565). Added to the final version is a three-quarter-page passage depicting Edmond's belated realization of his boys' knowledge of the situation and of his own ignorance. The emphasis is upon Roth's total surprise and rage:

> He stopped dead in his tracks. He whirled. He was not only about to perceive the whole situation in its complete and instantaneous entirety, as when the photographer's bulb explodes, but he knew now that he had seen it all the while and had refused to believe it purely and simply because he knew that when he did accept it, his brain would burst. . . . Edmonds couldn't hear it any more, drowned by a rushing in his skull which, had he been a few years older, would have been apoplexy. He could neither breathe nor see for a moment. Then he whirled again. He said something in a hoarse strangled voice and sprang on. [GDM, pp. 85–86]

27. Frederick J. Hoffman, *William Faulkner* (New York: Twayne, 1961), p. 26.

28. The earliest is a revised 17-page incomplete TS entitled "An Absolution" (with the title "Apotheosis" pencilled-in above it). "The Fire on the Hearth" is a complete, revised 20-page TS that incorporates the pencilled-in corrections of the earlier draft and includes additional amplification of character and scene. Additionally, a 24-page revised TS of chapter 3 was deposited with the materials in Item 9817-a.

29. Moreover, in a cryptic note at the side of page 1, Faulkner sketched the basis for further complexity in their relationship: "Mollie. Wet nurse and doctor, mother died. High water. Doctor delayed." Faulkner used the spelling "Mollie" throughout both TSS.

30. "Pantaloon in Black," *Harper's* 181 (October 1940): 503–13. A 24-page revised, complete, carbon TS of the story is on deposit in the Alderman Library.

31. Additionally, fragmentary revised pages (3 pages & 2 pages) were added to the Alderman Library collection under Item 9817-a.

32. "The Old People," *Harper's* 181 (September 1940): 418–25. Hereafter cited as OP in the text.

33. The *Go Down, Moses* version was also reprinted in *Big Woods*.

34. Faulkner also set the time of the final version of "The Old People" back about forty years in order to accommodate the story to the McCaslin genealogy. See Henry Alden Ploegstra, "William Faulkner's *Go Down, Moses:* Its Sources, Revisions, and Structure," Ph.D. diss., University of Chicago, 1966, p. 110, both for an excellent discussion of this change and for the probable time and probable composition dates of other stories.

35. Similarly, additions to the TS for the magazine story, although less extensive, also serve to emphasize Sam's tutorial role. The two longest of such additions are:

> "You got time," Sam said to me once. "We'll get there before he does."
> So I tried to go slower. That is, I tried to slow, decelerate, the dizzy rush of time in which the buck which I had not even seen was moving, which it

seemed to me was carrying him farther and farther and more and more irretrievably away from us even though there were no dogs behind him to make him run yet. So we went on; it seemed to me that it was for another hour. [OP, p. 422]

(Brackets indicate wording found only in the typescript; italics indicate wording added to the *Harper's* version.)

> "Wait" [, he said.]. *And I remember how I turned upon him in the truculence of a boy's grief over the missed chance, the missed luck.*
> "Wait?" I said. "*What for?* Don't you hear [Walter's] *that* horn?"
> *And I remember how he was standing. He had not moved. He was not tall, he was rather squat and broad, and I had been growing fast for the past year or so and there was not much difference between us, yet he was looking over my head. He was looking across me and up the ridge toward the sound of Walter's horn and he did not see me; he just knew I was there, he did not see me.* [TS, p. 14; OP, p. 423]

36. "The Bear," *Saturday Evening Post* 214 (May 9, 1942): 30–31, 74, 76, 77, reprinted in Francis Lee Utley et al., *Bear, Man, and God* (New York: Random House, 1964), pp. 149–64. Hereafter cited as B in text. "Lion," *Harper's* 172 (December 1935): 66–77, reprinted in *Bear, Man and God*, pp. 132–49. Hereafter cited as L in the text. (The 1971 second edition of *Bear, Man and God* deletes the two stories.) Although "The Bear" was published in the *Post* about the same time as the short story composite (in fact, *Publisher's Weekly* for May 9, 1942, lists *Go Down, Moses and Other Stories* among the books published in the previous week), the *Post* version was written before the completion of the five-part version. It was submitted to Harold Ober for publication in October 1941; the longer version was not completed until mid-December 1941, when Faulkner sent part 4 to Random House. The relationship between the two versions is complex, however, since the typesetting copy of part 1 of "The Bear" (which is the section that roughly corresponds to the detached story) was received by Random House July 25, 1941, and since Faulkner claims in a letter received by Harold Ober, November 10, 1941, that the shorter version "was a rewritten chapter of a book under way. The story I sent you was rewritten from the chapter in the novel, first draft and in haste because I need some money badly." If one takes Faulkner at his word, it would seem that the differences between the two versions are due to Faulkner's cutting and shaping of the story of magazine publication. Undoubtedly, he did revise the ending in accordance with the wishes of the *Post* editors (see Faulkner-Ober correspondence, November 5, 1931, and Blotner 2: 1085–88). Technically, then, the *Post* story is not "preexistent" in the same sense that the other stories under consideration here are. I was unaware of this fact when I wrote my article, "Revision and Craftmanship in the Hunting Trilogy of *Go Down, Moses*," *Texas Studies in Literature and Languages* 15 (Fall 1973): 577–92. Yet, we do not know what draft Faulkner was working from when he composed the *Post* story. It is possible that he was using an earlier version than the one sent to Random House July 25. If that is so, then the *Post* version may represent— imperfectly to be sure—an earlier stage of "The Bear." I suggest this because I

am reluctant to concede that Faulkner would trouble himself to make so many major and minor changes that serve to weaken his story. Ploegstra, pp. 333–40—who had neither the conflicting evidence of the Faulkner-Ober correspondence nor of Blotner's chronology of the approximate writing of the various parts of "The Bear"—was also convinced that the *Post* story represented an earlier draft than the *Go Down, Moses* version.

37. Unfortunately, very little unpublished material is available for study of "The Bear." In addition to the TS setting copy of *Go Down, Moses,* only one page (numbered 237 and corresponding roughly to pp. 237–38 of the printed version) from a corrected carbon TS is on deposit in the Alderman Library. Parts 1, 2, 3, and 5 of "The Bear" were reprinted in *Big Woods.*

38. O'Connor, pp. 125–34; Klotz, passim; Edward M. Holmes, pp. 68–71, notes the more "formal narrative manner," more "detail," and more profound "moral themes" in the revised story, although he sees hints of "themes yet undeveloped" in the two preexistent stories; James Early, *The Making of "Go Down, Moses,"* p. 31, unequivocally praises the "synthesis" of the final form of "The Bear."

39. O'Connor, p. 131.

40. Klotz, p. 15.

41. O'Connor, p. 129.

42. Early, p. 67.

43. "Delta Autumn," *Story* 20 (May–June, 1942): 46–55. Hereafter cited as DA in the text. The 18-page revised, complete TS is on deposit in the Alderman Library. Additionally, 5 pages of revised TS were added to the collection under Item 9817-a. Although the magazine version of "Delta Autumn" appeared after the publication of *Go Down, Moses and Other Stories,* it was written earlier. The story was received in Harold Ober's office December 16, 1940. Changes made would suggest that the TS was written first, then the magazine story, and finally the *Go Down, Moses* version. Part of the final version was revised and reprinted in *Big Woods.*

44. See Carol Clancy Harter, "The Winter of Isaac McCaslin: Revision and Irony in Faulkner's 'Delta Autumn,' " *Journal of Modern Literature* 1 (1970): 209–25, for a similar conclusion about the altered portrait of Ike effected by revisions of "Delta Autumn."

45. "Go Down, Moses," *Collier's* 107 (January 25, 1941): 19–20, 45, 46.

46. In addition to the change from Henry Coldfield Sutpen on page 1, page 2 of this 14-page complete TS has Carothers Edmonds crossed out and Samuel Worsham added in script. Apparently Faulkner felt that these names would suggest a too-obvious linkage to the McCaslin-Edmonds genealogy. A complete 17-page carbon TS and page 1 of another TS are also on deposit in the Alderman Library. Except for minor stylistic changes, these versions are very close to the published versions of the story.

47. The Molly of "The Fire and the Hearth" is inexplicably changed to "Mollie" in "Go Down, Moses." It is sloppiness about detail like this that annoys some critics.

48. I cannot share James Early's dissatisfaction with the characterization of Mollie who he says seems "to be almost a caricature rather than a believable human being. . . . In a final comic twist which pretty much erases any serious effect her

mourning has had on the reader, she insists in heavy dialect that instead of being protected from publicity, as Gavin Stevens and the editor assumed she desired, she wants a full account in the paper of Butch's reception in Jefferson and burial, 'all of hit' " (p. 105). Faulkner has shown earlier in "The Fire and the Hearth" that Molly has a fierce and simplistic belief in religion and the Bible. She condemns improper actions—like digging for gold—and approves proper rituals—like public burials—with moral conviction and biblical sanction. She is not sophisticated enough to think she ought to hide the infamous end of her grandson from public knowledge (and, in fact she is unaware of how he died). She only knows intuitively that Roth Edmonds "sold him in Egypt. Pharaoh got him''; and she is childlike and gauche enough (to middle-class scruples) to take pride in the public attention that is given to her and to her dead grandson on this occasion. Such attitudes are inscrutable to Gavin who with his overwrought sense of delicacy goes through unnecessary precautions to keep the truth from her, but such a character is neither unrealistic nor comic. What is comic and tragic about the story is the communication gap between people like Mollie and Gavin.

49. Early, p. 105.
50. "Address upon Receiving the Nobel Prize for Literature," *Portable Faulkner,* p. 724.

Conclusion

1. I should perhaps mention as a postscript that the altered pagination of the typescript setting copy of *Go Down, Moses* seems to indicate that Faulkner until a relatively late date placed "Delta Autumn" before "The Bear." Undoubtedly this differing spatial arrangement would have altered the structural design and the portrait of Ike in the volume. "Delta Autumn" would no longer function as a denouement to Ike's repudiation, and perhaps as a result would not serve as such a stinging indictment of it. The structural coherence of the final text is clearly preferable; Faulkner as usual is an astute revisionist.

2. *Faulkner in the University,* p. 45.

A SELECTED BIBLIOGRAPHY

BY WILLIAM FAULKNER

**Unpublished Materials in The
Alderman Library,
The University of Virginia.
Deposited under Item 6074 unless
otherwise noted.**

Go Down, Moses

1 p. manuscript—McCaslin genealogy; 411 pp. revised, complete typescript setting copy.

"Was": 22 pp. revised, complete typescript; 5 pp. revised typescript.

"The Fire and the Hearth":

"A Point of Law": 21 pp. revised, complete typescript; 25 pp. revised typescript of chapter one. Item 9817-a; 1 p. revised typescript of chapter one.

"Gold Is Not Always": 5 pp. typescript; 19 pp. revised, complete typescript; 1 p. typescript of chapter two.

"An Absolution" also entitled "Apotheosis": 17 pp. revised typescript.

"The Fire on the Hearth": 20 pp. revised, complete typescript. Item 9817-a: 24 pp. revised typescript of chapter three.

"Pantaloon in Black": 24 pp. revised, complete, carbon typescript.

"The Old People": 17 pp. revised, complete typescript. Item 9817-a: 3 pp. revised typescript; 2 pp. revised typescript.

"The Bear": 1 p. carbon typescript.

"Delta Autumn": 18 pp. revised, complete typescript. Item 9817-a: 5 pp. revised typescript.

"Go Down, Moses": 14 pp. revised, complete typescript; 17 pp. complete, carbon typescript; 1 p. typescript.

The Hamlet

210 pp. manuscript; 87 pp. manuscript; 18 pp. typescript; 85 pp. revised typescript; 35 pp. carbon typescript; 604 pp. revised, complete typescript setting copy.

"Father Abraham": 54 pp. carbon typescript; 51 pp. carbon typescript; 1 p. typescript. Item 9817-a: 54 pp. revised typescript; 6 pp. revised typescript; 3 pp. revised typescript; 1 p. typescript; 4 pp. carbon typescript.

"Abraham's Children": 2 pp. carbon typescript. Item 9817-a: 48 pp. complete typescript; 9 pp. typescript; 13 pp. typescript.

"As I Lay Dying": Item 9817-a: 17 pp. complete carbon typescript.

"As I Lay Dying": Item 9817-a: 22 pp. complete, carbon typescript.

"Aria Con Amore": Item 9817-a: 16 pp. complete typescript; 16 pp. complete, carbon typescript.

"The Peasants": Item 9817-a: 59 pp. complete, carbon typescript.

"Barn Burning": 17 pp. manuscript; 32 pp. complete typescript headed "Chapter One"; 32 pp. complete, carbon typescript headed "Chapter One."

"Fool About a Horse": 10 pp. manuscript; 21 pp. revised typescript; 33 pp. revised complete, carbon typescript.

The Mansion

592 pp. revised typescript; 569 pp. revised typescript. Item 9817-a: 13 pp. revised typescript; 1 p. revised typescript.

"Hog Pawn": Item 9817-a: 26 pp. revised, complete, carbon typescript; scattered pages of revised typescript on versos of 13 pp. typescript and 592 pp. typescript above.

"By the People": Item 9817-a: 4 pp. typescript on versos of 13 pp. typescript above.

The Town

171 pp. revised typescript: 488 pp. revised, complete typescript setting copy.

"Mule in the Yard": 10 pp. complete manuscript; 10 pp. revised typescript.

The Unvanquished

"An Odor of Verbena": 23 pp. complete manuscript; 54 pp. revised, complete typescript.

Published Texts and Stories

Absalom, Absalom! 1936. Reprint. New York: The Modern Library, 1951.

"Ambuscade." *Saturday Evening Post* 207 (September 29, 1934): 12–13, 80, 81.

"Barn Burning." *Harper's* 179 (June 1939): 86–96. Reprinted in *Collected Stories* and *Selected Short Stories*.

"The Bear," *Saturday Evening Post* 214 (May 9, 1942): 30–31, 74, 76, 77. Reprinted in *Bear, Man, and God.*

"By the People." *Mademoiselle* 41 (October 1955): 86–89, 130–39.

"Centaur in Brass." *American Mercury* 25 (February 1932): 200–10. Reprinted in *Collected Stories.*

Collected Stories of William Faulkner. New York: Random House, 1950.

"Delta Autumn." *Story* 20 (May-June 1942): 46–55.

Doctor Martino and Other Stories. New York: Smith and Haas, 1934.
"Fool About a Horse." *Scribner's* 100 (August 1936): 80–86.
"Go Down, Moses." *Collier's* 107 (January 25, 1941): 19–20, 45, 46.
Go Down, Moses and Other Stories. 1942. Reprint. *Go Down, Moses.* New York: The Modern Library, 1955.
"Gold Is Not Always." *Atlantic* 166 (November 1940): 563–70.
The Hamlet. 1940. Reprint. New York: Vintage, 1956.
"The Hound." *Harper's* 163 (August 1931): 266–74. Reprinted in *Doctor Martino.*
"Lion." *Harper's* 172 (December 1935): 67–77. Reprinted in *Bear, Man, and God.*
"Lizards in Jamshyd's Courtyard." *Saturday Evening Post* 204 (February 27, 1932): 12–13, 52, 57.
The Mansion. 1959. Reprint. New York: Vintage, 1965.
"Mule in the Yard." *Scribner's* 96 (August 1934): 65–70. Reprinted in *Collected Stories.*
"The Old People." *Harper's* 181 (September 1940): 418–25.
"Pantaloon in Black." *Harper's* 181 (October 1940): 503–13.
"A Point of Law." *Collier's* 105 (June 22, 1940): 20–21, 30, 32.
The Portable Faulkner. Edited by Malcolm Cowley. New York: The Viking Press, 1946.
"Raid." *Saturday Evening Post* 207 (November 3, 1934): 18–19, 72, 73, 75, 77, 78.
"Retreat." *Saturday Evening Post* 207 (October 13, 1934): 16–17, 82, 84, 85, 87, 89.
Selected Short Stories of William Faulkner. New York: The Modern Library, 1962.
"Skirmish at Sartoris." *Scribner's* 97 (April 1935): 193–200.
"Spotted Horses." *Scribner's* 89 (June 1931): 585–97.
The Town. 1957. Reprint. New York: Vintage, 1961.
"The Unvanquished." *Saturday Evening Post* 209 (November 14, 1936): 12–13, 121, 122, 124, 126, 128, 130.
The Unvanquished. 1938. Reprint. New York: Vintage, 1966.
"Vendée." *Saturday Evening Post* 209 (December 5, 1936): 16–17, 86, 87, 90, 92, 93, 94.
"The Waifs." *Saturday Evening Post* 229 (May 4, 1957): 27, 116, 118, 120.
"Wash." *Harper's* 168 (February 1934): 258–66. Reprinted in *Doctor Martino, Collected Stories,* and *Portable Faulkner.*

Secondary Sources

Backman, Melvin. *Faulkner: The Major Years.* Bloomington: Indiana University Press, 1966.
Bassett, John. *William Faulkner: An Annotated Checklist of Criticism.* New York: David Lewis, 1972.
Beck, Warren. *Man in Motion: Faulkner's Trilogy.* Madison: University of Wisconsin Press, 1961.
Blotner, Joseph. *Faulkner: A Biography.* 2 vols. New York: Random House, 1974.
———. *William Faulkner's Library: A Catalogue.* Charlottesville: The University of Virginia Press, 1964.
Bradford, Melvin E. "All the Daughters of Eve: 'Was' and the Unity of *Go Down, Moses.*" *Arlington Quarterly* 1 (Autumn 1967): 28–37.
Brooks, Cleanth. *William Faulkner: The Yoknapatawpha Country.* New Haven: Yale University Press, 1963.

Cowley, Malcolm. *The Faulkner-Cowley File: Letters and Memories, 1944–1962*. New York: The Viking Press, 1966.

Creighton, Joanne V. "The Dilemma of the Human Heart in *The Mansion*." *Renascence* 25 (Autumn 1972): 35–45.

————. "*Dubliners* and *Go Down, Moses*: The Short Story Composite." Ph.D. dissertation, University of Michigan, 1969.

————. "Revision and Craftsmanship in Faulkner's 'The Fire and the Hearth.' " *Studies in Short Fiction* 11 (Spring 1974): 161–72.

————. "Revision and Craftmanship in the Hunting Trilogy of *Go Down, Moses*." *Texas Studies in Literature and Language* 15 (Fall 1973): 577–92.

————. "Suratt to Ratliff: A Genetic Approach to *The Hamlet*." *Michigan Academician* 6 (Summer 1973): 101–12.

Dabney, Lewis M. *The Indians of Yoknapatawpha: A Study of Literature and History*. Baton Rouge: Louisiana State University Press, 1974.

Early, James. *The Making of "Go Down, Moses."* Dallas: Southern Methodist University Press, 1972.

Faulkner at Nagano. Edited by Robert A. Jelliffe. Tokyo: The Kenkyusha Press, 1956.

Faulkner at West Point. Edited by Joseph L. Fant, III, and Robert Ashley. New York: Random House, 1964.

Faulkner in the University: Class Conferences at the University of Virginia, 1957–1958. Edited by Frederick L. Gwynn and Joseph L. Blotner. Charlottesville: The University of Virginia Press, 1959.

Greet, T. Y. "The Theme and Structure of Faulkner's *The Hamlet*." *PMLA* 72 (September 1957): 775–90.

Gregory, Eileen. "Faulkner's Typescripts of *The Town*," *A Faulkner Miscellany*, Jackson: University Press of Mississippi, 1974, pp. 113–38.

Harter, Carol Ann Clancey. "The Diaphoric Structure and Unity of William Faulkner's *Go Down, Moses*." Ph.D. dissertation, State University of New York at Binghamton, 1970.

————. "The Winter of Ike McCaslin: Revisions and Irony in Faulkner's 'Delta Autumn.' " *Journal of Modern Literature* 1 (1970): 209–25.

Hoffman, Frederick J. *William Faulkner*. New York: Twayne, 1961.

Holmes, Edward M. *Faulkner's Twice-Told Tales: His Re-Use of His Material*. The Hague: Mouton, 1966.

Howe, Irving. *William Faulkner: A Critical Study*. New York: Random House, 1962.

Hunt, Joel A. "William Faulkner and Rabelais: The Dog Story." *Contemporary Literature* 10 (Summer 1969): 383–88.

Kazin, Alfred. "William Faulkner: The Short Stories." *Contemporaries*. Boston: Little, Brown, 1962, pp. 154–58.

Kibler, James Everett, Jr. "A Study of the Text of William Faulkner's *The Hamlet*." Ph.D. dissertation, University of South Carolina, 1970.

Klotz, Marvin. "Procrustean Revision in Faulkner's *Go Down, Moses*." *American Literature* 37 (March 1965): 1–16.

Langford, Gerald. *Faulkner's Revisions of "Absalom, Absalom!": A Collation of the Manuscript and the Printed Book*. Austin: The University of Texas Press, 1971.

Lion in the Garden: Interviews with William Faulkner, 1926–1962. Edited by James B. Meriwether, and Michael Millgate. New York: Random House, 1968.

Lisca, Peter. *"The Hamlet:* Genesis and Revisions." *Faulkner Studies* 3 (Spring 1954): 5–13.

Lytle, Andrew Nelson. "The Son of Man: He Will Prevail." *Sewanee Review* 63 (Winter 1955): 114–37.

Malbone, Raymond G. "Promissory Poker in Faulkner's 'Was.' " *English Record* 22 (Fall 1971): 23–25.

Massey, Linton R. *William Faulkner: "Man Working," 1919–1962: A Catalogue of the William Faulkner Collection at the University of Virginia.* Charlottesville: Bibliographical Society of the University of Virginia, 1968.

Mellard, James B. "The Biblical Rhythm of *Go Down, Moses." Mississippi Quarterly* 20 (Summer 1967): 135–45.

Meriwether, James B. *The Literary Career of William Faulkner: A Bibliographical Study.* Princeton: Princeton University Library, 1961.

———. "The Place of *The Unvanquished* in William Faulkner's Yoknapatawpha Series." Ph.D. dissertation, Princeton University, 1958.

———. "Sartoris and Snopes: An Early Notice." *Library Chronicle of the University of Texas* 7 (Summer 1962): 36–39.

———. "The Short Fiction of William Faulkner: A Bibliography." *Proof: The Yearbook of American Bibliographical and Textual Studies* 1 (1971): 293–329.

———. "William Faulkner: A Check List." *The Princeton University Library Chronicle* 18 (Spring 1957): 136–58.

Millgate, Jane. "Short Stories into Novels: A Textual and Critical Study of Some Aspects of Faulkner's Literary Method." Master's thesis, University of Leeds, 1962.

———. "Short Story Into Novel: Faulkner's Reworking of 'Gold Is Not Always.' " *English Studies* 45 (August 1964): 310–17.

Millgate, Michael. *The Achievement of William Faulkner.* London: Constable, 1966.

Mooney, Stephen L. "Faulkner's *The Town:* A Question of Voices." *Mississippi Quarterly* 13 (Summer 1960): 117–22.

Muste, John M. "The Failure of Love in *Go Down, Moses." Modern Fiction Studies* 10 (Winter 1964–65): 366–78.

O'Connor, William Van. *The Tangled Fire of William Faulkner.* Minneapolis: University of Minnesota Press, 1954.

Ploegstra, H. A. "William Faulkner's *Go Down, Moses:* Its Sources, Revisions, and Structure." Ph.D. dissertation, University of Chicago, 1966.

Reed, Joseph W., Jr. *Faulkner's Narrative.* New Haven and London: Yale University Press, 1973.

Roth, Russell. "The Brennan Papers: Faulkner in Manuscript." *Perspective* 2 (Summer 1949): 219–24.

Sultan, Stanley. "Call Me Ishmael: The Hagiography of Isaac McCaslin." *Texas Studies in Literature and Language* 3 (Spring 1961): 50–66.

Thompson, Lawrance R. *William Faulkner: An Introduction and Interpretation.* New York: Barnes and Noble, 1963.

Tick, Stanley. "The Unity of *Go Down, Moses," Twentieth Century Literature* 8 (July 1962): 67–73.

Trimmer, Joseph F. *"The Unvanquished:* The Teller and the Tale." *Ball State University Forum* 10 (Winter 1969): 35–42.

Utley, Francis Lee; Lynn Z. Bloom; and Arthur F. Kinney, eds. *Bear, Man and God: Seven Approaches to William Faulkner's "The Bear."* New York: Random House, 1964.

Vickery, Olga W. *The Novels of William Faulkner: A Critical Interpretation.* Baton Rouge: Louisiana State University Press, 1959.

Volpe, Edmund. *The Reader's Guide to William Faulkner.* New York: Noonday, 1964.

Waggoner, Hyatt H. *William Faulkner: From Jefferson to the World.* Lexington: University of Kentucky Press, 1959.

Walker, William E. *"The Unvanquished*—The Restoration of Tradition." *Reality and Myth.* Edited by W. E. Walker and R. L. Welker. Nashville: Vanderbilt University Press, 1964, pp. 275–97.

Watkins, Floyd C., and Thomas Daniel Young. "Revisions of Style in Faulkner's *The Hamlet." Modern Fiction Studies* 5 (Winter 1959): 327–36.

Watson, James Gray. *The Snopes Dilemma: Faulkner's Trilogy.* Coral Gables: University of Miami Press, 1970.

Wertenbaker, Thomas J., Jr. "Faulkner's Point of View and the Chronicle of Ike McCaslin." *College English* 24 (December 1962): 169–78.

Wills, Arthur. "A Study of Faulkner's Revisions." *Exercise Exchange* 10 (March 1963): 14–16.

Winn, James A. "Faulkner's Revisions: A Stylist at Work." *American Literature* 41 (May 1969): 231–50.

INDEX

Joanne V. Creighton, associate professor of English, Wayne State University, received her B.A. (1964) from the University of Wisconsin; her M.A. (1965) from Harvard University; and her Ph.D. (1969) from the University of Michigan. She has published several articles in scholarly journals.

The manuscript was edited by Marguerite C. Wallace. The book was designed by Mary Primeau. The typeface for the text is Times Roman, designed under the supervision of Stanley Morison in 1931; and the display face is Cheltenham bold extra condensed, originally designed by Bertram G. Goodhue in 1896.

The text is printed on Glatfelter offset paper and the book is bound in Columbia Mills Fictionette cloth over binders' boards. Manufactured in the United States of America.